LEADING FROM THE CENTER

*Scholars Press*

## *Studies in Theological Education*

| | |
|---|---|
| Christian Identity and Theological Education | Joseph C. Hough, Jr./ John B. Cobb, Jr. |
| Vision and Discernment: An Orientation in Theological Study | Charles M. Wood |
| The Arts in Theological Education: New Possibilities for Integration | Wilson Yates |
| Beyond Clericalism: The Congregation as a Focus for Theological Education | Joseph C. Hough, Jr./ Barbara G. Wheeler |
| The Education of the Practical Theologian: Responses to Joseph Hough and John Cobb's *Christian Identity and Theological Education* | Don S. Browning/ David Polk/ Ian S. Evison |
| Piety and Intellect: The Aims and Purposes of Ante-Bellum Theological Education | Glenn T. Miller |
| Religious Studies, Theological Studies and the University-Divinity School | Joseph Mitsuo Kitagawa |
| The President as Educator: A Study of the Seminary Presidency | Neely Dixon McCarter |
| Power, Powerlessness, and the Divine: New Inquiries in Bible and Theology | Cynthia L. Rigby, editor |
| Leading from the Center: The Emerging Role of the Chief Academic Officer in Theological Schools | Jeanne P. McLean |

# LEADING FROM THE CENTER
## The Emerging Role of the Chief Academic Officer in Theological Schools

by
Jeanne P. McLean

Scholars Press
Atlanta, Georgia

# LEADING FROM THE CENTER
## The Emerging Role of the Chief Academic Officer in Theological Schools

by
Jeanne P. McLean



The research project which led to the publication of this book
was made possible by a grant from
The Lilly Foundation, Inc.

**Library of Congress Cataloging in Publication Data**

McLean, Jeanne P.
Leading from the center : the emerging role of the chief academic officer in theological schools / by Jeanne P. McLean.
p. cm. — (Scholars Press studies in theological education)
Includes bibliographical references and index.
ISBN 0-7885-0542-4 (hardcover : alk. paper)
1. Theological seminary presidents. 2. Deans (Education)
I. Title. II. Series.
BV4166.M35 1999
230'.071'1—dc21 99-17246
CIP

Printed in the United States of America
on acid-free paper

For Jeff

## Table of Contents

# INTRODUCTION

The position of chief academic officer today has a centrality and importance in theological school administration that belies its short history. Although the office of academic dean was not widely established in theological schools until the 1950s and 1960s, it has grown steadily in its responsibility and influence. Today the chief academic officer plays a vital leadership role in developing academic programs, building and maintaining a quality faculty, meeting the academic needs of students, and creating a community with a clear sense of mission and purpose. In four decades, the office of dean has evolved from assistant to the president to senior administrative officer with significant responsibility for the academic leadership of theological schools.

Other developments, however, are troubling. Although the deanship has grown in responsibility and stature, attitudes toward administrative service remain ambivalent. While most educators value an effective dean, few actively seek the position and many take it reluctantly. During the past ten years, an average of 25 percent of chief academic officers in theological schools have left their positions annually.[1] Nearly half of the more than 200 member schools of the Association of Theological Schools in the United States and Canada (ATS) have had three or more deans during this ten-year period.[2] While desirable rates of turnover for academic officers may vary among schools and depend on many organizational factors, these data raise critical questions concerning the stability and continuity of academic leadership in theological education.

These trends invite serious inquiry into the nature and function of the chief academic officer position. They give urgency to questions about the work and workload of the office, about the roles, responsibilities, and relationships that define the position; about its stresses and rewards; about the preparation of deans and institutional practices for their recruitment and professional development; about who deans are, how they come to their positions, and why they leave; about how deans succeed or fail, and how academic communities support or fail their deans. These trends compel us to listen to academic officers and to those who work closely with them to learn what is needed for sustained and effective academic leadership in theological education. Such vital issues concerning chief academic officers and their work are the subject of this book.

To understand and address the challenges facing academic deans, the Lilly Endowment Inc. sponsored the Study of Chief Academic Officers in North American Theological Schools. This research provides the theological education community with its first, fully documented account of who academic officers are, what they do, and what role they play in the administration and governance of theological schools. As project director, I am pleased to present the findings of this study in this single volume and to add this more extensive and unified treatment of the research results to earlier publications on selected topics.[3]

This book aims to do more than construct a profile of chief academic officers and their work. Its more important task is to probe the research findings for the insight they offer into the challenges of the job, its singular potential for leadership, the cultivation and nurture of academic leaders, the problem of frequent turnover, and the meaning and value of administrative service. The exploration of such issues is intended to identify concerns critical to the deanship and to provide the information and analysis needed to address them. In doing so, this book seeks to stimulate fresh thinking about the reality and potential of the office, to convey what has been learned about effective administrative practice, and to renew efforts to strengthen academic leadership in theological schools.

## Purposes

Until recently, our knowledge of the work of chief academic officers was limited to a handful of personal accounts, an abundance of anecdotal evidence that was amusing and horrifying by turns, and studies of academic administration in higher education that applied only selectively to theological schools. Beyond the walls of individual schools, little was known about chief academic officers or the nature and scope of their administrative work. The first purpose of this book is to offer an informed understanding of the deanship in theological education based on the rich body of qualitative and quantitative data acquired through this research. An extensive survey, to which 75 percent of theological school deans responded, gives a reliable overview of the common features and variations among deanships in theological education. However, it is the personal interviews with chief academic officers and with the presidents, administrators, faculty members, students, trustees, and church leaders with whom they work that are the heart of this research. These conversations afford a multidimensional view of the work of chief academic officers, not in the abstract, but in the complex, dynamic context of institutional life and in relation to the many individuals and groups that comprise the academic community.

A second purpose of this book is to examine what constitutes effective practices, both on the part of deans in carrying out the responsibilities of office and on the part of theological schools in the hiring, evaluation, and professional development of academic administrators. Deans and their colleagues frequently expressed the need to know more about other theological schools and their administrative practices, about what has succeeded and failed. Through the experiences recounted in these pages, this book brings that conversation to every reader and provides a resource to all looking for guidance and perspective in their own situation.

Third, while this project clearly speaks to the current realities of academic administration, it does so in the hope that critical reflection on the present will be informed by the past and offer a reliable guide to the future. The evolution of the deanship from administrative assistant to the president to a position with broad managerial, leadership, and pastoral responsibilities signals the emergence of this new form of the office. This study urges theological school communities to consider how broadly or narrowly they are defining the dean's role and whether they are utilizing the potential of the office in ways that effectively address the needs of their institutions. Theological schools are encouraged to examine their own attitudes and practices in selecting academic officers, apportioning responsibilities, and tending to their professional growth and development. This book invites theological educators to think in new and constructive ways about the potential of the deanship and about the institutional policies and practices that support it.

Fourth, this book affirms the worthiness of the call to academic administration. The testimony of academic officers at diverse institutions and at various stages in their administrative service shows repeatedly that capable, committed people, many of whom never aspired to administration, can develop the skills and personal resources to serve successfully in the role. Everyone attests to the challenges of the job. Even the most skilled and experienced deans acknowledge their disappointments and failures; and even deans facing intractable personnel issues or daunting institutional problems speak of the job's satisfactions. This book seeks to render faithfully the balance between the challenges and rewards of academic administration and to show, in concrete and specific ways, how deans meet the challenges and find reward and meaning in administrative work.

## Themes

Several themes recurring throughout this book provide important clues to the enormous difficulty and promise of academic administration. These themes, introduced briefly here, are illustrated and amplified as the discussion progresses.

### *Complexity*

The complexity of the dean's work is evident initially in the responsibilities of office, which encompass virtually all aspects of the academic life. In fulfilling these duties, the dean works with the faculty, the president and senior administrators, the academic staff, students, board members, church leaders, and academic organizations. Each constituency has many members who have varied, sometimes conflicting expectations of academic officers. In working with these individuals and groups, the dean is called upon to serve as manager, leader, and pastor to the academic community. Each of these roles requires responsiveness to diverse needs, a range of personal aptitudes and skills, and an ability to maintain effective relationships with individuals whose personalities and concerns differ widely. The complexity of the dean's work is inherent not only in the broad scope of the dean's duties but in the multiple roles and relationships these duties require.

### *Centrality*

Another characteristic of the deanship confirmed in these chapters is the centrality of the office: its direct link to the mission of theological schools and its pivotal role in the daily conduct of institutional life. Despite impressive differences, theological schools have in common the purpose of educating students for various forms of religious ministry in the church and in the world. Within the schools, chief academic officers have the primary administrative responsibility for the academic programs and personnel on which these educational goals depend. In their leadership role, chief academic officers foster understanding and commitment to the mission and work with administrators, faculty, and other constituent groups to develop the curriculum, to build the faculty, to strengthen teaching, learning, and scholarship, and to nurture community life. This work is central to the distinctive mission of theological schools and the fundamental task of preparing men and women for religious leadership and service.

By virtue of these responsibilities, chief academic officers are located at the operational center of their institutions. Not only do chief academic officers have administrative responsibility for academic programs and personnel, they also serve as members of the senior administrative cabinet and, often, as "second in command" to the president. Since the majority of deans come from the faculty and maintain their faculty status through regular teaching and sometimes scholarship, they have dual citizenship as faculty members and administrators. The position is defined by their twofold allegiance to the faculty and the administration and by their service as representatives and advocates for both groups. The chief academic officer often is a vital link in the communication and cooperation between faculty and administrators, and among various constituent groups. Both the breadth of the dean's responsibilities and this intermediary role place the chief academic officer at the center of institutional life where relationships converge. This centrality underscores the complexity of the job and is fundamental to the leadership and pastoral work of the office.

In his book *Leadership Jazz*, Max DePree makes a distinction between being at the center of an organization and being at its heart. "CEOs and members of Congress and deans, by the nature of the power that accumulates around them, are at the center. They can't avoid it. Being at the center, being in control, differs from being at the heart."[4] Although this distinction is not fully elaborated in DePree's text, it is fertile in its potential to explain the difference between being at the operational center of the organization, which deans definitely are, and having the intellectual, emotional, and spiritual pulse of the group that makes leadership and community building possible. DePree acknowledges "rare and wonderful instances where a person is both at the center and at the heart."[5] The deanship has the capacity for both. This book is about "leading from the center," and also about the more intangible, but vital quality of "leading from the heart."

## *Link to the Presidency*

The history of the deanship in theological and higher education shows its direct and critical link to the presidency. The office of academic dean was created to assist the president by assuming administrative responsibility for the academic area and managing much of the daily operation of the institution in the president's absence. Throughout its history, the deanship has been defined in relation to the presidency, and the role and responsibilities of individual deans have taken shape according to the administrative style of their presidents and the needs of their institutions. The relationship of dean and president is foundational, and both the limits and possibilities of individual deanships are due largely to their presidents and the nature of the presidential office. As we shall see, the leadership potential of the chief academic officer position is dependent not only on the aptitudes and skills of particular officeholders but on a complex array of environmental factors and relationships. The dean-president relationship is foremost among them.

Changes in the presidency also have led to dramatic changes in the role and responsibilities of chief academic officers. As economic pressures have required presidents to become more externally focused and to spend a greater portion of their time on constituent relations and fundraising, chief academic officers have had increasing managerial and leadership responsibilities within their institutions. While individual schools may be at different stages in this process, the majority of executive and academic officers in this study attest to the prevalence and significance of this change. During its brief history, the position of chief academic officer has evolved from presidential assistant with well-defined clerical, record keeping, and organizational tasks to senior administrative officer with a broad range of managerial, leadership, and pastoral responsibilities. Our aim in this book is to examine this new form of the deanship and its implications for theological school communities, now and in the future.

## *Theological Context*

Many theological school deans have another important component to their work: its grounding in their own religious faith. Over half the theological school deans participating in the study found a sense of religious vocation or call important to accepting their administrative positions. Deans often spoke of their personal commitment to the church's ministry and to the seminary's mission of educating leaders for that ministry. Some felt their faithfulness to that ministry and mission sustained them in difficult times. Deans often referred to themselves as "servant leaders" whose primary role was to serve the faculty, the students, the seminary, and the church, and with them, to build the kingdom of God. Theological school deans frequently used concepts of vocation, service, and faithfulness to explain their administrative work and found much of its meaning and value rooted in their own religious beliefs. While having a religious anchor for one's personal and professional life is distinctive neither to members of seminaries nor to academic deans, its prevalence among academic officers in theological schools is noteworthy and essential to understanding their commitments and practices.

When a group of theological school faculty met during a site visit to discuss the dean's role, one faculty member admitted, "I really do think deans should walk on water." The others agreed. Colleagues often expect their deans to do the impossible and, as the biblical story suggests, to calm the turbulence of the waters and offer hope and reassurance. Deans, in turn, can sometimes feel that performing miracles is a real and definite part of their job description. If mastering the complexities and challenges of the job is tantamount to "walking on water," the stories of individual deans and their schools throughout this book confirm the persistence of such miracles.

## The Research

The Study of Chief Academic Officers in North American Theological Schools on which this book is based began in October 1993, with the data-gathering phase completed in June 1995, and analysis and writing concluded in December 1998. The project encompassed the broad and diverse range of institutions that had accredited, candidate, and associate status with the Association of Theological Schools in the United States and Canada (ATS). Of the 219 ATS-related schools in 1993–1994, 83 percent were denominational, 12 percent were interdenominational, and 5 percent were without denominational affiliation. Within this group, 14 percent were university-related, while the majority were freestanding or independent institutions. Throughout this book, the term "theological schools" is used inclusively to refer to the seminaries, divinity schools, theological colleges, schools of theology/religion, and other institutional members of ATS.

Relatively small compared to colleges and universities, theological schools have an average of 10 full-time faculty members and an average student headcount of 205.[6] While theological schools are similar in their basic structure and administration to other professional schools in higher education, they are distinguished by their mission of graduate education for ministry and, in many cases, by the direct relationship to churches and denominational bodies that requires.[7] This study of chief academic officers explores issues of academic administration and leadership in the distinctive context of theological schools.

The research was designed to collect both quantitative and qualitative information about the position, as well as ethnographic data on the institutional cultures that shape the role of the dean and provide the context for the dean's work. To achieve these goals, the project employed a variety of research methods:

- *Survey of Chief Academic Officers.* A survey dealing with a broad range of administrative issues was distributed to chief academic officers in all ATS-related schools. Theological schools in all categories of institutional size, type, affiliation, and location were well represented among survey respondents.
- *Site Visits.* The research team visited eleven theological schools in the United States and Canada to interview chief academic officers, presidents, and representatives of other constituent groups to gain multiple perspectives on the deanship and an understanding of the context for the deans' work.
- *Focus Groups.* To foster dialogue on the central issues of the research across institutional lines, the study sponsored five focus groups: two groups of chief academic officers and one group each of faculty members, presidents, and trustees.
- *Commissioned Essays.* The study commissioned six essays in which chief academic officers reflected on the daily work of academic administration, its rewards and challenges, and the lessons learned.

Appendix A provides a more complete account of each component of the study.

The research findings acquired from these sources are the basis for the analysis of the deanship that follows. These methods enabled us to record the impressive differences among individual deans and their institutions, as well as the common features of the position and how it functions in the schools.[8] While cognizant of the range and variety of deanships, this book focuses on the recurrent patterns, the shared characteristics and experiences that create a powerful, composite sketch of the dean's work. Just as this collective profile of the deanship is intended to inform individual experience, so the personal statements and stories of individual deans are intended to enliven and make concrete the generic data. I hope this interplay of the general and specific will be enriching in these ways.

In order to place results of this research in a broader context, this book draws upon related studies in theological education and literature on leadership and higher education administration insofar as they inform the central issues of this project. Unfortunately, there are few research-based studies of the deanship in higher education and none with recent data that can be meaningfully compared. Most fruitful are general studies of leadership and academic administration that deal with issues arising in theological school settings. A brief annotated bibliography of the most helpful sources is provided in Appendix C.

In the subsequent discussion, the term "chief academic officer" is used to refer to the administrator who has primary oversight of the daily operations of the academic area, including curriculum, academic programs, policy, and, in some cases, academic personnel and budgets. The title given to this office in theological education varies with institutional traditions and structures. In 1993, 66 percent of academic officers in freestanding theological schools were titled dean or academic dean, and 12 percent were academic vice president or provost. In most university divinity schools, the associate dean for academic affairs is the nearest equivalent.[9] In the small group of schools where an academic officer is not designated, we studied the single position in which academic and executive functions are combined. This book and other reports on this study use the most common terms "dean" and "academic dean" generically to refer to all who hold the chief academic officer position. Similarly, chief executive officers in theological schools are variously entitled president, rector, dean, or principal, depending on their institutional contexts. Consistent with other research, this book uses the term "president" to refer to all chief executive officers.[10]

Survey respondents and participants in site visit interviews were assured, as a matter of research policy, that their responses would remain confidential. Consequently, throughout this book, neither institutions nor individuals will be cited by name, and some incidental characteristics may be omitted or changed to protect their identities.

## Overview of Content

To appreciate the complexity of the dean's duties and the centrality of the office within academic communities, it is necessary first to understand the basic structure of the chief academic officer position. Chapter One discusses the historical and organizational contexts for the dean's work, the nature and scope of decanal responsibilities, and their cumulative effect on the workload of the office. Knowing what deans do is fundamental to understanding their role and how they carry out their broad responsibilities. Chapter Two examines the managerial and leadership functions of the office, with particular attention to concepts and practices of leadership within theological schools. An analysis of academic governance reveals that, while leadership typically is shared among various constituent groups, the chief academic officer has a distinctive role that derives from the nature of the office. This chapter examines the dean's leadership role within the institution and, based on site visit data, provides models of good leadership practice.

At the heart of the dean's administrative and leadership roles are relationships with the president or chief executive officer on the one hand, and with the faculty, individually and collectively, on the other. In Chapters Three and Four, theological school deans offer candid personal accounts of their efforts to develop strong, effective working relationships with the president and the faculty. Chapter Four adds to the earlier discussion of the dean's work with faculty in governance by examining the dean's pastoral role, specifically the dean's responsibility for building the faculty, supporting their professional growth, and creating community. Chapter Five considers the dean's role in working with senior administrators, board members, and church leaders on behalf of the academic area. This chapter underscores the breadth of the dean's constituent relationships and the challenge of coordinating the needs and interests of these diverse groups.

The second part of the book shifts from concerns of institutional leadership to personal issues of vocation and professional development. Chapters Six and Seven examine three institutional practices—hiring, evaluation, and professional development—and show their critical importance in securing and maintaining effective academic leadership. Chapter Eight discusses prevailing attitudes toward administrative work in theological schools and the reasons why individuals choose to enter and to leave administrative service. The book concludes with an assessment of challenges facing the theological education community, with particular attention to where academic leaders will come from and what they will need to deal with the increasing complexity of theological school administration.

## Audience

The Study of Chief Academic Officers in North American Theological Schools was undertaken to address the need for an informed understanding of academic administration and leadership among both the internal constituents and external publics of theological schools. This book, therefore, has several audiences. First and most importantly, it offers theological school deans a comprehensive account of the work of the office and critical assessment of its costs and rewards, its limitations and possibilities. The response of theological school deans to a variety of issues will enable individual officeholders to gain perspective on their daily work and reassurance that their experience is widely shared. In the words of their colleagues, deans will find conversation partners whose practical advice and personal reflections may enhance the meaning and value of their own ministry.

This book also aims to contribute to the discernment of prospective deans and of theological schools in search of academic leaders. To candidates for the deanship, it offers a realistic account of the dean's work and the aptitudes and skills it requires, which may help individuals assess their personal call to administrative service. To theological schools in search of deans, it stresses the importance of clarifying the role and responsibilities of the office and developing appropriate methods for the recruitment and professional development of academic officers. This book will have succeeded if it helps prospective deans choose administration knowingly and theological schools choose their deans wisely.[11]

To presidents, senior administrators, and faculty who work closely with deans, this book gives a clear view of the interdependence of their roles and what is needed to develop effective working relationships. Faculty, in particular, will gain insight to their relationship to the chief academic officer, their respective roles in governance, and their shared responsibility for collegial decision-making practices. In addition to exploring the dynamics of the dean's relationship to senior administrators, this book examines the distinctive role presidents play in defining the dean's work, developing the potential of the office, and creating the partnership on which effective academic administration and leadership depend. Understanding chief academic officers in relation to their colleagues is essential to appreciating the interdependence of administrators and faculty within the academy and the importance of maintaining cooperative and mutually supportive working relationships.

To advisory and governing board members, church leaders, and others associated with theological schools, this study aims to demystify the role of the chief academic officer and to underscore the vital leadership of the office in creating quality theological education. Based on personal interviews with seminary personnel and members of these groups, this study examines how boards and church leaders work with the dean and faculty to shape academic decisions and to influence the direction of their institutions. Board members without firsthand experience of theological education will gain perspective on their role in academic governance and will discover ways to make a positive contribution to the decision-making process.

This book also is addressed to academic administrators and researchers in other areas of higher education. While there are several current books on the presidency, there are few on the deanship and none in recent years based on empirical research with a broad population. I hope this study will inform the experience of deans in colleges and universities whose work differs in scale but whose challenges and satisfactions may be remarkably similar. Finally, I hope this project stimulates further research on the deanship, within and outside of theological education, to extend, confirm, and correct the findings of the present study.

## Notes

[1] Data on the turnover of chief academic officers is obtained from the Association of Theological Schools in the United States and Canada (ATS). The ATS *Directory and Membership List*, published in September of each year, contains the only continuous record of chief academic officers and chief executive officers in theological schools. Analysis of this information from 1987 to 1997, when the number of ATS-related schools ranged from 205 to 229, shows the average annual rate of change in the chief academic officer position is 25 percent, with a high of 31 percent in 1992 and a low of 18 percent in 1994. This is considerably greater than the 16 percent average annual rate of change for chief executive officers. These figures may be conservative, since changes of short duration occurring between the reporting dates are not recorded.

These rates of administrative turnover in theological education are comparable to those in U.S. colleges and universities. In 1987–1988, at the beginning of this ten-year period, the turnover rate for college and university chief academic officers was 24 percent and for presidents 17 percent. See D. E. Blum, "24 Pct. Turnover Rate Found for Administrators: Some Officials Are Surprised by Survey Results," *The Chronicle of Higher Education* (March 29, 1989), A1-A14.

[2] Among the theological schools with accredited, candidate, and associate status with ATS, 48 percent had three or more deans in the ten-year period from 1987 to 1997, and 22 percent had four or more deans.

[3] The study is described briefly later in the Introduction and more fully in Appendix A. Other publications on this research are listed in Appendix C.

[4] Max DePree, *Leadership Jazz* (New York: Dell Publishing, 1992), 35.

[5] DePree, 35.

[6] This data is provided by the Association of Theological Schools. In 1993–1994, theological schools ranged in size from 1 to 90 full-time faculty members (mean of 10), with a faculty full-time equivalent (FTE) ranging from 1 to 134 (mean of 13). Student headcount ranged from 14 to 3,458 (mean of 205), with a student FTE ranging from 13 to 2,507 (mean of 130).

[7] Of the 57 different denominations listed by the Association of Theological Schools in 1993–1994, all were within the Christian tradition.

[8] Throughout this book, all reports of differences among deans based on survey data are statistically significant at a level less than or equal to .05, unless otherwise indicated. Survey responses to most questions were subjected to statistical analysis based on institutional differences of size, denominational affiliation, and type (freestanding or university/college affiliated) and on differences among respondents based on gender, race, and years in position. Most of the statistically significant differences are reported.

[9] The significance of these different titles for the work of the office is discussed in Chapter One.

[10] Neely Dixon McCarter, *The President as Educator: A Study of the Seminary Presidency*, Studies in Theological Education (Atlanta, GA: Scholars Press, 1996), 6.

[11] I am indebted to Project Advisory Committee member, James Hudnut-Beumler, for this formulation.

# 1 The Nature and Scope of the Dean's Work

*"When a theological community really works—and serves—you can be certain that a creative dean is at the center of it."*

*James L. Waits*

Nothing more clearly establishes the complexity of the deanship, its potential for leadership, and its centrality within theological schools than the broad responsibilities that define the office. These responsibilities, in turn, account for the multiple roles and relationships at the heart of the dean's work. To understand the managerial, leadership, and pastoral roles of the office, to understand the dean in relation to the many individuals and groups that comprise theological school communities, we must first understand what deans are called upon to do. Examining the responsibilities of office and their implications for the dean's daily work affords a first glimpse of both the burdens and deep rewards of the job.

The duties of current theological school deans are rooted in both an historical and organizational context. This chapter begins by examining the origin of the deanship in American higher education over a century ago. How the office was created, how duties were defined, and how the first deans were chosen shed considerable light on the chief academic officer position today. This brief account of the evolution of the deanship establishes the fundamental character of the office and, somewhat paradoxically, reveals both the continuity between its early history and current practice and significant changes in the nature of the dean's responsibilities. Theological school deans are a product of that history and, in many cases, models of a new form of the office for which academic leadership and community building are basic requirements.

The chief academic officers, who are the subject of this research, carry out their responsibilities in the context of graduate theological schools. While the character of theological school communities is elaborated throughout this book, this chapter deals with two of their fundamental features: the mission of the schools, which not only defines their distinctive purposes but establishes the dean's central and critical role in fulfilling them; and their administrative structures, which locate the deanship relative to the larger organization and its primary constituents. As our analysis shows, the importance of the chief academic officer position derives less from its senior administrative status than from the direct connection between the responsibilities of office and the purposes of graduate theological education. These historical and organizational considerations provide a framework for understanding the role and responsibilities of chief academic officers in theological education today.

The principal focus of this chapter is on the specific duties of theological school deans. Based on findings of the Study of Chief Academic Officers, we examine the nature and scope of the deans' responsibilities, their implications for the total workload, and the range of relationships they require. Our concern is twofold: to assess the cumulative effect of the responsibilities, workload, and relationships on individual officeholders and to identify the conditions that make the dean's leadership possible. As we shall see, the dean's pivotal position within the theological school community and capacity for academic leadership are an outgrowth of the broad responsibilities that accrued to the office from its earliest days. This general profile of the context and content of the dean's work will provide the foundation for exploring, in Chapter Two, the role of deans and how they carry out their multifaceted responsibilities.

## Evolution of the Deanship

The office of academic dean has a remarkably short history. As John Wesley Gould explains, there were no deans in the seventeenth and eighteenth centuries when American higher education was in its infancy. "It was in the latter half of the nineteenth century, when presidents began to feel the need for someone to relieve them of record- and housekeeping chores, that deans were designated."[1] In 1870, when the office of the Dean of the College Faculty was created at Harvard, the president explained that "both the Governors and the Alumni thought that the President had too much to do, and that he should be relieved of the immediate charge of the College administration."[2] The dean was appointed from the faculty to assist the president and, while remaining actively engaged in teaching, took on a broad range of administrative responsibilities.[3] By 1885 only fifteen deanships had been established, but by 1913 the office was already "quite universal."[4]

From the beginning, the deanship was derived from the presidency and its duties were defined in relation to that office. As institutions grew in size and complexity, the president's responsibilities expanded and changed. When schools were small, the president typically handled all matters pertaining to faculty and students. Gerald E. Dupont explains, "With the growth of enrollments after 1900, the president found himself more and more engaged in making contacts and raising funds. His frequent absences from campus obliged him to delegate certain functions to members of the staff, to committees, or to other officers of the college."[5] The position of dean was created to handle the overflow of duties from the president. As a result, the responsibilities of deans were broad and inclusive. According to Dupont,

> . . . the dean was not only the head of the faculty and the director of the instructional work of the college, but very often performed the disciplinary functions, now ordinarily assigned to the deans of men and women, and the functions of admissions, record keeping, and advising, now most often assigned to deans of admission, registrars, and guidance counselors.[6]

Not surprisingly, the dean's office also became overburdened in time, and additional administrative layers were added to handle the load. The first deans were precursors not only of present-day academic officers but of registrars, deans of students, directors of admissions, advisors, and counselors.

The deanship in theological schools originated much later than in other areas of higher education but followed a similar pattern. Although deans were appointed in university divinity schools near the turn of the century, the deanship did not become widely established in freestanding Protestant seminaries until the 1950s and in Roman Catholic seminaries until the 1960s.[7] As in higher education generally, the office of academic dean was created in theological schools to provide administrative assistance to the president. Since the addition of administrative offices is linked historically to growth in the size and complexity of institutions, the fact that theological schools remained relatively small compared to colleges and universities may help to explain the late arrival of the deanship and other administrative offices. However, since the mid-1960s, enrollment declines in some schools and decreasing contributions from sponsoring denominations necessitated that even presidents of small institutions focus on external relations and fundraising.[8] As presidents' responsibilities broadened, they had to rely on other administrators for help in managing the institution. Foremost among those administrators was the academic dean.

Even this brief sketch reveals several characteristics of the deanship that are significant for the subsequent development of the office. First, historical accounts show that the evolution of the dean's office runs parallel to developments in the presidency. Since the deanship was defined in relation to the presidency, the dean's duties from the outset were both academically focused and broadly institutional. In the president's absence, the dean often served as stand-in for the president on campus and shared responsibility for the daily, internal operation of the school. The current trend of having academic officers serve as chief operating officers has its roots in the original purpose for which the office was created.

Second, in light of the differences among individual presidents and their institutions, deans' offices tended to lack uniformity in their organization and structure. The dean's duties were susceptible to changes with the changing needs of the presidency. In a review of studies of the dean's office between 1929 and 1947, Dupont confirms significant differences among schools in the structure of the office and in the configuration of responsibilities.[9] While the dean's work had some common features across institutions, the specific duties of deans also varied from one position to another.

A third characteristic of the deanship is that officeholders traditionally were selected from among the faculty and retained some of their faculty duties while serving as academic administrators. Accounts of the early years of the deanship at Harvard indicate that trustees were concerned to keep their dean's administrative work at a reasonable level so that he could maintain his teaching responsibilities. As an active scholar/teacher, the dean gained credibility as leader of the academic area. Since growing administrative demands on the executive office made it increasingly difficult for presidents to maintain their scholarship and teaching, deans who typically were chosen from senior faculty ranks served as models of academic vitality and accomplishment. The early practice of appointing academic deans from among the faculty has persisted with some modifications to the present day. Colleges, universities, and theological schools continue to seek chief academic officers who have experience in the professoriate and an established academic record.[10] Consequently, the majority of deans have dual citizenship, as faculty members and as administrators, and much of their work is within and between those worlds.

Despite these continuities in the development of the office, the change in the nature of the deans' responsibilities has been dramatic. The majority of chief academic officers in theological schools today seem only distantly related to their forebears. While deans continue to have important managerial duties, they also have significant responsibility for academic leadership and governance, for developing the faculty, and for building community life. The office has changed not merely quantitatively with an expansion of duties, but qualitatively with the addition of duties of a different kind. The enormity of this change is evident when early descriptions of the dean's "record- and housekeeping chores" are compared to current responsibilities and the full range of managerial, leadership, and pastoral skills they require. The profile of theological school deans today, based on data from the Study of Chief Academic Officers, documents nothing less than the emergence of a new form of the office.

The evolution of the deanship from administrative assistant to a position of significant institutional leadership often is linked to increasing organizational complexity and changing demands on the presidential office. Despite differences in the rate of change among individual schools, seminary presidents commonly report that in recent years their responsibilities have shifted steadily from direct involvement in the academic life of the institution and daily contact with faculty and students to resource development and work with the board, civic and denominational leaders, and other constituents outside the school. As discussed more fully in Chapter Three, one result of this shift has been delegation of operational duties to senior administrators and significant growth in the administrative and leadership responsibilities of academic officers.

## Organizational Context

The work of chief academic officers is inevitably shaped by many organizational factors, ranging from institutional history and traditions to organizational structure and culture to current economic and social realities. Two aspects of the theological school context serve to place the chief academic officer within the larger organization: the distinctive mission of the schools and their organizational structure. The former establishes the basic purposes of theological education and their direct connection to the work of the chief academic officer; and the latter locates the chief academic officer position relative to other senior administrators and faculty.

*Institutional Mission*

Robert K. Greenleaf begins his essay, "Mission in a Seminary," by observing: "One of the easiest to ask and hardest to answer of all questions is, *What are you trying to do?*"[11] In their mission statements, theological schools attempt to answer this question by articulating their fundamental aims and purposes. Among the diverse group of North American theological schools in this study, mission statements reveal the common goals of graduate theological education and, in doing so, establish the central role of chief academic officers in achieving them.

The mission of theological schools, most generally stated, is to prepare students for various forms of religious ministry in the church and the world. While individual schools may focus on particular types of ministry, the representative group of schools in the study, collectively, aimed to educate students to serve as ordained pastors of the church, denominational leaders, educators, researchers, pastoral counselors, chaplains, church musicians, spiritual directors, community workers, and missionaries. As theological schools prepare men and women for religious leadership and service, they also strive to *be* communities that exemplify these values. Both through their members and graduates, theological schools seek to lead, to serve, and to contribute to theological, moral, and spiritual discourse in the church, in the academy, and in public life. These several related purposes of the schools reveal their intended reach to the larger society beyond their own walls.

Because theological schools so directly influence the quality of religious thought and religious life, the work of chief academic officers in fulfilling the mission of the schools becomes vitally important. Theological schools accomplish their educational purposes primarily through their academic programs and personnel. Chief academic officers work closely with faculty to develop and maintain the curriculum and academic programs and to create an environment in which student learning and formation can flourish. Academic officers have significant responsibility for the hiring of faculty, for their development as teachers and scholars, and for support of their service to the academy and the church. As senior academic officers, their responsibility is to keep the community focused on the mission and goals of a theological education and to bring constituents together in an effort to fulfill them. Chief academic officers, by virtue of their roles and responsibilities, are charged with guarding and enhancing the quality of all facets of the academic life. Nothing could be more central to the mission than this.

*Administrative Structure*

This critical link between the work of academic officers and the mission of their institutions is supported by their location within the larger organizational structure of theological schools. When the Association of Theological Schools in the United States and Canada (ATS) classifies its member institutions as either independent/freestanding or university/college-affiliated, it is signaling a structural difference that has important implications for administration and governance.

Freestanding schools, which account for approximately 85 percent of the ATS membership, are structured to function independently, and each typically includes its own governing board and president or chief executive officer. While freestanding schools may develop cooperative relationships with other institutions and share some resources, their funding and governance processes tend to be independent. In these schools, the chief academic officer reports directly to the president and serves with other senior administrators (e.g., vice presidents for business, development, student affairs, etc.) as a member of the president's administrative team or cabinet. In turn, the chief academic officer typically oversees a group of division, department, and/or program heads who represent the principal areas of the academic program. In a few of the larger theological schools, there may be an additional administrative layer wherein a provost or academic vice president is the chief academic officer to whom deans, representing academic divisions or schools, report.

The 15 percent of theological schools that are university/college-affiliated are described by ATS as "integral parts of larger institutions that possess at least two other professional schools or departments at the graduate level."[12] While the university/college-affiliated theological schools may resemble freestanding schools in their internal organization and procedures, they differ markedly in their dependence on university approval for their funding and governance. In the university context, the chief executive officer is the dean of the school who, in turn, reports to the university provost or academic vice president and represents the school to the university administration and its governing board. While the theological school may have an advisory board or board of visitors and administrative officers of its own, its governance and administration are subject to university oversight. In many schools, the theological school dean is assisted by an associate academic dean whose function approximates that of the academic dean in a freestanding school. In schools without a designated academic officer, the dean is considered both the executive and the academic officer.

Given the distinctive histories and traditions of theological schools, structural variations may exist within the broad categories of freestanding and university-related institutions. However, in both types of schools, the chief academic officer reports to the chief executive officer and, in turn, oversees the administrative heads of academic divisions, departments, and programs. In schools with other senior administrators, the chief academic officer serves as a member of the president's team or cabinet and often is designated as "first among equals" within that group. Chief academic officers also serve the faculty as their institutional representative and have administrative responsibility for the academic area, including academic programs, policy, and planning, and various activities relating to faculty recruitment, evaluation, and professional development.[13]

In all types of institutions, the chief academic officer is a senior administrator who works closely with the president, other administrative officers, and the faculty in the academic governance of the school. The chief academic officer's central role in the conduct of academic life and in the fulfillment of the institutional mission are requisite to understanding the multifaceted responsibilities of the office and the complexity of the dean's work.

## Responsibilities

Appreciating the daily life of the academic dean requires an imaginative leap for those without direct experience of the office. As this chapter describes the dean's responsibilities sequentially, the reader must imagine their cumulative effect—the variety and sheer quantity of tasks, the range of skills they require, the pace of the work, the stresses, the inevitability of long days, sometimes sleepless nights, and almost always too much to do. Getting inside an average day in the life of a dean requires that we keep the several components of this linear description of duties in mind at once, that we be attentive not only to the work but to the workload, not only to the content of the job but to its implicit pressures and demands. Our concern is both the responsibilities of office and their effect on the daily life of the academic dean.

The story of one particular dean, who for six years served as the chief academic officer of an urban, denominational seminary, introduces in a concrete and personal way the central themes of this chapter. His account reveals the multifaceted nature of the dean's work and the difficulty of balancing its competing demands.

> "I didn't start out to be an academic administrator," he begins. After twenty-one years in theological education and five years on the faculty at his present seminary, he was asked to be dean following the resignation of his predecessor. In addition to his administrative work, he teaches half of a full-time faculty load and spends one day a week off-campus to do his scholarly work and to edit a professional journal. Despite his best efforts, he admits, "I am not at the same place in the scholarly pecking order that I was ten years ago. There's a sense of grief," he adds, "but most of the time I think it's worth the sacrifice."
>
> His daily schedule is full to overflowing. "I am responsible for all the academic programs and activities," he explains, including curriculum, faculty hiring and evaluation, academic planning, and budgets. He estimates that a full ten hours per week are spent in committee meetings alone, with another ten or more hours spent meeting individually with other administrators, faculty, and students. Twenty-five percent of his time is spent on paperwork. He also is the senior administrator primarily responsible for the daily operations of the school and for cooperation with a consortium of area seminaries—a time-consuming part of his workload.
>
> His office is understaffed. He would like an administrative assistant to help with scheduling and other tasks, and he believes that academic advising could be handled elsewhere in the school. "Too many days," he explains, "I am caught up in putting fires out. I think it's a full-time job." He laments how little time remains for strategic issues. "The trouble with delegation is that everyone delegates up, so you have to guard against that."
>
> "The difficulty is that you're thrust into the position without much preparation and with no training." He has found "there's twice as much work as you think there is and you need to protect your time, learn how to say no." He has a conflict of values in trying to keep up with his teaching and scholarly work, while at the same time trying to be an effective administrator. "The job is taxing physically, and there's lots of stress. The challenges are so significant that the job requires every minute of waking life seven days a week." In balance, however, he feels good about administrative work and has enjoyed being part of institutional change. "I've been a new person during the last six years, and it's something I never imagined myself doing."

This story, with a few minor changes, could be the story of countless other seminary deans. It raises questions about the nature and scope of the dean's responsibilities, about the balance of academic and administrative duties, about the total workload, and about the sacrifices and rewards of the job.

Describing the responsibilities of chief academic officers seems a straightforward task, until one considers the many factors that complicate such description. The first and most obvious factor is the difference among theological schools in their size, structure, denominational affiliations, histories, and cultures, as well as in their current needs and priorities. Such institutional characteristics can determine how responsibilities are distributed among senior administrators, what particular configuration of duties is assigned to the chief academic officer, and what areas of responsibility are the primary focus at a given time. Consequently, the responsibilities of deans can vary from one institution to another.

In the Study of Chief Academic Officers in Theological Schools, 87 percent of survey respondents indicated that institutional documents defined their responsibilities. However, site visit interviews revealed that the priority given to specific duties and the overall balance among them was considerably more fluid than job descriptions suggested. At the time of our visits, several of the deans interviewed were eager to reconfigure their duties to eliminate registrar and advising functions, for example, or to increase their involvement in faculty hiring, advancement, and salary decisions. At several institutions, presidents and deans noted the difficulty of keeping job descriptions current. The content of the dean's work in any given year was susceptible to staffing and budgetary changes, new institutional priorities, increasing demands on the president, and a variety of other planned and unplanned changes. Responsibilities often shifted subtly and gradually. As one president observed, "Although there are no changes structurally, the dean's office now is more harassed in terms of the amount of administration. It now feels like the dean is responsible for more things."

The effort to keep job descriptions fluid can also be deliberate in recognition of both changing conditions within the institution and the dynamic character of the relationship between the executive and academic officers. Not only are the dean's duties defined in relation to the presidency, but the individuals occupying both offices work out many of the particulars of their responsibilities and authority continuously in the course of their daily work. As one seminary president explained, his own strong involvement in shaping the institution required that the relationship with the chief academic officer remain dynamic: "It's going to be difficult to have job descriptions that spell it all out. Some of it has to work out in terms of the evolving of the interpersonal relationship—trust, really good communication. . . ." The dean conveyed the same idea a bit differently: "If you're dealing with persons with multiple gifts and/or interests, they're not going to have segmentalized job descriptions and roles. You need to work collegially . . . have trust. Without trust, you'd better have clearly defined boxes."

Any account of the work of the dean's office must acknowledge the organic nature of the president-dean relationship and the fact that some responsibilities may be defined by implicit understanding rather than explicit description. This is not to deny, however, the advantages of well-defined duties and expectations or the dangers inherent in operating with a vague sense of the parameters of the job. We will consider this topic more fully in the context of the dean-president relationship in Chapter Three.

While recognizing that differences exist in the specific responsibilities of deans from different theological schools, the 1993 survey conducted as part of the Study of Chief Academic Officers enables us to create a composite sketch of the responsibilities of the office. Although a general profile cannot capture the varied combinations of duties in individual positions, it does afford an overview of the type and range of responsibilities that characterize the chief academic officer position.

The following description of what deans do focuses on three interrelated areas of responsibility: the dean as scholar/teacher, the dean as academic administrator, and the dean as senior officer of the institution. These categories are not intended to rigidly compartmentalize duties that frequently overlap in actual practice, but to highlight broad, distinguishable areas of the dean's work. These responsibilities provide important clues to the paradoxical nature of the job. On the one hand, the sheer quantity of these duties and the challenge of balancing their competing demands on a daily basis contribute to the overload and job-related stresses commonly reported by deans. On the other hand, the breadth of these responsibilities and the range of relationships they require establish the centrality of the chief academic officer position and ultimately account for its distinctive leadership role within the schools.

### *Dean as Teacher/Scholar*

What we learn from the early history of the deanship in higher education and from this research on theological school deans is that the majority of chief academic officers come to their positions directly from the faculty and remain active as teachers and/or scholars during their administrative service. While deans have personal reasons for maintaining a significant level of teaching and scholarship, many consider it essential to their credibility and effectiveness as administrators. For the majority of deans, these activities are not incidental to academic administration but an integral and necessary part of it.

The profile of chief academic officers serving in theological schools during the 1993–1994 academic year shows the strength and character of their faculty citizenship. According to survey data, 88 percent of academic deans had experience as full-time faculty members prior to assuming their administrative positions. It may not be surprising, then, that over 98 percent of these deans had doctoral degrees and, in schools granting rank and tenure, over 87 percent had rank and over 75 percent were tenured. Having served as full-time faculty members for an average of eight years, deans tended to be ranked at the Associate or Professor level. In 1993, the majority of theological school deans (65 percent) came to administration directly from faculty positions.[14]

The activities of deans once in office indicate they not only come *from* the faculty but remain *of* the faculty. In 1993, 93 percent of academic officers continued to teach while serving as administrators, and, of those who taught, 77 percent taught every term, and 95 percent taught at least once a year.[15] Credit-hour reports suggest that most deans were teaching standard courses, with some carrying a half-time faculty course load. In addition, 43 percent of deans indicated that scholarship was expected or required of them as academic administrators, and among those for whom it was optional, several remained committed to an active scholarly life. Of the eleven deans interviewed for this study, seven dedicated time to their scholarly work and were writing and publishing on a regular basis.

What these data do not fully reveal are the myriad duties that come with regular teaching and ongoing scholarship. In addition to classroom hours, teaching also includes course preparation, grading, student conferences, and advising. Deans who strive to remain current in their scholarship require time for study, writing, and sometimes travel to do their research and to meet with colleagues. Although only 38 percent of deans surveyed are *required* to teach, and only 3 percent are *required* to be productive scholars, many more see these activities as essential to their administrative role and to their personal and professional vitality.[16] Ten of the eleven deans interviewed for the study consider teaching critical to their administrative effectiveness. They note that teaching keeps them involved with their disciplines, mindful of the challenges of the classroom, and in touch with students and their needs. They find that teaching and scholarship keep them engaged in the academic life and give them credibility with their faculty colleagues.

In site visit interviews, several deans who were trying to maintain their teaching and scholarship felt that both tended to suffer with the press of other demands. One dean, who continued to teach, said that if he also tried to keep up with his scholarship, he would "be completely crazy." In his view, a dean must have a commitment to faculty growth and development and "a willingness to subjugate one's own academic ambitions vis-à-vis publications, etc., so that others might be able to [publish]." Another dean continues to teach because, he says, "it's very central to my own self-worth"; he also tries "to maintain some kind of life as a scholar." He highly values both teaching and scholarship and admits he "cannot do the job without them." Yet another dean feels pressured to continue his scholarship, since his own reputation is critical when judging faculty scholarship for hiring and retention decisions. Thus, he devotes much of the summer to his own scholarly work. While deans vary in the balance they personally achieve between teaching/scholarship and the demands of academic administration, their ability to find that balance can be important to their tenure in the role.

Despite the personal challenge of coordinating academic and administrative responsibilities, most deans readily acknowledge the value of their ongoing faculty work. While deans report that their move into administration often distances them from their faculty colleagues, their continued identification with faculty and understanding of their needs and concerns are critical to their own effectiveness as academic officers. When a dean works with colleagues to shape curriculum and academic programs, to build the faculty, and to uphold standards of teaching and scholarship, the dean's active presence as a teacher/scholar gives evidence of a personal commitment to and understanding of the academic life. Often, it is as a respected member of the faculty that the dean earns credibility as an academic administrator.

### *Dean as Academic Administrator*

While most chief academic officers (93 percent) are engaged in teaching and many continue their scholarship, it is their administrative responsibility for the academic area that constitutes the central work of the office. As the senior administrator whose primary responsibility is oversight of academic programs, policy, personnel, and planning, the chief academic officer works with the president, other administrators, faculty, staff, and students in carrying out the educational mission of the institution. A closer look at the principal areas of responsibility shows that, as numerous and varied as those responsibilities may be, there is considerable commonality among deanships in theological schools.

On the 1993 survey of theological school deans, respondents were asked to identify those academic areas for which they had the primary administrative responsibility at their institutions. Table 1 below lists those areas and gives the percentage of survey respondents who indicated primary responsibility in each area. Significant in this listing is the sizable percentage of deans from diverse institutional contexts who have similar responsibilities. While many of these duties are combined and weighted differently in individual positions, there is considerable congruence among deans from different types of schools.[17] In the first seven areas listed, more than 80 percent of deans have the same general administrative responsibilities.

**Table 1**
**Areas for which Deans have Primary Administrative Responsibility**

| | % of deans with primary responsibility |
|---|---|
| Academic priorities and planning | 96% |
| Curriculum and academic programs | 95% |
| Academic policy | 93% |
| Preparing for accreditation | 85% |
| Faculty evaluation | 83% |
| Faculty development | 83% |
| Academic budgets | 82% |
| Hiring academic personnel | 71% |
| Faculty promotion and tenure | 68% |
| Daily internal operations | 60% |
| Academic advising of students | 39% |
| Faculty salaries | 37% |
| Spiritual advising/formation | 17% |
| Fundraising for academic programs | 10% |

Virtually all deans have the primary administrative responsibility for academic priorities and planning, curriculum and academic programs, and academic policy.[18] When survey respondents were asked which of their responsibilities was most important and central to their work, 80 percent identified "curriculum and academic programs." In this area, deans also felt they were "most prepared and effective" and had "worked most successfully with faculty." Confidence in dealing with curriculum and academic programs may reflect the fact that most deans had experience as faculty members prior to their administrative appointments.

In their work with faculty, over 80 percent of deans are responsible for evaluation and development; approximately 70 percent for faculty hiring, promotion, and tenure; but only 37 percent for faculty salaries. In financial matters, a far greater percentage of deans are responsible for departmental and program budgets in the academic area (82 percent) than are responsible for determining faculty salaries (37 percent). While presidents may consult with their chief academic officers about faculty salaries, the majority still retain control of this sizable part of the institutional budget.

Worth noting, however, is an increase in academic planning and a decrease in spiritual advising/formation among deans who have been in their positions less than five years.[19] While these data cannot be fully interpreted without a longitudinal study, they seem to signal a shift in the dean's role toward decreasing responsibility for student services, for which specialized personnel are often hired, and increasing involvement in institutional administration with attention to priorities and planning. A significant 60 percent of deans consider themselves primarily responsible for the daily internal operations of the school. This reflects both the breadth of the duties of the office and the currency of one of the purposes for which the deanship was originally created, to oversee operations in the absence of the president.

Deans vary considerably in the amount of direct interaction they have with students. Thirty-nine percent of survey respondents indicated they had primary responsibility for academic advising. Interviews further indicated that deans perform a variety of tasks relating to the academic status of students: evaluating transcripts, granting waivers and exemptions, dealing with academic problems and concerns, monitoring academic progress, certifying students for graduation, and the like. These academic matters are the dean's responsibility, even if others are in charge of nonacademic student services and spiritual formation. Deans in schools with an active and organized student government tend to have frequent interaction with student leaders and appoint student representatives to faculty and institutional committees. Through their teaching, deans have regular contact with students enrolled in their courses and frequently cite the opportunity to stay in touch with students as one of the principal benefits of continued teaching. One dean explained, however, that he knows many fewer students now; when he was teaching full-time, he knew almost everyone in the school.

Several of the deans interviewed lamented their limited opportunities for positive contact with students. As one dean explained, "I now see students only when they have problems or are in trouble."

Not only do chief academic officers work with the heads of academic departments and programs, but many supervise other professional administrators whose work is related to the academic area (e.g., director of the library, director of continuing education, registrar, assistant dean, etc.). When asked on the survey about the number of administrative staff reporting directly to them, deans indicated an average of 3.2 administrators, with as many as 12 reported by some deans.[20] While some of these administrators, such as associate or assistant deans, may be assisting with the work of the dean's office, others have separate areas of responsibility but are accountable to the dean. In either case, the chief academic officer must be concerned with personnel, operations, and budgets of these units on a regular basis. Depending on the number of administrators reporting to the dean, these supervisory responsibilities can be substantial.

What this brief overview of the responsibilities of the office does not convey are the many appointments, calls, committee meetings, informal conversations, memos, reports, and other activities that these administrative duties require. Each area of responsibility entails numerous tasks and regular contact with individuals and groups at all levels of the organization. These duties and relationships have significant implications for the total workload of the office.

### *Dean as Senior Officer of the Institution*

In addition to the administrative responsibilities for the academic area that define the deanship, a second administrative role figures prominently in the work of the office. The dean reports to the president, serves as a member of the president's administrative team or cabinet, and often is designated as "second in command" to the president with broad operational responsibilities in the president's absence. The chief academic officer, by whatever title, has a group of administrative peers, usually consisting of directors or vice presidents of development, business, student affairs or formation, administrative services, and the like. These individuals constitute the senior administrative staff of the school. Since virtually all other areas are related to the academic area in some way, the chief academic officer has frequent substantive dealings with other administrators. In the daily life of the dean, this means taking part in numerous meetings, conversations, and negotiations on an array of academic and other institutional issues.

Although senior administrators have certain duties that define the distinctive work of their offices, responsibilities for the overall functioning of the organization typically are shared by the president, the chief academic officer, and other administrators. Activities such as building support for things that need to be done, solving short-term problems, stimulating creative thinking and change, promoting cultural diversity, building cooperation and trust rarely are the sole responsibility of any one person but are carried simultaneously by several individuals. This is not to suggest, however, that such responsibilities are distributed evenly. On the survey, deans were asked to identify the individuals and groups at their institutions who had the primary responsibility for such organizational tasks. Seventy-six percent of deans felt they had the primary responsibility for developing faculty leadership, and 56 percent for interpreting policies and procedures to others. Survey responses show that presidents and deans in about equal numbers have the primary responsibility for building support for things that need to be done, stimulating creative thinking and change, and promoting cultural diversity, and about an equal number of deans and other administrators have primary responsibility for solving short-term problems. However these duties are distributed among administrators at particular institutions, they are a significant component of senior administrative service and constitute a very real, if immeasurable, part of the dean's work.

Also difficult to calculate are the dean's responsibilities in relation to the external publics of the institution. Meetings with alumni/ae, donors, denominational representatives, bishops, and vocation directors, visits to congregations, work with accrediting agencies, contact with peer institutions, attending professional and civic events on behalf of the school—all represent a commitment of countless hours that are seldom measured or adequately reflected in a job description. Such meetings and appearances may frequently occur during evening hours and weekends, which are over and above the full daily schedule of administrative work and teaching. While many of these activities are directly related to the chief academic officer position, others may occur when the dean is called upon to represent the institution in the president's absence.

Thus, the dean is a citizen in a larger administrative world that comes with its own set of responsibilities and expectations. Add these to the full load of academic administrative responsibilities and to the continuing work of teaching and possibly scholarship, and one can begin to appreciate the cumulative effect of the dean's duties. While these spheres of responsibility are not unrelated, each has its own distinct and considerable demands. Taken together, they establish the complex, multifaceted nature of the dean's work and the centrality of the dean's office in the daily operation of the school. They also raise questions about the total workload of the office.

## Workload

Workload studies suggest that the number of hours actually spent in work-related activity and the distribution of those hours among an array of particular duties is virtually impossible to determine with accuracy.[21] Short of keeping a detailed log of one's daily work, any report will be, at best, a rough estimate of how time is used. The survey data on the workload of theological school deans, therefore, should be viewed as an approximation rather than as an accurate accounting of how time is distributed among their various duties. Nonetheless, the deans' reports give perspective on their work and are particularly useful in determining an apportionment of time that would be optimal.

On the survey, deans were asked to estimate the percentage of time dedicated to various types of work during a typical week of the academic year. Table 2 summarizes the deans' workload.

**Table 2**
**Estimated Use of the Dean's Time**

| | % of time during the week |
|---|---|
| Paperwork, correspondence, and reports | 25% |
| Teaching, professional reading, and writing | 20% |
| Attending committee meetings | 20% |
| Working with individual faculty, administrative staff, and students | 18% |
| Attending church-related functions and other activities | 17% |

In performing these activities, theological school deans on average spend 13 percent of their time off-campus.

The survey also asked deans for their *preferred* use of time in each of the above categories. As a group, deans would prefer to reduce substantially the amount of time spent on paperwork and committee meetings, and to increase time for their teaching and scholarship and for their work with the president and with individual faculty and students.[22] Deans tend to feel that a disproportionate amount of their time is spent on administrative detail and meetings, and not enough time is spent on their own academic work and in direct personal dealings with colleagues and students. Site visit interviews reveal that individual deans struggle to attain a workable balance that meets both their own professional needs and the multiple requirements of the job.

A critical factor in the ability of deans to manage their administrative workload is the availability of capable support staff. During site visits, deans frequently remarked that their administrative assistant or secretary was invaluable to them in conducting the business of the office. Survey respondents reported an average full-time equivalent of 1.4 secretarial or support staff working directly for them.[23] Site visits disclosed, however, that in some cases the dean's secretary not only handled paperwork and routine office tasks but developed course schedules, served as registrar, was an information resource on academic policy and procedures, and provided informal advising to students. A detailed study of secretarial workloads is needed to determine how much support-staff time is dedicated to functions that in some schools are handled by other administrative personnel (e.g., registrar, academic advisor). In schools where deans are without adequate assistance, informational inquiries and record-keeping duties take valuable time from their other professional responsibilities. In survey comments, approximately 30 percent of deans cited budget limitations and about 16 percent cited staff shortages as hindrances in carrying out the responsibilities of their office.

Much of the dean's administrative work requires direct, personal interaction with other individuals and groups related to the school. To obtain a sense of how much of the dean's time is spent in direct contact with others, survey respondents were asked to estimate the number of hours per week they spend "in substantive conversation" with the persons listed below. Then they were asked to determine, in each case, whether the time spent was adequate for them to perform their job effectively. Table 3 reports the deans' estimates of the time spent on these professional interactions each week.

**Table 3**
**Estimated Time Spent with Individuals and Groups**

| | Average number of hours per week in substantive conversation |
|---|---|
| Faculty in committees or groups | 5.4 |
| Students | 5.3 |
| Individual faculty | 4.0 |
| Administrative colleagues other than the president | 3.6 |
| President/chief executive | 2.2 |
| Church leaders | 1.2 |
| Peers at other institutions | 1.1 |
| Members of board of trustees | .6 |
| Total | 23.4 |

According to these estimates, deans spend an average of 9.4 hours per week working with faculty, individually and as a group; this is almost twice as much time as they spend with other administrators, including the president, or with students. While the majority of deans consider this apportionment of time "about right," over 30 percent would like more time with students and individual faculty, and 25 percent would like more time with the president. In other categories, 37 percent of deans would like more time with peers at other institutions, and about a quarter of the deans would prefer more time with board members and church leaders. Currently, deans spend an average of more than 23 hours per week with all constituents. Deans clearly value frequent and direct engagement with colleagues on substantive issues and consider these personal relationships critical to their administrative effectiveness.

## Relationships

Forming and maintaining professional relationships at all levels of the organization, dealing with countless individual needs and concerns on a daily basis, and frequently interacting with a wide range of persons within and outside the institution account for much of the time deans spend fulfilling the basic responsibilities of office. In one of the six essays written for this study, Jane I. Smith offers an apt description of the various relationships that typically engage chief academic officers.

> While it is the president who has ultimate responsibility for the institution, *on a day-to-day basis it is often the dean who is at the center of the operations.* One might envision two concentric circles of persons and groups with whom he or she is

> in some contact. In the inner or closer circle are the faculty, students, trustees, senior administrators, staff, alumni/ae, and various advisory councils of the institution. Included in the wider circle of those relating to the school often directly to or through the dean are the university with which one's own institution is affiliated (if relevant); other educational institutions, including theological schools; one's own administrative and academic peers, and colleagues at those institutions; denominational officials . . . ; local pastors; and occasionally representatives of other faith traditions with whom one interacts personally or in connection with institutional commitments. (Italics mine)[24]

Smith observes that "[a]ll these relationships can be, and . . . must be, direct ones between the dean and other first-hand parties." Whereas the "dean is not the only representative of the institution to make these connections . . . it is often that person's responsibility to initiate, foster, and maintain them."

This expansive network of internal and external relationships is necessitated by the variety and scope of the dean's responsibilities. Initiating, fostering, and maintaining these relationships is no small task. Whether they are nurtured through personal conversation or by telephone, in meetings, through e-mail, letters, or reports, the task of keeping people involved and informed about the school, working with them on issues, and responding to their concerns is a significant component of the dean's work. These contacts also are advantageous to deans, enabling them to stay on top of things and remain current with what others are thinking, for better or worse, about the school. The ongoing task of maintaining effective relationships with various constituents is among the principal challenges of the job.

The highly relational character of the dean's work also affects the schedule and pace of the workday. During site visit interviews, deans remarked on how often their days were filled with back-to-back meetings and appointments, with unexpected problems needing immediate attention, with frequent interruptions. The steady, sometimes hectic, pace of events tends to exacerbate the difficulty of keeping the many tasks in balance, some of which require quick turnaround and others that necessitate a block of uninterrupted time to think and to write.

Henry Rosovsky, who served eleven years as dean of the faculty of arts and sciences at Harvard University, describes his daily schedule in terms familiar to many theological school deans.

> Both professors and students have in their possession uninterrupted time. Time to write, read, think, dream—and to waste. A dean's schedule—any administrator's schedule—couldn't be more different: half-hour appointments lasting all day and not infrequently beginning with breakfast. Indeed, most meals require an official character. Learning to make little speeches while

> eating is essential. Once I compared myself to a dentist: twelve to fourteen interviews a day, frequently accompanied by pain. That resulted in an angry letter from an official of the dental profession![25]

Rosovsky's analogy is a useful, and amusing one. As deans inevitably discover, all too often they are carried along by the steady stream of meetings and appointments, not all of which are pleasant or easy. The work-day is fragmented and busy, allowing few opportunities for reflection.

In an essay on her experience as a seminary dean, Elizabeth Nordbeck vividly describes the same dilemma. "Even for those of us who are comfortable with a demanding and unpredictable workday, administration is not without real frustration."[26] In a seminary "small enough for everyone to know each other and to feel comfortable walking in on everyone else," she explains,

> the initial and overriding frustration was my seeming inability to complete even the shortest, simplest task without interruption. A closed-door policy violated the institutional ethos, as well as my own convictions about accessibility and sociability; an archaic telephone system routed every call to the dean's office straight through to my desk. Trips to the restroom resulted in extended, unscheduled conversations about school business. Blessed days with no writing on my calendar miraculously metamorphosed into strings of spontaneous one-on-one meetings. For a time I ceased to go out for lunch, but people quickly learned that I could be found alone at my desk between noon and one.[27]

After relating this familiar scenario, Nordbeck tells the story of a graduate whose enthusiasm for ministry in a needy, rural parish was dampened by deep frustration. The student felt she "wasn't doing ministry at all" because every time she tried to plan something, she got interrupted. "Until," she said, "I realized that the interruptions *were* the ministry." Nordbeck found this wisdom applied equally to academic administration. "The interruptions *are* the work—indeed, the ministry—for that, as Paul knew, is what administration surely is."[28] This insight, however, did not solve "the real problem of getting routine tasks done in an efficient and timely way" or, we might add, for tending to larger projects where sustained attention is required. To address this need, Nordbeck arranged to absent herself from the office one day each week for the purpose of completing work that demands a block of time without interruptions.

The breadth of the dean's responsibilities and relationships account in large part for the practical problem of having sufficient time both to be available to others and to complete other tasks. Even deans who are efficient in handling the routine business of the office face the challenge of balancing two quite different requirements: on the one hand, the need to be present and responsive to others, understanding that "the interruptions *are* the work," and, on the other hand, to capture time to complete larger tasks and to engage in the personal reflection that effective administration requires. While some deans find the variety and pace of the job exhilarating, others experience job-related stress and burnout.[29] One dean explained that he often works "from 8 a.m. to 10 p.m. pretty much doing what has to be done." He continued, "There's a certain crisis-management feeling I have about the job because of the total workload." On the survey, nearly two-thirds of theological school deans indicated the job was very stressful. One contributing factor is long hours and the persistent feeling that there is never enough time to do all that needs to be done. Commenting on the time-consuming nature of the work, one dean observed that "administration seems to be a voracious beast which is never satisfied."

Another dilemma for some deans are the different, even conflicting expectations that these various groups and their members may bring to the relationship. For example, board members may view the dean as an advocate for the administrative agenda, faculty may consider the dean their staunch ally and defender to the administration, while church leaders see the dean as a gatekeeper whose task is to insure faculty compliance with church teaching. In those settings where expectations diverge, deans face the formidable challenge of navigating a minefield. As we shall discuss more fully in Chapter Three, academic officers unable to achieve clarity regarding their role and responsibilities may be held to impossibly diverse standards, defined not by the dean or the seminary, but by the needs and interests of particular groups. Although different expectations to some extent are inevitable, it is incumbent on deans and their schools to reach agreement concerning the dean's primary role and to communicate that understanding to all concerned.

## Conclusion

The deans' numerous responsibilities, the total workload, and the range of relationships these duties require establish several salient features of the office. First, as their responsibilities indicate, the majority of deans hold *dual citizenship* as faculty members and as administrators, and their work is principally, though not exclusively, within and between those worlds. The common practice of selecting chief academic officers who not only have administrative aptitude but experience as faculty members recognizes their responsibility to serve both groups. As noted previously, the majority of theological school deans hold tenure and faculty rank and actively engage in teaching (and sometimes scholarship) while serving as the senior academic administrator of their institutions. With this dual status, chief academic officers often become the link between administrators and faculty, representing each to the other, serving as liaison between them and advocate for both.

Second, the dean's broad responsibilities and relationships place the office at the *center* of daily operations and of institutional life. Chief academic officers have administrative responsibility for the academic programs and personnel essential to the educational mission of the schools. Since virtually all other programs and activities of the institution intersect in some way with the academic area, deans play a pivotal role in coordinating the work of various constituents to achieve their common goals. Consequently, the dean's effort to maintain effective constituent relationships is not limited to administrators and faculty but extends to relations between faculty and students, faculty and faculty, board members and faculty, administrators and staff—in short, to all constituencies in any combination. The dean not only relates personally to these and other individuals and groups but provides a connection between them as they seek to communicate ideas, resolve differences, and give voice to their needs and concerns.

During a focus group of theological school deans, participants agreed that the dean is "the one person in the system who interacts with the greatest number of people." "If persons have respect for the dean's office, then everything comes to the dean."[30] During a site visit interview, another dean explained that the dean's office is "the heart of the educational institution . . . it touches everything and becomes a kind of linchpin for the operation of the institution." After seven years in office, another dean finds that "the dean is responsible for all parts of the operation, except development, and fosters conversation among units, holding together the various units." The dean is uniquely positioned to facilitate these conversations and relationships and to build the networks of communication essential to community life.

Findings from the Study of Chief Academic Officers show that deans view themselves not so much "caught in the middle" but "positioned at the center." Their broad responsibilities place them at this juncture, and this centrality is essential to understanding their roles.[31] From this relational center, the dean is afforded both a comprehensive and intimate view of the whole. From this vantage point, the dean is able to serve not only as an interpreter and broker of ideas but as a catalyst for strengthening communication, coalescing divergent points of view, and creating an integrated sense of mission and purpose. As we shall see, the centrality of the dean's position creates distinctive opportunities and responsibilities for academic leadership.

Third, the *complexity* of the dean's work is evident even in this brief consideration of basic responsibilities and relationships and their effect on the total workload of the office. To understand the daily life of academic administrators, we must imagine for each of their duties the array of individuals and groups involved, the pace of the work, the time and versatility it requires, and their cumulative effect on officeholders. The fact that 65 percent of the deans surveyed find the job stressful raises important questions about how realistic and manageable the deanship has become. Perceptions of the dean's work as high pressured, frenetic, and prone to burnout are unlikely to aid efforts to recruit and retain able academic administrators. Although there are many different reasons for frequent turnover in the chief academic officer position, the issue of job overload must certainly be included among them.[32]

Paradoxically, the same characteristics of the deanship that can have such unfortunate consequences also account for the positive and creative potential of the office. Its broad responsibilities, its blend of academic and administrative tasks, its opportunities for frequent interaction with a wide range of people, all contribute to the richness, the excitement, and reward of the dean's work. Based on conversations with deans in the course of this research, the ability to balance these duties and to effectively maintain multiple relationships are among the principal challenges of the job. Deans often describe their work by analogy to a juggler whose success depends on keeping several things in the air at once, who must have flawless concentration and timing, and who must never lose sight of the continuity among the separate parts.[33] Based on this research, the metaphor is very apt.

## Notes

[1] John Wesley Gould, *The Academic Deanship* (New York: Teachers College Press, Columbia University, 1964), 6.

[2] Gerald E. Dupont, "The Dean and His Office," in *The Problems of Administration in the American College,* Roy J. Deferrari, ed. (Washington, DC: The Catholic University of America Press, 1956), 53.

[3] Dupont, 53–54.

[4] Dupont, 55.

[5] Dupont, 55.

[6] Dupont, 53.

[7] Robert Wood Lynn, "Living on Two Levels: The Work of the Academic Dean in North American Theological Education," *Theological Education* 24 (Autumn 1987), 79–80. An exception to this general trend is noted by Gerald E. Dupont. In Roman Catholic Jesuit institutions, the office of prefect of studies was established in 1565 and closely corresponded to the present office of dean. Dupont states that Jesuit institutions changed the title from prefect to dean as early as 1919. Dupont, 54–55.

[8] Two recent studies of the seminary presidency provide helpful descriptions of changes in the presidency: Robert J. Wister, "The Effects of Institutional Change on the Office of Rector and President in the Roman Catholic Theological Seminaries—1965–1994," *Theological Education* 32 (Supplement I 1995), 98–101; and Erskine Clarke, "Leadership: The Study of the Seminary Presidency in Protestant Theological Seminaries, *Theological Education* 32 (Supplement II 1995), 98–101. See also Katarina Schuth, *Reason for the Hope: The Futures of Roman Catholic Theologates* (Wilmington, DE: Michael Glazier, Inc., 1989), 84–87.

[9] Dupont, 51–52, 56.

[10] This also has been true of seminary presidents. See Mark Allyn Holman, *Presidential Search in Theological Schools: Process Makes a Difference.* Distributed by agreement with the Association of Theological Schools in the United States and Canada. (Oakland, CA: 1993), 5.

[11] Robert K. Greenleaf, *Seminary as Servant* (Indianapolis, IN: The Robert K. Greenleaf Center, 1980), 27.

[12] Gail Buchwalter King, ed., *Fact Book on Theological Education 1993–1994* (Pittsburgh, PA: The Association of Theological Schools in the United States and Canada, 1994), 2. The description was updated by the ATS in the 1996–1997 *Fact Book* as follows: "*University-Affiliated:* This designation identifies schools of theology that are integral parts of larger teaching or research universities with multiple professional schools and graduate programs, typically offering research doctorates in more than one area. *College-Affiliated:* This designation identifies schools of theology that are integrally related to four-year undergraduate comprehensive colleges that have limited graduate or professional programs other than the theological school." Jonathan Strom and Daniel Aleshire, eds.,

*Fact Book on Theological Education 1996–1997* (Pittsburgh, PA: The Association of Theological Schools in the United States and Canada, 1997), 3.

[13] To emphasize the dean's responsibility for developing the faculty and representing their concerns, some schools prefer the title Dean of Faculty to the more general designation of Academic Dean.

[14] This and subsequent data on the faculty citizenship of theological school deans was first reported in a monograph on the research findings: Jeanne P. McLean, *Leading from the Center: The Role of Chief Academic Officer*, Monograph Series on Academic Leadership, vol. 1 (St. Paul, MN: University of St. Thomas, 1996).

[15] Among the 7 percent of deans who did not teach, the majority were new to their positions (0–3 years in office) and served in mid-sized seminaries (student FTE 76–150) that were predominantly Roman Catholic.

[16] Although the percentage of theological schools that *require* teaching and scholarship of their deans is relatively small, an additional 38 percent of schools *expect* their deans to teach and an additional 40 percent *expect* them to produce scholarly work. Such institutional requirements and expectations provide incentive to deans to remain active as teachers and scholars. The reasons some schools have these explicit requirements and expectations and other schools do not merit further investigation.

Analysis of survey data reveals notable differences between university-related and freestanding theological schools in their teaching and scholarship requirements for academic officers. Teaching is *required* of 43 percent of deans in freestanding schools, but of only 16 percent of deans in university schools. However, teaching is *expected* of 58 percent of university deans, compared to 37 percent in freestanding schools. Scholarship is required or expected of 70 percent of university deans, compared to only 40 percent of deans in freestanding schools.

Analysis of responses according to institutional size shows that teaching is *required* of 60 percent of deans in small schools (1–75 student FTE), compared to 37 to 43 percent of deans in mid-sized schools (76–300 student FTE), and only 19 percent of deans in large schools (over 300 student FTE). Deans in small schools also teach more frequently than their counterparts in larger schools.

[17] Analysis of survey data concerning the dean's primary administrative responsibilities reveals no statistically significant difference among deans based on gender, length of service, or type of institution.

[18] The small percentage of deans who indicated they did not have the primary administrative responsibility for academic priorities and planning, curriculum and programs, and academic policy are located predominantly in small seminaries (student FTE 0–75) where presidents may be more fully involved in these areas.

[19] In Roman Catholic seminaries, fewer academic deans have responsibility for spiritual advising/formation than do their counterparts at other seminaries. Based on her research on Roman Catholic theologates, Katarina Schuth reports: "Of the fifty theologates in our study, all except eight designate a person who is responsible for personal and spiritual formation. In situations where no one is listed, this aspect of formation is usually the responsibility of religious communities or diocesan houses of formation." Schuth, *Reason for the Hope*, 145.

[20] Analysis of these data by denominations indicates the highest average number of academic administrators reporting to the dean is 4 in mainline Protestant seminaries, and the lowest average number is 2.5 in Roman Catholic seminaries. Not surprisingly, the number of administrative staff reporting to the dean varies with institutional size, ranging from an average of 1.7 in small schools (student FTE 1–75) to 4 in larger schools (student FTE 151 and above).

[21] Harold E. Yuker, *Faculty Workload: Research, Theory, and Interpretation*, ASHE-ERIC Higher Education Report No. 10 (San Francisco: Jossey-Bass, 1984), 15, 25. While Yuker's concern is with faculty workload, he makes useful observations about the validity of self-reported data.

[22] Analysis of survey responses based on school size indicate that for the activities of teaching and of professional reading and writing, deans in small schools (student FTE 1–75) spent the greatest percentage of time (an estimated 23 percent), whereas deans in large schools (student FTE 300 or more) spent the lowest percentage of time (an estimated 15 percent). However, both groups preferred that a greater portion of their time be dedicated to this work: deans in small schools 36 percent, and deans in large schools 27 percent.

[23] Compared to the overall mean of 1.4 support staff, deans in mainline Protestant seminaries and mid-sized seminaries (student FTE 76–150) averaged 1.9 and 1.6 support staff respectively. The lowest averages were among deans in interdenominational/non-denominational seminaries with .75 support staff, deans in small seminaries (student FTE 1–76) with .8, and deans in university-related schools with .9.

[24] Jane I. Smith, "Academic Leadership: Roles, Issues, and Challenges," *Theological Education* 33, Supplement (Autumn 1996), 2.

[25] This excerpt from Rosovsky's book, *The University: An Owner's Manual*, was published in: Henry Rosovsky, "Deaning: A Short Course," *In Trust* 2, no. 1 (Easter 1990), 19.

[26] Elizabeth C. Nordbeck, "The Once and Future Dean: Reflections on Being a Chief Academic Officer," *Theological Education* 33 (Supplement Autumn 1996), 24.

[27] Nordbeck, 24.

[28] Nordbeck, 24.

[29] An earlier publication, based on research findings of the Study of Chief Academic Officers, discusses the stresses of the job and ways in which some deans have dealt with them. Karen M. Ristau, *Challenges of Academic Administration: Rewards and Stresses in the Role of the Chief Academic Officer*, Monograph Series on Academic Leadership, vol. 2 (St. Paul, MN: University of St. Thomas, 1996). Chapter Eight of this book will return to the topic of job-related stress and burnout.

[30] These remarks were part of a focus group of theological school deans held in conjunction with the ATS Biennial Meeting in Atlanta, Georgia, on June 12, 1994. Eight deans from theological schools in the United States and Canada were invited to participate.

[31] In Neely McCarter's recent study of the seminary presidency, that office also is described as "central" by virtue of the president's interaction with all constituencies of the institution. (See Neely Dixon McCarter, *The President as Educator: A Study in the Seminary Presidency*, Studies in Theological Education [Atlanta, GA: Scholars Press, 1996], 32–38.)

Claims to the centrality of the deanship and the presidency are not mutually exclusive. While both presidents and deans are linked through their broad responsibilities to the internal constituents and external publics of the school, many presidents are increasingly focused on external relations and resource development, while chief academic officers are most directly involved with daily operations and internal constituents. While this general trend may be more evident in some schools than in others, it has evolved to the point where 60 percent of theological school deans responding to the 1993 survey indicated that they had the primary administrative responsibility for the daily operation of their schools.

[32] The several issues related to turnover in the position will be taken up in more detail in Chapter Eight.

[33] Jane Smith effectively applies the juggler image to the dean's work. See Smith, "Academic Leadership," 8.

# 2 MANAGERIAL AND LEADERSHIP ROLES

*"I really do think deans should walk on water."*
*Theological school faculty member*

The leadership role of the chief academic officer is elusive. In theory, it can be described and distinguished from other forms of institutional leadership. In practice, it is firmly embedded in a complex network of roles, relationships, and processes that obscures its distinctiveness, while providing the context for its understanding. Leadership also is closely related to the managerial functions of the office. Although leadership and management capture different facets of the dean's work, they tend to blur as deans carry out their daily administrative duties. Recognizing the complexity of organizational life and of administrative work within it, this chapter seeks to delineate the managerial and leadership roles of chief academic officers in theological schools.[1]

Against the background of Chapter One, which describes the responsibilities of deans, this chapter examines *how* deans fulfill their multiple responsibilities. Given the importance of institutional context, we begin by considering the salient features of theological school cultures and their implications for academic leadership and governance. Within these cultures, chief academic officers perform two closely related functions of manager and leader. While managerial tasks frequently occupy the greater portion of the dean's time, it is the leadership role that accounts for the distinctive contribution of the office to theological education. Following discussion of the managerial role, we turn to an analysis of leadership, first explicating the concepts of leadership held by academic officers and their colleagues and then applying those concepts to specific practices in the schools. While acknowledging variations in these concepts and practices due to differences in individual officeholders and their organizational cultures, the goal is to identify the common character of the dean's leadership role that underlies these variations and to assess its importance to theological education.

Participants in the Study of Chief Academic Officers provide the conceptual framework for this examination of academic leadership. Through the survey, site visits, focus groups, and commissioned essays, this study reveals how a broad and representative group of theological educators conceive of leadership and identify its practice. Other leadership and organizational theories are brought to bear on these primary data only as they serve to sharpen analysis and to situate these findings in terms of recent research. There is no attempt here to offer a thorough review of this vast literature. Rather, related theories of academic leadership and culture are introduced only to provide concepts and models that illuminate results of the study of chief academic officers in theological schools.

## The Context

North American theological schools are notoriously diverse. Even the most general descriptions of the schools point to significant differences: their denominational or interdenominational affiliations, their geographical locations, variations in institutional size, their status as freestanding or university-related, and the like.[2] During site visit interviews, participants frequently referred to such basic facts to explain the prominent features of their institutional cultures. Whether a school's decision-making process tended to be hierarchical or collegial, formal or informal, whether the school was entrepreneurial or administratively conservative often was attributed to the school's ecclesial identity or to the influence of regional customs. Theological schools also are differentiated by their particular histories and traditions, and by the continuous interaction of persons and events that influence the development of organizational culture. In light of these variables, the "collective, mutually shaping patterns of norms, values, practices, beliefs and assumptions" that come to define a culture and guide the behavior of its members differ from one institution to another.[3] As institutional cultures differ, so does the role of chief academic officer within them.

In their 1988 study, *Collegiate Culture and Leadership Strategies,* Ellen Chaffee and William Tierney explain: "The most fundamental construct of an organization . . . is its culture. An organization's culture is reflected in what is done, how it is done, and who is involved in doing it. It concerns decisions, actions, and communication both on an instrumental and symbolic level."[4] How deans fulfill the duties of their office is determined, in part, by cultural norms concerning "what is done, how it is done, and who is involved in doing it." One seminary president recounted his experience coming from the North to a southern seminary where "everything was done by word of mouth." He immediately began to ask for written policies. Although some policies were developed, he acknowledged, "there was an informal style when I came and there will be an informal style when I leave. . . . Culture is very important, very powerful." Studies show that the ability of administrators to understand such culturally accepted practices and to adapt to them are critical to their effectiveness.[5] Situational factors and events shape the behavior of individual leaders, and, because situations differ, the measure of leadership effectiveness can vary from one institution to another.

The relationship between the individual and the organizational culture, however, does not end there. Individuals also shape and influence cultural patterns. The personality, working style, and modes of communication adopted by an institutional leader, for example, can significantly affect what the community considers acceptable practices. Site visits conducted for this study reveal that a particularly strong president or dean can have considerable influence on how decisions are made and who participates in the process. In one instance, a dean whose personal style was informal and conversational made that the primary mode of deliberation on important issues. While academic decisions were discussed and approved at faculty meetings, substantive and often decisive consultations took place in hallways and offices outside the formal structure. Therefore, even as organizational cultures define and limit the dean's role, they too are susceptible to individual influence. Academic cultures both shape and are shaped by their individual members.[6] The role of chief academic officer is contextually and individually defined.

Similarities among theological schools and their deans, however, are easily as compelling as their differences. Acknowledging organizational differences does not preclude the possibility of describing common characteristics of theological school cultures and of the dean's role within them. Recognizing differences among individual officeholders does not deny basic similarities in the way deans fulfill their responsibilities. During the site visits and focus groups conducted for this research, deans from diverse institutional settings discussed their roles in remarkably similar language. The cultural dynamics they described, the challenges they confronted, and the issues they dealt with on a daily basis formed a common ground among them despite obvious personal and cultural differences. A closer look at some of the widely shared features of their organizational cultures is helpful in understanding this common ground.

In their landmark study, *Modern Approaches to Understanding and Managing Organizations,* Lee Bolman and Terrence Deal consolidate organizational theories into four typologies that serve as "frames" through which to view the complexities of organizational life and to understand the managerial problems they present.[7] Each of these frames captures the dominant characteristics of particular organizational cultures; taken together, the four frames provide multiple lenses that afford a comprehensive and multidimensional view of any organization. Based on their analysis, the four frames can be described as follows: in the *structural frame,* an organization exists primarily to accomplish goals, and structures are designed to coordinate and control activity toward meeting those goals; the *human resources frame* emphasizes the interdependence between people and organizations and sees the organization as existing to serve human needs; the *political frame* views organizations as coalitions of individuals and interest groups and is characterized by power, conflict, and the distribution of scarce resources; and in the *symbolic frame,* the focus is on the meaning of events, and organizational cohesion is achieved, not through power or rational design, but through shared images and values.[8]

When Estela Bensimon and her colleagues applied the theoretical frameworks of Bolman and Deal to higher education, they concluded that an integrated use of all four frames was necessary to understand the complex dynamics of colleges and universities and that, when the frames were considered separately, the human resources, political, and symbolic frames were most useful in accounting for the dominant features of academic cultures.[9] Theological schools, as a subset within higher education, have even more pronounced cultural similarities. Although elements of the four organizational types were found in the eleven theological schools visited for this study, the human resources frame most adequately described the forms of interaction, decision making, and leadership in the majority of these schools. The general characteristics of the human resources frame, while nuanced differently in different institutions, capture the most prominent and pervasive features of theological school cultures.

In *Making Sense of Administrative Leadership: The 'L' Word in Higher Education,* Bensimon, Neumann, and Birnbaum describe the human resources frame in the context of higher education:

> [T]he human resource orientation is best exemplified by considering the institution (or at least the faculty of the institution) as a collegium, a community of equals, or a community of scholars. . . . In a collegium, where differences in status are de-emphasized, people interact as equals in a system that stresses consensus, shared power and participation in governance, and common commitments and aspirations. . . . Leaders in collegial systems are selected by their peers for limited terms and are considered "first among equals" as they serve the interests of the group members. Rather than issue orders, they try to mold consensus and to create the conditions under which the group will discipline itself by appealing to the group's norms and values. Leaders are more servants of the group than masters, and they are expected to listen, to persuade, to leave themselves open to influence, and to share the burden of decision making.[10]

In this view, leaders place emphasis on decision-making processes and see their role as working collegially to promote consensus within the community. They work with respected colleagues and recognize that talent, expertise, and leadership are diffused throughout the organization. Bensimon et al. explain that "effective collegial leaders gain authority by demonstrating the ability to orchestrate consultation rather than relying on authoritarian tactics. Collegial leaders do not act alone; they use processes and structures to involve those who will be affected by the decisions made."[11] As Bolman and Deal emphasize in their account, the human resources frame "starts from the premise that people are the most critical resource of the organization."[12] The organization and its members are interdependent. Involving individuals in decision making and addressing their needs and concerns are core values in the human resources perspective.

While the human resources frame affords an apt description of many academic cultures with participatory forms of governance, its applicability to theological schools is further strengthened by the relatively small size of their faculties and their rootedness in the Judeo-Christian tradition. Given these characteristics, theological schools tend to foster respect and concern for the individual and to be intentional in their efforts to develop a community with shared values and purposes. The usual criticism of the human resources frame, that collegial decision making is unrealistic in light of the distinct faculty and administrative cultures of most institutions, is largely offset by the communitarian ethos of theological schools and the common practice of combining administrative and faculty responsibilities in the same positions.[13]

Theological school administrators and faculty interviewed during site visits most frequently described the reality and aspirations of their academic communities in terms of the collegium. Several presidents and chief academic officers considered themselves servant leaders who seek to fulfill the mission of their institutions by facilitating the work of faculty and students. While participatory governance and shared decision making were not perfectly realized in all instances, these clearly were the normative values and practices.[14] Chief academic officers, in particular, sought to develop consultative processes that fostered broad participation and encouraged the input and leadership of colleagues. As our subsequent analysis will reveal, the managerial and leadership roles of theological school deans are carried out in cultural contexts in which shared leadership, participatory decision making, and collegial relationships are highly valued. These cultural norms define the limits and possibilities of the deanship and account for the forms of academic leadership characteristic of the office in theological education.

With these cultural affinities, it is not surprising that theological school deans from diverse institutional settings described their roles in remarkably similar language. They viewed themselves as functioning in two predominant modes, as managers and leaders.[15] While both roles were variously configured and took many forms, the deans had considerable agreement about these two dimensions of the job and what constituted effectiveness in each.

## The Managerial Role

When chief academic officers report that their jobs are more management than leadership, they are employing a distinction that is commonplace in corporate and higher education literature. The two terms are usually defined in contrast to one another, as in the oft-quoted list provided by Warren Bennis in his 1989 book *On Becoming a Leader.* Whereas the leader is innovative and visionary, the manager administers and carries out operations within a defined structure. "The manager has a short-range view; the leader has a long-range perspective. . . . The manager asks how and when; the leader asks what and why. . . . The manager does things right; the leader does the right thing."[16] Madeleine Green puts this distinction in the context of higher education: "Leadership stresses vision—the ability to set goals and to define mission in accordance with the followers' sense of their own needs, values, and purposes. Management connotes the mundane, the operational, the ability to get things done in order to accomplish a predetermined goal."[17]

Theological school deans find that much of their daily work and the greater percentage of their time is spent on managerial tasks. With oversight of the academic area comes responsibility for the smooth operation of programs and for monitoring and enforcing academic policies and procedures—serving as "traffic manager," as one dean described it. Many dealings with students involve advising on requirements, clarifying policies, granting exemptions, and managing admissions and dismissals. In working with faculty and administrative colleagues, academic officers are regularly involved in hiring, staffing, scheduling, organizing, evaluating, negotiating, problem solving, and planning. Deans staff and often chair committees, document decisions, distribute resources, prepare calendars, send announcements, and keep records. In short, they "take care of the details." As one dean explains, "Administration is a maintenance job." Another dean summarizes what is expected of his office: "that the curriculum, academic decision making, and the maintenance of the academic year will be done decently and in order."

While the conduct and the quality of teaching, learning, scholarship, and the academic life depend heavily on effective organizational management, many view the managerial role of administrators as less worthy than teaching or scholarship and often fail to appreciate its importance until it is poorly practiced. Because effective managers facilitate the smooth and organized running of the institution, their contributions may go largely unnoticed and unappreciated; the dire effects of poor management, however, become immediately apparent. As Joseph C. Rost observes in his discussion of the management/leadership distinction:

> People love to work for well-organized managers who facilitate getting the job done by coordinating the work of various people, and they hate to work for managers who are ineffective, uncoordinated, or incompetent. Most human beings crave order, stability, well-run programs, coordinated activity, patterned behavior, goal achievement, and the successful operation of an organization. . . . That is the attraction of having the trains run on time. On the other hand, people become frustrated when they encounter poor or ineffective management, when the proverbial trains do not run on time.[18]

Academic officers who organize operations, resolve problems, and remove barriers so that "the trains run on time" are providing an administrative service that, however invisible, makes the daily work of countless others possible. To perform these managerial tasks effectively requires an ability to stay organized while balancing multiple tasks and to be skilled in dealing with crises, conflicts, and a range of personalities and temperaments, needs and concerns. At the heart of academic administration is the need for highly skilled managers who are able to approach a complex and varied array of tasks with fairness, equilibrium, and efficiency. To do this well, with little or no formal preparation in management, is the challenge facing every theological school dean every day.

The variety and sheer quantity of such tasks, while invigorating for some, can be stressful and burdensome for others. One long-term dean described the job as "holding it all together." While the dean expressed genuine enthusiasm for "working with lots of people in lots of capacities," she also described the weariness that comes with "arms that are tired from trying to gather everyone in, and legs that are tired from straddling things that are sliding apart." Some version of this ambivalence was common among the deans interviewed for the study.

Another tension deans experience is balancing their managerial and leadership roles. Deans typically find that routine administrative duties and dealing with crises that arise unexpectedly command much of their attention each day. While deans are hired to perform these duties and manage these crises, they often find there is insufficient time to undertake the more visionary thinking and planning also important to their work. Several deans and presidents in the study lamented how rarely they find opportunities to work together on the broader, long-range issues that are at the heart of their leadership roles.

Some of the tension between managing and leading may derive from the polarization of those concepts in leadership studies based on the corporate model. When managerial and leadership roles are defined in opposition to one another, the emphasis is on their separateness and difference rather than on their relationship and interdependence. Unlike corporate cultures, where management and leadership positions can be distinct and roles sharply defined, academic cultures have more participatory forms of governance that tend to combine management and leadership functions in the same positions and to find both of these roles carried out at various levels of the organization. In the deanship, these roles are combined and more intimately related than may at first appear. Faculty at one of the larger seminaries in the study articulated this connection:

> The provost is more of an implementer, a manager, who makes sure the troops are in order, that they are fed, clothed, and in their right mind. The provost makes the schools work together in the same direction. . . . The provost does not articulate a vision but does the managing and consolidating to achieve it. The provost has to be both leader and manager.

Conscientious performance of managerial duties facilitates the essential work of the institution, thereby creating conditions in which leadership can flourish. In the discussion of leadership that follows, implementing the corporate vision, which is part of leadership, depends on managerial skills for its accomplishment. Clearly, effective management makes leadership possible.

Recent studies of leadership also reveal a second and quite opposite difficulty: that the concepts of management and leadership are conflated so that the difference between them is blurred.[19] In this view, strenuously opposed by Rost, leadership is equated with "effective management," so the distinction between them is one of degree, not of kind. In other words, good managers are considered leaders simply because they perform their managerial tasks well. While interviews for this study gave some evidence of this thinking, most viewed managerial and leadership roles as distinct but related, and often coexisting in the position of the chief academic officer. A closer look at the meaning of leadership and how academic officers exercise leadership may serve to clarify the relationship between these two basic roles.

## Leadership

To understand how leadership is conceived and practiced in theological schools, the eleven site visits conducted for this study included interviews with the chief academic officer, the chief executive officer, administrators, faculty, students, and board members at each institution. All were asked to articulate their concept of leadership and then to identify leaders and leadership practices within their schools. The result was remarkable agreement across institutional lines about the defining elements of leadership and, within a given school, consensus concerning the individuals and groups who provide leadership. Those interviewed also offered similar descriptions of the dean's leadership role despite differences in personality and style among the deans, differences in their specific contexts and in the issues confronting them.

To explicate the dean's leadership role, we begin by examining the general concept of leadership advanced by participants in the study and their perception that leadership is exercised, formally and informally, by persons at various levels of the organization. Then, using that concept, we examine general leadership practices in theological schools and the particular role of the chief academic officer.

### *Concepts of Leadership*

Definitions of leadership acquired during site visits include descriptions of leadership traits, behaviors, and relationships. The majority of definitions emphasize the behavioral elements of leadership, what leaders *do,* and discuss the relationship between leaders and followers as fundamental to these practices. Personal qualities or traits of leaders, such as integrity or trust, for example, do not so much define leadership as indicate elements essential to an effective leader/follower relationship. To organize these various ideas of leadership, our analysis centers on the notion of leadership as an activity or process that is rooted in the relationship of leaders to their communities. These concepts provide the lens through which theological educators view leadership and identify its practice in the schools; they also provide the framework for understanding the distinctive leadership role of the chief academic officer.

Central to most definitions of leadership were the two primary ideas stated here by a seminary dean: "In exercising leadership, an individual has a vision of what the institution is and may become and has the gifts to put that vision into concrete reality, engaging people to share in the vision." In this view, leadership involves two things: developing a vision of organizational mission and goals that is supported and owned by the community; and implementing the vision through the program, policy, and personnel decisions of the institution. While these activities are distinguished for purposes of analysis, they typically are less separate and sequential, and more interrelated in actual practice. Fundamental to this process is a relationship between leaders and followers that makes the vision and its support, ownership, and implementation possible.

*Creating the Vision.* In the leadership literature, "vision" generally refers to a coherent view of the direction and goals of the institution. A vision worthy of community support is rooted in the institutional mission and serves to articulate its significance and promise. To be responsible, such vision must be informed by a knowledge of the past—the institutional history—and grounded in a clear, realistic discernment of the present.[20] As a university dean explains, "Vision is not just blue sky; it's being able to articulate with great clarity what the particular mission and understanding is of the institution."

Those who were perceived as architects of the institutional vision varied in the eleven sites visited for this study. While most looked to the president or chief executive to be involved in creating and articulating a vision, some believed that the president and governing board or the president and dean shared that task. Others thought the institutional vision was shaped and carried by the faculty, and the dean's task was "to put wings and feet on faculty visions." In four schools, presidents considered it their responsibility to articulate the vision and the dean's responsibility to implement it. One dean explained, somewhat facetiously, "The dean is the person who makes the school become what the president already says it is." In two schools, presidents took responsibility for developing a corporate vision and expected the dean to shape an academic vision consistent with it. In another school, there was almost universal agreement, and considerable discomfort, that there seemed to be no vision to unify and guide the school.

Whichever individuals or groups are viewed as primarily responsible for the institutional vision, it is virtually impossible for the vision to be fashioned in a vacuum. In academic cultures that rely on collegial relationships and shared governance, a vision of what the institution is and may become is influenced, directly and indirectly, by the many participants in the dialogue. In the words of one dean, "An effective leader must have a genuine openness and recognition that others who serve with you . . . have both a right and a responsibility to dialogue about that mission, to struggle with that mission and its implications." In schools where faculty, administrators, and other constituents have such dialogue, vision is dynamic and evolves in response to changing conditions and new ideas. Those who articulate a coherent, compelling view of the mission and direction of the school and who can frame issues accordingly are perceived as leaders. Participants from a broad spectrum of theological schools found leaders among all constituent groups and noted that different persons emerge as leaders on different issues and at different times.

The notion of the leader as a solitary, charismatic figure who literally "goes out ahead to show the way" tends to minimize the rootedness of vision in community dialogue and experience. When those interviewed were asked to identify campus leaders, almost all named faculty and students who exercised leadership informally, as readily as they named administrators, trustees, or others who held formal leadership positions. In one university school, the dean and faculty were so collegial and cohesive that most cited the group as a whole, rather than specific individuals, as the primary source of leadership. Whether leadership was exercised by individuals or groups or, in rare instances, by no one at all, the constituents of each school tended to agree in their overall assessment of leadership and in their identification of who their leaders were.

While various persons may share in the task of developing an institutional vision, the positional leaders, particularly the executive and academic officers, bear special responsibility. By virtue of their formal leadership roles, they are well positioned to elicit ideas and to draw them together in a coherent view of what the institution is and where it is going. As faculty in one seminary observed, "The president and dean articulate a vision for theological education—their own and what they hear from faculty—and give voice and embody the vision." Creating the institutional vision often is attributed to positional leaders, not because they fashion it independently, but because their administrative roles afford regular opportunities for them to publicly articulate the collective vision.[21]

The breadth and strength of the ownership of that vision can depend on how firmly it is rooted in the community's own self-understanding and how compelling is its sense of the institution's purpose and possibilities. In the words of an experienced seminary president, "A leader has to articulate the institution's reality and goals, its present and future, in such a way that it is persuasive and reflective of a broad, broad community." The ability to understand and articulate the community's best sense of its shared identity and direction is fundamental to the exercise of leadership.

*Implementing the Vision.* The strength of community support and ownership of the institutional vision is tested when specific proposals for a change in programs, policy, or personnel come before the faculty, students, administrators, and governing boards. An institutional goal that may be widely supported in its general formulation may be vigorously challenged when it is embodied in a specific proposal. For example, two of the schools participating in the study had the goal of increasing the racial and gender diversity of the faculty. In both instances, debate became contentious, and in one instance divisive, when the acceptance of specific candidates appeared to entail endorsement of unconventional career paths or less traditional forms of scholarship. In these instances, achieving the goal of gender or racial diversity required accepting candidates whose path to the doctorate was lengthy and indirect or whose work dealt with topics outside of mainstream, traditional scholarship. When the general goals became concrete, when they were embodied in specific persons whose work did not fit the usual categories, the meaning and implications of the goals became more evident. The vision was tested anew and served either to strengthen or weaken the original resolve.

Implementation is the realization of vision and its true test. Implementation is not something that occurs once a vision is fully formulated; rather, vision evolves and is defined in the very process of developing programs or policies, or making hiring and retention decisions. The governance process, through which specific proposals are considered, debated, and ultimately accepted or rejected, is the arena where the institutional vision is defined and made real. Leadership involves not only articulating a vision to which there is community assent but achieving support for its implementation. The work of the leader is well summarized by another participant in the study: "A leader shapes a vision, not in isolation, but in dialogue with the group led and puts words to the best goals of the group. *A leader constantly negotiates [the vision], building consensus and enlisting support.*" (Italics mine)

When some participants defined leadership in terms of the personal qualities of leaders, it reflected their sense of what it takes to successfully negotiate the vision and build consensus and support. The traits most frequently mentioned were trust, honesty, and integrity—all of which are necessary for an effective leader/follower relationship. Participants also cited attributes such as strength of character, maturity, self-esteem, and humor needed to withstand the pressure and controversy associated with change, and other traits, such as organizational skill, decisiveness, and efficiency, that are essential to handling the managerial tasks that support leadership activities.

Those identified by their colleagues as leaders tended to focus less on specific traits than on the defining elements of leadership—the work of creating a vision and building support for its implementation. Since individual leaders differ in their personal traits, and since leadership requires different qualities in different settings and at different times, such characteristics appear not to define leadership so much as to indicate the qualities most desirable in a leader at a particular place and time.[22] The frequent association of leaders with specific traits, however, recognizes the importance of personal strengths and abilities to the exercise of effective leadership.

This concept of leadership, creating and implementing a vision with the support and ownership of the community, reflects the culture of collegiality and shared governance characteristic of theological schools: 1) in this process, leadership is dispersed throughout the institution and exercised by various persons with and without formal leadership positions; and 2) leadership is fundamentally relational, as leaders work with members of the community to achieve widespread ownership of decisions. With these basic principles established, there remains the question, How do leaders lead? How do they accomplish the task of bringing the community together in reaching shared goals? More specifically, in theological school contexts where there are multiple leaders and complex, participatory decision-making processes, what forms of leadership characterize the role of chief academic officer?

### *Leadership Practices*

The process of academic decision making or governance most clearly reveals how faculty, administrators, students, and board members work to implement specific institutional goals. The two examples below illustrate in some detail the type of formal and informal leadership strategies evident in several sites visited for this study. The first example, set in a denominational evangelical seminary, shows how a new academic dean works with colleagues and provides leadership in curriculum revision through a formal, four-year process of consultation and decision making. The second example, set in a university divinity school where the dean functions as both executive and academic officer, reveals how an experienced dean effectively utilizes informal methods of working with faculty and university administrators. At the time of this study, the two schools were similar in size, each with 15 full-time faculty members, and both described their institutional cultures as congenial, consultative, and collegial. Despite impressive differences in their institutional missions, histories, traditions, and governance structures, both had effective means of working collegially and exercising leadership in systems of shared governance.

*Example 1.* At this seminary, the president invited the dean to direct the curriculum revision while still serving as a faculty member. In preparation for this task, administrators and faculty reviewed and refined the mission statement and formally approved changes that were subsequently endorsed by the board. When the dean took office, she designed a broad-based planning process that, over four years, would involve faculty, administrators, students, board members, and denominational leaders. That process would be guided by a shared vision of institutional mission and goals, would result in changes in program requirements, course offerings, and teaching methods, and would provide for regular evaluation of these changes once they were underway.

In the first stage, the faculty used their fall retreat to examine the strengths and weaknesses of the old curriculum and to work within departments to develop a statement of the goals for each program consistent with the school's mission statement. Following the retreat, the president and dean appointed a curriculum committee, composed of faculty members, two students, and the dean (ex officio) to work with results of the curriculum assessment and departmental statements and to begin developing a new curricular model. Broad consultation was undertaken in the second year. With outside funding, the seminary sponsored a denominational symposium held on campus to help determine appropriate areas of focus for the new curriculum, and distributed a survey to students and alumni/ae to assess the outcomes of current programs and to elicit ideas for curriculum change. At the fall retreat in the third year, the faculty adopted a conceptual model of the new curriculum and worked throughout the year in interdisciplinary teams of faculty and students to discuss the specific course changes the model required. By December of that year, the curriculum committee had received recommendations from the teams and had submitted a plan for the revised curriculum to the faculty for final approval. Although an individual faculty member raised objections late in the process, the new curriculum was approved by the faculty on schedule. The curriculum committee and the dean met with students to explain the changes, and the new curriculum was implemented in the fourth year. The plan was to monitor the impact of these changes through evaluation during the first years of the new program and to make refinements and adjustments as needed.

All constituent groups were invested in the process. On the recommendation of the administration and the faculty, the board had approved a strategic plan calling for curriculum review and had endorsed the revised mission statement. As the chief academic officer, the dean's role was to initiate, design, and lead the decision-making process to a successful conclusion. Although the president gave the dean "a free hand" in conducting the curriculum revision, the dean kept senior administrators informed at their weekly cabinet meetings and consulted with the president about specific concerns. Faculty were the primary agents of change and, through the use of departmental and interdepartmental teams, were full participants at every stage of the process. As faculty worked through the substantive changes in course content and the overall structure of the seminary's core program, the dean served as interpreter, mediator, and negotiator. In the give-and-take that curricular changes required, the dean became the go-between and often negotiated the compromise. When difficulties arose late in the process, the dean worked with the department chair and one-on-one with the faculty member who strenuously objected to a specific provision in the final proposal. Students and church leaders, some of whom served on the seminary board, were consulted early and involved at appropriate stages throughout the process. The dean solicited the input of board members and informed them of progress on the project at their regular meetings.

In this example, the dean provided leadership by designing a process that fostered clear articulation of institutional mission and goals and insured broad constituent participation and ownership. While individual faculty members did provide leadership in gaining support for specific program changes, it was the dean who worked with individuals and groups at all levels of the organization and kept the project on track by mediating differences, resolving controversy, and effectively pacing the rate of change. As the dean explained, she was a go-between who did a lot of mediating and "negotiating about trade-offs." The faculty credit the open dialogue and broad participation the dean encouraged for the smooth progress of their work. The project successfully concluded, as the dean observed, "with everyone intact, on board, and of one mind."

*Example 2.* During his nine years in office, this university dean has worked closely with the religious studies faculty to incorporate global, non-Christian perspectives in the curriculum and to broaden the gender and ethnic diversity of the faculty. As the sole administrator of the school, the dean serves as the executive officer who represents the school to the university, to the denominations, and to external constituents, and also as the chief academic officer who oversees the academic life of the school and helps to set its agenda. The faculty council, composed of faculty, denominational representatives, and students, is the principal governing body of the school whose decisions, in turn, are subject to review and approval by the university senate and its governing board. The faculty council is supported by an elaborate faculty committee structure organized around the principal degree programs.

In the curriculum development and faculty hiring that realize the vision of a strong comparative religion program, the decision-making process has tended to follow a consistent, but informal pattern. Those interviewed reported that the impetus for change can come from the university, from the dean, from committees, or, as some suggested, "it can come from anywhere." Typically, on a given issue, the dean solicits opinions informally through conversation at the school's regular afternoon tea, as well as formally through the faculty council. The dean explained his strategy this way: first, "you start building toward issues one-on-one, discuss informally, and have individual faculty on board before taking them to the whole faculty"; second, "you try to put an issue on the table and to be as transparent as possible—to be open, transparent with all information and with the decisions that have to be made." From the outset, the dean tries to define and clarify the issues, as well as to set out the process by which they will be dealt with and decided.

When issues eventually come before the faculty council, they are presented and discussed at the first meeting but not placed on the agenda for formal action until the second meeting. Between meetings, faculty talk informally and sometimes circulate memos regarding the issues raised. During this process, the dean poses questions, generates discussion, and monitors the progress of the group toward some measure of agreement. When faculty disagree on an issue, it tends to be resolved by continuous and sometimes lengthy discussion. Faculty explain that issues are talked through by everyone until they arrive at consensus. Committees put things on record, but saying yes occurs informally. The work of reaching agreement often takes place outside the formal structure, although ultimately decisions are formalized and go through faculty council. As one faculty member observed, we have "a villagey way of making decisions."

In this environment where "the machinery of decision making is not well defined," as another faculty member put it, the dean does a lot of consultation one-on-one, keeps everyone well informed on a casual level, and provides many opportunities for discussion. The dean "facilitates decision making so it appears seamless," a colleague noted. The dean also is an active participant in this dialogue and, while having only one voice and one vote, clearly influences the deliberations. As one long-term faculty member explained, "Decisions are made in the open, but influence is exerted informally." One of the denominational leaders affiliated with the school believed that the trust and good will among the faculty, the absence of turf battles and acrimony, is due in large part to the dean's consultative, collegial approach: "The ethos has something to do with who the dean is."

Many also remarked on "the tradition of civility" that has long characterized the faculty and makes shared governance possible.

Beyond the school, the dean described his work with university administrators in similar fashion. Although he has contact with university executive and chief academic officers through committee meetings and a handful of appointments scheduled through the year, he does a lot of business at luncheon gatherings or during conversation over cocktails. The dean likes these interactions and finds things are accomplished more efficiently. Widely considered an effective dean, he views his role as advocating for the needs of religious studies to the university and communicating the university regulations and budget parameters to the religious studies faculty. In this university setting, the dean provides the link between the faculty and programs of the school and the larger university of which the school is a part.

These two examples of leadership practices illustrate how the institutional vision comes to be supported and owned by the academic community through distinctly different processes that nonetheless have several common features. While the first process is decidedly more prescribed and the second more informal, both are directed by deans who explicitly encourage the participation of all constituent groups. Both directly involve all members of the faculty at every stage and provide for appropriate consultations with other groups in the formative phase of the project. In such participatory processes, ideas for change may come from anywhere, but it is the dean and the faculty who are most directly involved in developing proposals, negotiating differences, and successfully achieving faculty, president, and governing board approval. In these examples of academic governance, the dean in direct and subtle ways guides the process and serves as the link among the various constituents of the school.

In such contexts where decision making is shared, leadership depends on the relationships among individuals and groups and the influence those relationships make possible. During site visits, participants identified as leaders those individuals who, by virtue of their insight, expertise, status, or personal persuasiveness, helped to move the group closer to owning and implementing their common goals. In the two schools above, the deans were considered effective leaders, as were selected faculty members and students. Whether such individuals were highly visible and articulate or a quiet presence within the community, they were individuals to whom others listened and were persuaded and followed. Their leadership was a leadership of influence. At various stages in the decision-making process, their influence enabled the group to reach agreement and move forward together.

In his study of the seminary presidency, Neely McCarter finds that Joseph Rost's theory of leadership, centered on "an influence relationship among leaders and followers," is among the most useful in accounting for leadership practices in higher education.[23] In this view, influence is noncoercive, and "the relationship is fluid; influence shifts back and forth between active followers and leaders."[24] This fluid quality of leadership, where at different times leaders become followers and followers become leaders, is consistent with the findings of this study. It similarly confirms the applicability of influence-based leadership theories to the systems of shared governance prevalent in theological schools.

This general discussion of leadership practices only partially illuminates the particular forms of leadership characteristic of chief academic officers. Given their location within the organizational structure and their broad responsibilities, theological school deans have distinctive opportunities and mechanisms for exercising leadership that flow directly from the nature of their positions. Drawing from the two examples above and from several other schools participating in the research, we turn now to a closer examination of their leadership role and the specific strategies deans employ in fulfilling it.

### *The Leadership Role of the Chief Academic Officer*

Among the multiple players in the arena of academic decision making, the chief academic officer is positioned to play a significant role. As discussed in Chapter One, the breadth of the dean's responsibilities and the relationships they entail place the office at the center of institutional life. The dean is a member of the senior administrative team and works closely with faculty and administrative colleagues to manage all aspects of the academic area. In fulfilling these responsibilities, deans have frequent, even daily, interaction with individual faculty members, faculty committees, the president, other administrators, and students; most deans also have regular, though less frequent, contact with board members, denominational leaders, and others associated with the school. The centrality of the office and the substantive relations it makes possible at all levels of the organization give it a distinctive reach and access. The dean's responsibility to work with and among these groups is fundamental to the leadership of the office.

Research findings further reveal that theological school deans, despite variations in individual personalities and circumstances, exercise leadership in ways that reflect common practices tailored to cultures of shared governance. The following analysis of their leadership practices focuses on the dean's role in setting the academic agenda and in directing the decision-making process. The dean's work includes: organizing the process, exercising influence, empowering others, dealing with conflict and controversy, and securing final approval. To more clearly identify the forms of leadership embedded in these practices, we conclude with brief consideration of two theories of leadership that provide a useful framework for understanding the role of the chief academic officer.

*Setting the Academic Agenda.* In schools where chief academic officers are effective members of the administrative team and have responsibility for developing the academic vision, they can have considerable, if not decisive, influence in determining priorities and setting short- and long-term goals for the academic area. Several deans in the study talked about the power conferred by their positions to set the academic agenda—to decide which issues are truly important and worthy of serious consideration. After six years in office, one dean believed that the opportunity to introduce ideas, to send them out as a "trial balloon" in his weekly newsletter, gave him the singular opportunity to widely disseminate his proposals and to be heard. While the dean also championed the ideas of others, the selection of certain ideas from the many circulating within the community was itself an important step in shaping the conversation and, thereby, defining the direction of the school. Several deans interviewed for the study were surprised by the power of their office to focus discussion and to command the attention and energy of others.

Senior administrators, including the dean, also have considerable latitude in determining which decisions can be made administratively and which need to proceed through the formal governance process.[25] That judgment, too, can have far-reaching consequences for the institution. In one instance, the president almost singlehandedly pursued plans for a new retreat and conference center that would enable the expansion of the school's ecumenical and continuing education programs. At the time of the site visit, he was in the process of securing the support of the board and the faculty, many of whom remained ambivalent about the center, concerned about its leadership and about the apparent lack of ownership of the president's vision. The opposite problem faced a university dean early in her administration. She firmly believed in consultation with faculty on all important issues and was surprised to discover their indifference to some issues and their preference that she make most administrative decisions herself. More commonly, however, faculty tend not to feel adequately informed and consulted about administrative decisions that may have an impact, directly or indirectly, on the academic area. In the schools visited for this study, constituents placed high value on collegial decision-making processes and preferred to be overconsulted, rather than underconsulted, on important institutional decisions. Determining which decision-making processes are appropriate to which issues is, in itself, a significant administrative decision.

*Directing the Decision-Making Process.* Although academic decision making is governed in large part by a process of formal approvals that takes the familiar path through faculty committees, the faculty body, the president, and the governing board, the chief academic officer often plays the principal role in developing and directing that process. As the preceding example of curriculum revision shows (Example 1), the dean can influence the process in several ways. First, the dean, usually in consultation with the president, appoints some or all members of the planning committee and is seated either as chair or ex officio member of that group. This selection implicitly determines how representative the working group will be and what skills, attitudes, and beliefs will be brought to the table. Through this selection, the dean also may choose to include or exclude individuals who are notoriously critical or resistant to change. One experienced dean always wanted the opposition on the committee, because it was in the committee that the case had to be won. When deans also serve as members or chairs of such committees, they become influential in shaping many of the committee's strategic and substantive decisions.

Second, as chief academic officer and/or as member of the working group, the dean can determine how consultative and collegial the process will be. Who is involved and at what stages can significantly affect the specific content of the plan and its ultimate support and approval. In the previous example of curriculum revision, the decision to include denominational leaders early in the process enabled their needs and concerns to surface at a formative stage. Whether or not specific ideas are incorporated, consulting interested parties while drafting the plan helps to avoid unforeseen objections late in the process and serves to develop a sense of community ownership.

Failure to include interested groups at appropriate stages can be costly. At another school, the denomination advised its seminaries to develop a two-year pre-theology program for students entering without adequate preparation. After intensive work over a full year to revise the curriculum, the faculty designed "a Cadillac" two-year program that was strongly and enthusiastically endorsed by faculty members, administrators, and trustees of the school. On the verge of its final approval, the president learned from bishops and vocation directors their decided preference for a shorter, one-year program. "Based on data they didn't have," the president persuaded the faculty and the board they needed to go back to the drawing board and begin again. In the second round, bishops and vocation directors were included in the consultations. Faculty understandably were frustrated that their considerable time and effort in developing the two-year program came to naught.

At another seminary, insufficient consultation with faculty defeated a proposal for an extension program in Hispanic Ministry. In this case, the director of racial and ethnic ministries worked with the president, dean, two other seminaries, and an advisory committee of Hispanic church leaders to develop the plan for an off-site Hispanic ministries program. When the proposal came to the faculty for approval, they rejected it. Their ideas about cooperation and concerns about staffing had not been heard. At that point, however, they were confident the president and dean would appoint a planning committee and "put faculty on the committee who can sell it to the faculty." In instances such as these, who is included in planning and at what stage they enter the process become critical to its ultimate success.

Third, deans usually are responsible for establishing an appropriate pace for the process, deciding when there has been sufficient discussion and resolution of issues to bring matters to a vote. Some schools routinely present an item for consideration at one meeting, but postpone the vote until the second meeting to allow time for adequate discussion. On larger projects, like curriculum or handbook revision, for example, when decision-making processes are more protracted and complex, the pacing of committee work, consultations, and decisions requires careful planning. An instructive example is the seminary working to change its course schedule to include a four-day week and evening classes. An experienced dean, who practiced his belief that "you can never consult too much," had guided the proposal through the executive committee of the faculty, two student forums, several faculty committees, the academic divisions, and finally presented it to the whole faculty. The pace of the process accelerated at the end, since the dean stipulated a March deadline for the decision so he could prepare the course schedule before leaving on sabbatical. The faculty felt rushed. When it came to the faculty for a vote at the eleventh hour, it seemed railroaded even though it had gone through faculty committees. Some faculty described it as a fait accompli and had little ownership of the new schedule. The pace of the process, along with its inclusiveness, can determine whether worthy proposals are successful and, as importantly, whether they are approved with enough support to be effectively implemented.

In addition to leading faculty and other constituents through the decision-making process, deans also perform a variety of managerial tasks to facilitate the work of committees and of the faculty as a whole. When deans serve on committees where proposals are drafted and planning occurs, they often handle organizational tasks, such as scheduling meetings, preparing agendas, providing relevant data and information, keeping others informed of the committee's progress, and coordinating their work with that of other groups within the school. As deans structure and guide the decision-making process and handle many of the administrative tasks associated with it, the leadership and managerial roles of the office come together.

*Exercising Influence.* While deans exert considerable influence in appointing committee members and guiding the decision-making process, they find that few, if any, decisions ultimately rest with them. In matters of academic and institutional governance, it is the faculty or the president or the president's cabinet who makes the final decisions that then are subject to board approval. An associate academic dean of a university divinity school noted that the only areas in which he had authority to make decisions without involving the dean/executive officer or faculty were granting permissions and excuses and assigning classrooms. The academic officer "has more power than authority," he explained, "and in many instances either the faculty or the dean [executive officer] has the final say."

Paradoxically, several of the deans also recognize that their position has considerable power and authority, more than they anticipated and sometimes more than they would like. The authority of chief academic officers, the power or rights delegated to them by virtue of their positions, goes well beyond the handful of administrative decisions they make on their own. As noted above, deans have the right to initiate projects, to appoint committees, to orchestrate decision-making processes, and to influence decisions. In fulfilling their duties, deans also enforce compliance with policies and procedures and enlist the cooperation of others on a range of institutional activities.

Of these and similar powers that comprise the authority of the deanship, none is more important than the dean's ability to influence academic and institutional decisions. An experienced university dean described that influence as both personal and positional. Deans may influence decisions in personal ways by their knowledge, expertise, and persuasiveness. Deans who have a comprehensive view of the curriculum, or a realistic sense of budgetary constraints, or a detailed knowledge of accreditation standards and trends in theological education may gain support for ideas through such expertise. Personal characteristics, such as honesty, fairness, integrity, can elicit the trust and respect of colleagues and enhance the dean's influence. Some deans also are personally persuasive, able to present ideas cogently and convincingly to various groups.

Somewhat more complex is the power and influence that accrue to deans by virtue of their office. Deans often report having influence that goes well beyond the one voice and one vote they have on committees and in meetings. With few exceptions, deans who come to their positions from the faculty experience a palpable change in how their words and actions are weighed and perceived by colleagues. As dean, one speaks not merely as an individual but as senior officer of the institution, as representative of the faculty or administration or both, and as one who has close and influential relationships with members of these groups. Through the position, the academic community confers authority on its officeholders, and many members are prepared to be influenced and guided by their ideas. Mindful of the power of their positions, several deans and presidents interviewed for the study reported some hesitation about brainstorming with colleagues or floating very preliminary ideas, since their comments often became widely circulated and interpreted as official statements. Particularly deans new to their positions were surprised, and somewhat chagrined, to discover that even casual remarks can assume an unintended weight. As a seminary provost explains, "I really hold ideas quite loosely but, because I'm provost, they're heard quite tightly."

The power of the deanship, then, lies not in de facto decision-making authority or having "the final say," which is limited in systems of shared governance, but in the influence on major decisions that the position makes possible. Academic communities confer on positional leaders, like the chief academic officer, both the mechanisms and opportunities to shape the decision-making process and to influence its outcomes. Directly, through committee appointments and consultative practices for example, and indirectly, through personal relationships and conversations, deans have a power and authority that exceeds that of nonpositional leaders. Effective chief academic officers understand the leadership potential of their office and use the power it confers to guide the community in defining and accomplishing its goals.

*Empowering Others.* As the preceding discussion has shown, the leadership capacity of the deanship lies not in the authority to decide *for* others but in the opportunity to work *with* others toward shared goals. In the process of academic governance, effective deans create formal and informal opportunities for colleagues to participate fully in discussions and deliberations, and they explicitly invite other interested groups to consult at appropriate stages in the process. While some may invite participation reluctantly or half-heartedly, the deans perceived as effective leaders elicited ideas in a timely way and genuinely took them into account. In such instances, even those who disagreed with the final decision felt informed and included in the process.

Beyond insuring broad and effective participation in governance, deans also are positioned to create leadership opportunities for others, particularly for members of the faculty. At one school, a faculty member who assisted the dean with special projects was appointed head of the curriculum revision committee and director of a high-profile initiative in faculty development. The dean made these appointments with obvious conviction about the skill and leadership potential of the faculty member; and the faculty member discovered that his creativity, organizational skills, and thoroughness were helpful to colleagues and effective in moving the process along. In this case, the dean set the general direction for the process, then empowered the faculty member to organize planning and see it through. On the survey conducted as part of this study, 76 percent of theological school deans felt they had the primary responsibility for developing faculty leadership. Clearly, the leadership of chief academic officers consists, in large part, in empowering others to exercise leadership and to contribute their talent and best thinking for the benefit of the community.

In *Leadership Without Easy Answers,* Ronald Heifetz recognizes the tendency of groups to turn to their leaders for solutions to their problems, rather than engaging in the difficult work of confronting and solving the problems themselves.[26] In this view, an essential task of leadership is to awaken the community to its critical issues and to enable them to engage those issues and work together toward their resolution. In one seminary where revision of the M.Div. curriculum was politicized and particularly difficult, the dean resisted efforts by the faculty to have him shoulder responsibility for the controversial changes the committee recommended. The dean explained that he "brokered the process" but was careful to keep ownership in the committee, even when no one wanted to take leadership responsibility. As the dean explained, "I had to be on top of [the review process] and broker it, but I always felt that any suggestion that was made was made in the name of the committee." He was vigilant in keeping the work squarely within the committee. "I kept saying [to the committee], 'You have to talk and you have got to sit down and do this together.' . . . I had more than enough to do and I wasn't going to manage that for them." By resisting the temptation to take charge, the dean kept the work of resolving issues with the primary stakeholders, the faculty. Keeping faculty on task also served to maintain and strengthen their ownership of the final product.

Several deans spoke with conviction about the importance of empowering others and avoiding the top-down exercise of power from the dean's office. The chief academic officer of a large evangelical seminary explained:

> I succeed to the degree that people think it's their idea. So my role is to have as little of that seemingly come from me as possible and, nevertheless, to shape and direct and plant seeds such that it happens well and in a coordinated way and accomplishes [something]. To the degree that it's perceived as top-down, resentment builds, and you pay the price at some point. . . . You run out of chips if that's your approach.

After six years in office, another dean constantly reminds himself "not to force change from the office but to consult way beyond the call of duty." He tries to make sure that "the leadership is out there in the faculty, not in the dean's office all the time."

An important aspect of the dean's leadership, then, is to empower others, to draw forth their strengths and gifts for the good of the whole. In addition to encouraging the full participation of faculty and other constituent groups in academic governance, the dean is instrumental in tapping individuals for leadership positions, thereby developing their skills and enhancing their influence on the process. Some deans measure their success as administrators by the extent to which colleagues become seriously engaged in academic planning and decision making. As evident in the examples above, experienced deans are intentional in their efforts to keep the ownership of academic decisions within the faculty. As participants and guides in these processes, deans exercise their leadership, in part, by developing the leadership of others.

*Dealing with Conflict and Controversy.* In the arena of academic decision making, differences of opinion are inevitable. Decisions about faculty hiring or curriculum changes, for example, can require difficult choices and trade-offs and even, in some cases, can test the core values of the institution. Whether different viewpoints are mediated civilly or erupt into major conflicts can depend on the ability of the chief academic officer, who directs the process, to diffuse controversy, to mediate opposition and build alliances, and to bring the community to some measure of agreement. While many participate in making academic decisions, the dean serves as the overseer and guide of the process and, given the centrality of the office, serves as the critical link among faculty members, among departments, and between the faculty and the president, other administrators, and students. When dealing with controversial issues, effective deans use this broad network of personal relationships to persuade, mediate, negotiate, and bring disparate parties to a common ground. This task is rarely easy. Even experienced deans consider dealing with conflict and controversy one of the most difficult, yet critical, aspects of their job.

In theological schools with longstanding cultures of civility, deans and faculty report that disagreements still exist but tend to be expressed rationally and respectfully. At one university divinity school, faculty and administrators always stated their differences early in the process and then simply kept talking until those differences were resolved. As a faculty member observed, if decisions were forced, things would be more contentious. But "civility characterizes this faculty . . . there is a strong culture of decorum that eases stress points." In such fortunate circumstances, the dean participates and brokers ideas, but essentially helps to pace and monitor the group's progress toward agreement.

In theological schools with well-established traditions of propriety and decorum, disregard for cultural norms can be self-defeating. At one seminary, it was considered a violation of group norms "to air dirty laundry publicly" or to disregard established channels in voicing one's objections. When a tenure case became controversial and a faculty member circulated to church officials his objections to the candidate, his action was a clear violation of the tenure review process and of the authority of the dean and the faculty. The controversy over his violation of cultural norms became more significant than the substance of his objections. As the case attracted campus publicity, the dean instructed faculty and staff to keep the matter in-house. Even when this admonition went unheeded, the dean was strongly supported by group norms that were intolerant of such practices.

More commonly, however, heated controversy can erupt unexpectedly and lead to difficult, emotional, and potentially damaging exchanges. As noted previously, one strategy deans can use to reduce the heat and move the group forward is to regulate the pace of the process. The chief academic officer at a large seminary with multiple layers in the decision-making structure explains how he deals with controversy: "You talk a lot. You never try to cram through a decision, so you float. . . ." When an issue, like scheduling change, is stressful for the faculty, "you float it with them, but you're not asking for a decision. Three months later you bring it back for a vote. You let it percolate, you get new ideas, and you let the animosity drain off. . . ."

Deans frequently find that time is on their side. To keep faculty talking, to allow time for the animosity to drain off can be more effective than direct intervention in resolving issues. Two deans in the study postponed decisions for a year because of too much disagreement. At a seminary where a new program was on the verge of defeat, the dean requested additional time to gather more information and, though not publicly acknowledged, to mold opinion. Sometimes, faculty simply need more time for discussion and debate. During a particularly difficult curriculum revision process, the dean got angry letters from a couple of faculty members. Their concerns were resolved "through some honest and open discussion at a faculty meeting where people were able to say what they thought." The fact that people were able to be forthright in their criticisms of the curriculum proposal, and to express them publicly, enabled the dean and committee to address them. Taking time with the decision-making process also allows deans to take indirect approaches to achieving faculty cooperation. Several deans planned regular social events for faculty in part to nurture friendships and make it easier for them to talk openly with one another when dealing with difficult issues.

Many of the deans and presidents in the study acknowledged that they and their institutions tend to be conflict-averse. The sentiments expressed by this chief academic officer were typical: "Personality-wise I'm not great at digging into conflict. I tend to try to wish it away, to give it a positive spin and come up with a synthesis that somehow makes everybody happy." But, as he admits, "that doesn't always work." In those instances, some deans use personal persuasion to ameliorate conflict and move people toward agreement. One seminary dean, who had served twelve years in his position, had been caught in the middle of conflicts many times and had developed a strategy for dealing with them: "I attempt to hear both sides, to hear what is nonnegotiable, to present creative alternatives, to determine achievable outcomes if the original goal is unattainable, and to let go if an issue is not resolvable." He believed that "politics is the art of the possible." His preference was to have opposing views represented on committees. He was convinced that if the strongest objections could be heard and resolved within the committee, if compromises could be forged there, then the proposal would move more easily through the faculty.

Other deans arbitrate in larger forums. One, for example, believed controversy could best be defused at open all-school meetings, where differences could be aired and everyone heard. The president at the same school preferred to deal privately with difficult matters, working one-on-one with those directly involved. The difference in these approaches shows how closely they are linked to individual personality and style. Deans in the study considered effective by their colleagues used approaches for dealing with controversy that played to their personal strengths, were appropriate to the issues at hand, and were well adapted to the culture and ethos of the institution.

However, even with skilled and experienced deans, some issues engender conflicts so divisive they cannot be resolved by customary measures. Two examples from the study involved faculty hirings. The first seminary had a strong commitment to diversity, and the campus became sharply divided between "a white female finalist with traditional, highly regarded credentials, and the second finalist, a male of color, with less orthodox credentials." In the words of participants, the issue in the final stages of the search was "the weight given to racial identity over against other academic values." The conflict, which was deep and painful, alerted the campus to the limits of their problem-solving skills and methods. The seminary hired outside consultants to work with faculty and administrators on revising search process guidelines and on developing conflict-resolution skills.

In a similar case at another seminary, the campus split between a white male and a woman candidate whose theological views were problematic for the majority of faculty. The dean felt caught between factions, and increased faculty animosity when he finally took sides. When the faculty sent their recommendation to the board without consensus, the board sent it back for further discussion. The board held hearings with students and faculty and was able to achieve an acceptable compromise. This rupture, however, so seriously divided the faculty and the community that it resulted in a breakdown in institutional trust. As the dean explains, "It was like an earthquake went through the place in terms of loss. We came very close to just dissolving." They spent over a year recovering with the help of outside consultants and a retreat.

The responsibility to mediate differences in the course of academic decision making can be formidable, and even respected, experienced deans may be unable at times to resolve deep-seated conflicts of ideology and of values. Based on the diverse schools visited for this study, however, deans generally are in regular dialogue with individual faculty members and other constituents who afford perspective on the issues and tensions to be resolved. Whatever insight others bring to the process, however, the dean often is personally required to undertake the difficult tasks of negotiating and mediating disagreements. Deans who are conflict-averse by temperament or who lack mediating skills may be strengthened in their efforts by formal training in conflict management.[27] An ability to deal constructively with conflict, to resolve contentious issues, to facilitate agreement, or to recognize when issues are not resolvable are among the foremost skills required of chief academic officers.

*Securing Final Approval.* When such efforts culminate in the vote of the faculty to recommend a particular proposal or course of action, deans still may need to advocate for the proposal to the president and senior administrators, or the dean may be called upon to assist the president in presenting it to university committees or to the seminary board of trustees. If the dean has kept the president and administrators well informed and if the process of deliberation has been truly consultative, the need for advocacy in the final stages of approval should be minimal. As the need arises, however, it is the chief academic officer who is responsible for clearing the path through the administration for final approval by the board. The dean is liaison among these groups and both represents and advocates for the academic area. In fostering communication and finding common ground among diverse constituencies, chief academic officers help to bridge differences and strengthen ties within the community.

*Conclusion*

The preceding description of the dean's leadership role differs from the traditional view of the singular charismatic leader whose own compelling vision rallies followers and transforms communities. The leadership we have described is less grandiose and heroic. The dean works within the community to articulate a shared vision and to engage colleagues in its implementation. The dean designs and oversees the process by which various individuals and groups work to resolve their differences and reach agreement. With broad responsibilities and a network of relationships that reaches many individuals among all constituent groups, the dean works from the center of the organization to bring divergent views and voices together. Serving as facilitator, negotiator, and guide, deans exercise leadership by enabling others to participate in governance and to achieve their common goals.

Two theoretical models most notably capture facets of this distinctive form of leadership. In their review of leadership theories as they apply to higher education, Bensimon, Neumann, and Birnbaum find transactional theories useful in explaining the type of leadership prevalent in systems of shared governance. Transactional theory "views leadership as a mutual and reciprocal process of social exchange between leaders and their followers. The ability to exercise leadership is seen as highly dependent on the group's willingness to accept the leader."[28] The emphasis here is on the relationship of social exchange between leaders and followers, the two-way communication and mutual influence that befits participation in a collective decision-making process. Transactional theories find that "the leader's role is more appropriately seen as servant than as controller," as facilitator rather than as director; leaders are viewed "as coordinators of ongoing activities rather than as architects of bold initiatives."[29] These portrayals are consistent with our analysis of the leadership role of theological school deans. As Bensimon et al. rightly observe, "Good leadership in higher education may not necessarily consist of doing the work of the organization but of helping the organization do its own work. . . ."[30]

The theory advanced by Ronald Heifetz in *Leadership Without Easy Answers* is even more powerful in its ability to explain the leadership practices of chief academic officers. According to Heifetz, "[P]rogress on problems is the measure of leadership; leaders mobilize people to face problems, and communities make progress on problems because leaders challenge and help them do so."[31] Heifetz sees adaptive work that requires "a change in values, beliefs, or behavior" as the heart of leadership. "Adaptive work consists of the learning required to address conflicts in the values people hold, or to diminish the gap between the values people stand for and the reality they face."[32] Like deans who work with colleagues on curricular changes or hiring decisions, the central task of the leader is "to get people to clarify what matters most, in what balance, and with what trade-offs."[33] "The hardest and most valuable task of leadership," according to Heifetz, "may be advancing goals and designing strategy that promote adaptive work."[34] This view of leadership, as working within community to mobilize its members to clarify their values and purposes and to solve their problems, speaks directly to the leadership role of the chief academic officer.

"Advancing goals and designing strategy" is precisely the work of the dean. As noted earlier in our discussion, vision is developed with and through others, and it is the task of the dean, as a positional leader, to identify and articulate the collective vision.[35] The strategies for implementing change employed by theological school deans incorporate several of the strategic principles set out by Heifetz: 1) leaders identify the adaptive challenge, the gap between beliefs and reality, and focus attention on specific issues; 2) leaders pace the rate of change and give structure to the process; 3) leaders have the power to frame issues and to influence the terms of the discussion; they keep attention focused on the relevant issues; 4) leaders shift responsibility for the problem to the primary stakeholders; they give the work back to people; 5) leaders have the power to choose the decision-making process itself.[36] The authority of officeholders, according to Heifetz, is a resource because it provides the instruments and power to hold the process together, and when the leader does not know the answer or outcome, the task is to manage the process by which people with the problem achieve the resolution.[37]

While these leadership practices are found among deans in schools visited for this study, there are at least two respects in which Heifetz's model is somewhat less applicable. Heifetz emphasizes the task of solving problems rather than directing change more generally, and he suggests that leaders intentionally provoke conflict as a strategy to mobilize people to face their problems rather than seeking to avoid conflict and minimize disagreement which, as noted previously, is the common tendency in theological school cultures.

Even with certain points of divergence, the theories cited briefly here provide models of leadership practices that capture the essential role of the chief academic officer. As leaders, deans work collegially to guide the community through the processes by which it defines itself and achieves its purposes. To insure participation, to allow disparate voices to be heard, to ameliorate conflict, and to find the common ground is a form of leadership with an "enormous, and yet nearly invisible, influence."[38] A saying of Lao Tzu, posted in the office of a seminary dean, describes this type of leader: "Fail to honor people, they fail to honor you; but of a good leader, who talks little, when his work is done, his aim fulfilled, they will all say, 'We did this ourselves.'"

## Notes

[1] The pastoral role of the dean will be discussed in Chapter Four.

[2] Description of institutional characteristics is provided in the Introduction, 7.

[3] George D. Kuh and Elizabeth J. Whitt, *The Invisible Tapestry: Culture in American Colleges and Universities.* ASHE-ERIC Higher Education Report No. 1 (Washington, DC: Association for the Study of Higher Education, 1988), 12–13. Kuh and Whitt's definition of culture in higher education is stated here in abbreviated form.

[4] Ellen Earle Chaffee and William G. Tierney, *Collegiate Culture and Leadership Strategies* (Washington, DC: American Council on Education/Macmillan, 1988), 7.

[5] Contingency theories of leadership claim that effective leaders adapt their style of leadership to situational factors. A concise summary and critique of contingency theories is provided in: Estela Bensimon, Anna Neumann, and Robert Birnbaum, *Making Sense of Administrative Leadership: The 'L' Word in Higher Education,* ASHE-ERIC Higher Education Report No. 1 (Washington, DC: School of Education and Human Development, The George Washington University, 1989), 14–20, 45–49.

[6] Kuh and Whitt, iv.

[7] Lee G. Bolman and Terrence E. Deal, *Modern Approaches to Understanding and Managing Organizations* (San Francisco: Jossey-Bass, 1984).

[8] Bolman and Deal, 2–3, 31–32, 65, 109, 149–150.

[9] In their analysis of leadership and organizational theories as they apply to higher education, Bensimon and her colleagues conclude that, while effective leaders need to develop cognitive complexity by understanding the various theories of leadership and various conceptual models of organizations, some theories are more fruitful than others in explaining the realities of academic leadership and organizations. Specifically, they urge renewed attention to transactional theories of leadership and the cultural, symbolic frame of organizations. Bensimon, Neumann, and Birnbaum, 67, 69–80.

[10] Bensimon, Neumann, and Birnbaum, 54–55.

[11] Bensimon, Neumann, and Birnbaum, 56.

[12] Bolman and Deal, 64.

[13] Bensimon, Neumann, and Birnbaum, 57.

[14] This finding is corroborated by research on theological school cultures conducted independently of this project. See Mark N. Wilhelm, "Good Places to Work," *Tending Talents,* The Second in a Series of Reports from a Study of Theological Faculty. Auburn Studies, No. 5 (March 1997), 24–35.

[15] These two roles describe the deans' administrative functions, but deans also may fulfill teaching, pastoral, and mentoring roles depending on their situations.

[16] Warren Bennis, *On Becoming a Leader* (New York: Addison-Wesley, 1989; Paperback Edition, 1994), 45.

[17] Madeleine F. Green, "Developing Leadership: A Paradox in Academe," in *Academic Leaders as Managers.* Robert Atwell and Madeleine Green, eds. New Directions for Higher Education, no. 36 (San Francisco: Jossey-Bass, 1981), 12.

[18] Joseph C. Rost, *Leadership for the Twenty-First Century* (Westport, CT: Praeger Publishers, 1991), 142.

[19] One study of the managerial roles of chief academic officers in comprehensive colleges and universities employs the Mintzberg typology, which considers "leader" one of ten managerial roles. In other respects, the careful delineation of the various managerial roles of chief academic officers in this article is quite useful. See Terrence Mech, "The Managerial Roles of Chief Academic Officers," *Journal of Higher Education* 68, no. 3 (May/June 1997), 283–298.

[20] Two leaders in theological education have explored the meaning of "vision," emphasizing respectively its rootedness in "a good view of the distant past" and in the "capacity to perceive what is present." The former is discussed by Robert W. Lynn, "Living on Two Levels: The Work of the Academic Dean in North American Theological Education," *Theological Education* 24 (Autumn 1987), 75–87. The latter is discussed by Craig Dykstra, "Vision and Leadership," *Initiatives in Religion* 3, no. 1 (Winter 1994), 1–2.

[21] In a theory of leadership rich in its ability to explain academic leadership, Ronald Heifetz makes the point that leadership is not creating a vision oneself but identifying and articulating the vision within the community. In an analysis of former President Lyndon B. Johnson's effective leadership on civil rights, Heifetz states: "We often think that leadership means having a clear vision and the capacity to persuade people to make it real. In this case, Johnson had authored no vision. Events acted on him to shape the vision to which he then gave powerful articulation. He *identified the nation's vision* and put it into words." Heifetz's theory will be discussed more fully later in this chapter. Ronald A. Heifetz, *Leadership Without Easy Answers* (Cambridge, MA: The Belknap Press of Harvard University Press, 1994), 148.

[22] As Bensimon, Neumann, and Birnbaum observe, "Analysis of literally hundreds of studies performed over decades indicate that no traits have proven to be essential for successful leadership . . . and trait theories are no longer a major focus of organizational research." See p. 8.

[23] Neely Dixon McCarter, *The President as Educator: A Study of the Seminary Presidency* (Atlanta, GA: Scholars Press, 1996), 68–69. While the concept of influence is usually a component of leadership theories, it is the defining character of the leadership relationship in Rost, *Leadership for the Twenty-First Century.* Rost's full definition of leadership as "an influence relationship among leaders and followers who intend real changes that reflect their mutual purposes" is explicated in both texts and emphasizes the intent to bring about real or significant change to achieve shared goals. This is consistent with the general conception of leadership advanced by participants in this study.

[24] McCarter, 69.

[25] While academic decisions concerning curriculum, subject matter and methods of instruction, faculty status, and the like are governed in higher education by formal standards, there is greater latitude in the area of nonacademic administrative decisions. Most accredited institutions have governance documents that either replicate or

approximate the standards adopted by the American Association of University Professors (AAUP) in the 1966 "Joint Statement on Government of Colleges and Universities." While the faculty clearly has primary responsibility in all academic matters, the guidelines state only that "the broadest possible exchange of information and opinion" should be the rule in nonacademic areas such as long-range planning, physical resources, and budgeting.

[26] Heifetz, 14–15, 129–129, 250–252.

[27] A helpful starting point for thinking constructively about conflict management is Susan A. Holton, ed., *Conflict Management in Higher Education,* New Directions for Higher Education, no. 92 (San Francisco: Jossey-Bass, 1995). In addition to offering practical advice on common forms of conflict in higher education, such as faculty-to-faculty conflicts, student conflicts, administrator-faculty conflicts, and the like, the book includes a list of conflict-management programs available in the United States.

[28] Bensimon, Neumann, and Birnbaum, 74–75.

[29] Bensimon, Neumann, Birnbaum, 39–40, 75. Implicit here is the contrast between two social-exchange theories: the transactional theories described in the text, and the transformational theories in which leaders are directive and, through their motivation and inspiration, have an impact on their followers. In this manner, leaders fundamentally transform their organizations.

[30] Bensimon, Neumann, Birnbaum, 75–76.

[31] In an essay commissioned for this project, Brian McDermott discusses Heifetz's leadership theory and the challenges of adaptive work as they apply to his role as dean at Weston Jesuit School of Theology. See Brian O. McDermott, "Of Force Fields and Aspirations: Being an Academic Dean in the Nineteen Nineties," *Theological Education* 33 (Supplement Autumn 1996), 47–59.

[32] Heifetz, 22.

[33] Heifetz, 22. Adaptive work, which requires a change in values, beliefs, or behavior, is contrasted with technical work, in which problems are readily defined and amenable to clear-cut solutions.

[34] Heifetz, 23.

[35] Heifetz, 23, 148. Heifetz explains that he does not forsake the image of leadership as a visionary activity, but "places emphasis on the act of giving clarity and articulation to a community's guiding values."

[36] Heifetz returns to these principles in somewhat different configurations throughout the book, citing them as tools or strategic principles of leadership, 99–100, 104–122, 128–129.

[37] Heifetz, 84–88.

[38] I borrow the phrasing of Elizabeth Nordbeck who, in an essay written for this project, states, "Deanships are positions of enormous, and yet nearly invisible, influence." Elizabeth C. Nordbeck, "The Once and Future Dean: Reflections on Being a Chief Academic Officer," *Theological Education* 33 (Supplement 1996), 32.

# 3 The Dean-President Relationship

*"Trust is the coin of the realm."*

*Theological school dean*

In a 1994 case that received considerable public attention, a board of trustees demanded the resignation of both the seminary's academic dean and development officer for their alleged efforts to remove their president from office.[1] Few crises in the dean-president relationship have been of such magnitude or elicited such reaction. When the president resigned amidst claims of grave ineffectiveness, the board subsequently charged the two administrators with disloyalty to the president and, by extension, to the seminary.[2] The president had been hampered, the board felt, by inheriting senior administrators not of his choosing, and they wanted the next president to have freedom in selecting an administrative team. After formal hearings, a committee found the board's accusations to be insubstantial, and both administrators were reinstated to their positions.

During this same period, at another seminary, a dean and president were becoming increasingly aware of differences in their approaches to decision making and were having difficulties coordinating their respective roles. Both were dynamic individuals with strong personal commitments to the academic life of the institution and to a vision of its future. This relatively new administrative team was publicly perceived as ushering in a new era for the seminary and working compatibly toward shared goals. Privately, however, the president and dean were struggling. They were beset by persistent tensions over differences in their working styles and were searching for ways to remedy their role confusion, particularly regarding their leadership in academic matters. The relationship, while promising, was troubled.

Although these examples are specific to the politics and personalities in particular settings, they reveal the complexity of the dean-president relationship and the intentional effort required to establish and sustain it. Factors such as the circumstances of hiring, respect for professional competencies, the quality of communication, the compatibility of working styles, and mutual understanding of roles can determine the strength and durability of the relationship. So interdependent are the president and dean that serious problems between them not only affect the work of their respective offices but, as occurred in the instances above, can have a disruptive, destabilizing effect on the institution as a whole. On the other hand, effective partnerships can have a salutary effect on the sense of well-being and stability within the school.

This interdependence of president and dean is rooted in the history of both offices and is dramatically evident in current administrative and leadership practices within theological schools. While history tells the story of the structural relationship between the two positions, their interdependence is most apparent in the actual working relationships between particular presidents and deans. How roles are defined, how work is divided and shared between the two positions, how understandings are reached and differences resolved, in short, how presidents and deans work in partnership to manage and lead the schools, is the primary focus of this chapter.

After revisiting briefly crucial aspects of the recent history of both offices, we will draw principally on site visit interviews and focus groups to explore the working relationship of presidents and deans. These findings will enable us to identify characteristics of effective dean-president relationships and to discover how, in the absence of these qualities, relationships become problematic. Central to this discussion is analysis of several partnerships distinguished by their delineation of roles and by the personal dynamics of their interactions. This chapter concludes by exploring the challenge deans face in maintaining their dual allegiance to presidents and to faculty.

## Interdependence of the Offices

The offices of president and dean are historically interdependent. As discussed in Chapter One, the position of academic dean was created to take on the overflow of duties from the president. With the growing size and complexity of institutions, the dean provided general administrative assistance and had particular responsibility for the academic program.[3] As the position has evolved, the nature and scope of the dean's work has changed relative to changes in the presidency. Most notably in recent years, the need for financial development has caused presidents to focus externally on constituent relations and fundraising; in most instances, this has meant that chief academic officers take on a broader range of administrative tasks and become more central to the internal management and leadership of the schools.

A seminary president participating in the study reflected on his sixteen years in office:

> The president's job has changed. Now it is more administrative and includes more resource development and fundraising. . . . The president is now spending more time off-campus. It feels like the dean is responsible for more things, and the president's priority is in another place.

Another president similarly observed that "the dean used to be the faculty secretary and registrar, and the president was like the dean. The dean now has become more of the in-house academic leader and the president less." He noted the "emergence of the active dean" who shapes the curriculum, builds the faculty, responds to the environment, and is knowledgeable about educational developments and new technologies.

Deans and presidents commonly reported the trend toward presidents being the representatives and leaders of the school *externally* and deans the managers and leaders of the school *internally*.[4] "Deans are taking on many of the roles presidents traditionally had, and presidents are increasingly removed from faculty and students and do more with development and business people," as a dean in the study observed. In a 1997 article, William E. Lesher, president of Lutheran School of Theology in Chicago, noted that during his nineteen years in office the time spent on development steadily increased from about 10 percent of his workload to 60 percent. He described two by-products of this change: "[A]dministratively, I've gone from about twelve people to supervise to two. The whole development role has become much more prominent for me, and the kind of teacher-administrator that I was at the beginning has waned."[5]

This experience is replicated in many theological schools with similar consequences: as a president directly supervises fewer people, the chief academic officer and other administrators supervise more; as the president becomes less the teacher-scholar among administrators, the dean becomes more prominent in that role. Another president reported to his board of trustees that, since the early 1980s, the pendulum has shifted from the president as "scholar-administrator" to the president as "educator-manager-administrator." This change, so pervasive in higher education, he acknowledges is also "quite commonplace in American theological schools."[6]

While changes in the presidency and the "emergence of the active dean" may occur gradually, even subtly, over time and at different rates in different schools, the diverse group of executive and academic officers participating in this study described these parallel changes in their roles in similar terms. As presidents experience, often with dismay, the gradual shift away from academic responsibilities toward public relations and development, many deans find the steady accretion of administrative and supervisory responsibilities can further diminish their teaching and scholarship and lead to job overload. Changes in the presidency clearly have a ripple effect. If "taking on the overflow of duties from the president" continues to be a principal means of defining the deanship, regular assessment of workload and creative thinking about the apportionment of duties among senior administrators become increasingly important.

Even as the role and responsibilities of chief academic officers have changed relative to the presidency, other features in the structural relationship between the two positions have remained constant. To the present day, most presidents play a decisive role in the hiring of deans; they define the specific duties of the office; and they determine, through the differentiation of roles, the administrative and leadership parameters of the dean's work. The majority of deans serve at the pleasure of their presidents or chief executive officers to whom they directly report.[7] Presidents usually set the conditions of the dean's appointment and, given their supervisory role, attend to their evaluation and professional development. (The president's responsibility in these areas will be examined more fully in Chapters Six and Seven.)

In the daily work of academic administration, however, the reciprocal and interdependent nature of the dean-president relationship becomes most evident. The subsequent discussion of this relationship shows the level of shared understanding, the patterns of communication, the complementarity of gifts, and the mutual confidence and trust that must exist for them to fulfill their respective roles effectively. While the chief academic officer works for the president and the powers of their offices differ, in practice they depend on one another in matters large and small for advice, counsel, and support. Extensive interviews with presidents and deans conducted for this study enable us to examine ten administrative partnerships that afford insight into the complex interdependence at the heart of their working relationship.[8]

## Effective Dean-President Relationships

On the survey conducted for this project, 91 percent of theological school deans rated the relationship with their presidents "good" to "excellent," and 92 percent agreed or strongly agreed with the statement: "I believe I serve with the full support of the president/chief executive."[9] This high level of confidence in the quality of the relationship was borne out in the majority of sites visited for this study. Interviews revealed that such relationships are complex and highly nuanced, and the process of establishing and maintaining strong relationships is not always an easy one. Site visit evidence suggests that these positive appraisals of the relationship are less an indication of the absence of difficulties and challenges than that both parties can work together to deal effectively with them.

Clearly, there is no single formula for success. Among the factors that contribute to effective long-term working relationships, many are personal and context-specific. The compatibility of personalities and working styles, the match between individuals and their institutional cultures can be idiosyncratic and impossible to replicate. Other characteristics of these relationships, however, can be generalized, since deans and presidents in diverse settings identified the same basic elements of effective working relationships. The following analysis, based primarily on site visit interviews, is indebted to the deans and presidents who spoke openly and candidly of their hopes and concerns, their successes and difficulties.

Analysis begins with the fundamental issue of the delineation of roles. While there are various ways in which duties are distributed and management and leadership tasks are shared, clarity regarding that arrangement is a critical first step in establishing an effective working relationship. Interviews with presidents and deans also explored what it takes to maintain a partnership that is strong enough to withstand external pressures, yet flexible enough to adapt to the changing requirements of their positions. How experienced administrators sustain their relationships will be examined through several closely related topics: communication practices, compatibility of working styles, ability to deal with conflict and disagreement, and other relational qualities, such as trust, support, and friendship.

*Delineation of Roles*

Unquestionably, mutual understanding of the responsibilities and roles of both offices, how they differ and where they intersect, is the foundation of a successful dean-president relationship. Defining the principal duties of presidents and deans is easier and more straightforward than describing their roles. During site visit interviews, presidents and deans confidently discussed their major areas of responsibility. Even while acknowledging a certain fluidity in the way tasks are distributed between them and recognizing that institutional documents listing their duties may not be up-to-date, they demonstrated current and compatible understandings of the responsibilities of both offices.[10]

While presidents and deans found it relatively easy to define their respective duties, describing their roles, separately and relative to one another, proved to be a more complex and uncertain task. The managerial role was least problematic, since senior administrators typically are the principal managers of programs and personnel in their areas of primary responsibility. The president, for example, manages trustee and constituent relations; the dean oversees the smooth and organized functioning of the academic area; the financial officer manages the institutional budget, and the like. Although managerial tasks can be delegated and shared, the principal managerial roles tend to be assigned to senior administrators and to be aligned with their primary duties.

The leadership roles of presidents and deans, particularly in academic matters, can be considerably more difficult to describe and distinguish. Drawing examples from the study, we will consider various ways in which the chief academic officer role is defined vis-à-vis the president, then we will examine the challenges arising when both take an active role in the academic leadership of the schools.

*Defining the Dean's Role.* In discussing the responsibilities of theological school deans in Chapter One, we noted that the particular combination of duties can vary considerably from one institution to another.[11] Some deans, for example, may have a narrowly defined set of responsibilities that focus mainly on the curriculum and academic programs, with little or no administrative responsibility for personnel or budgetary decisions. Other deans may have the full range of responsibilities for academic programs, policy, personnel, and budgets and have considerable autonomy in administering these areas.

Curiously, the scope of duties assigned to the dean is not always consonant with other expectations concerning the dean's role. For example, the associate dean of a university divinity school and the dean of a small freestanding seminary both have positions primarily defined by their responsibility for planning, maintaining, and evaluating the curriculum and academic programs. The chief executive officers of both institutions work directly with the faculty in the areas of faculty hiring and evaluation, and financial matters relating to salaries and academic budgets. In the first case, however, the associate dean has significant responsibility for academic leadership: he is expected to articulate the academic vision and to oversee its implementation in the curriculum and programs of the school. In the other case, the dean is considered the administrative assistant of both the president and the faculty. As this president explains, the dean's role is "to assure that degree programs are well defined, interpreted, managed, and monitored. He is not called upon to be the director of faculty; the [president] is." Due in part to institutional tradition, to the president's own envisioning of the dean's role, and to the perception that the dean is not properly credentialed for a leadership position, the role of this particular dean remains almost exclusively managerial.

The roles of chief academic officers with broad institutional responsibilities are similarly varied. In two of the larger freestanding seminaries, the chief academic officers had the full range of academic administrative duties. In one instance, the president expected the dean to work with the faculty to develop an academic vision for the school; in the other instance, the president had responsibility for developing the vision, and the provost was expected to guide its implementation. In the first case, the president "trusts the chief academic officer to have the academic vision, since he [the president] is just a preacher." In the second example, the president explained, "If I had to use simple terms I'd talk about the difference between the visionary and the manager. I need a provost who does more managing and really understands my vision."

Clarification of presidential expectations concerning the role of the chief academic officer and the dean's acceptance of that role are critical to their working together successfully. Where the role is misunderstood by either party, missteps and confusion can result. Findings of the study suggest there is considerable clarity and agreement between presidents and deans regarding the duties of office, which are commonly specified in writing and discussed, but there are less well-defined and more implicit understandings of their respective administrative roles and areas of formal and informal authority. Most problematic is their leadership in academic matters where the roles of president and dean converge. Presidents in the study differed in their views of how leadership is shared with academic officers and others within their schools. Consequently, mutual understanding of this role by individual presidents and deans cannot be presumed.[12]

*The Dilemma of Academic Leadership.* During a focus group discussion of seminary presidents, one participant described a dilemma many presidents face:

> The best presidents are those who really essentially are academics, who are committed to the academic enterprise as the reason they are in the job. . . . One of the most difficult things emotionally is to hand over to somebody else the work that you love to do, that brought you into this whole affair to begin with.

Another president and former dean added: "Presidents want to have an academic vision and not just be out there for the money." A recent study of the seminary presidency confirms that 63 percent of presidents once served as faculty members and 32 percent served as academic deans.[13] Some presidents with prior experience and strong ties to the academic life struggle to balance their own commitments with the need to delegate significant portions of the academic administration and leadership of the school to someone else.

Presidents interviewed for the study dealt with this issue in different ways. At one end of the spectrum is the president who seeks to "hire good people and give them free rein." He believes that "the roles [of president and dean] can be foggy," and the president "must take care not to infringe on the academic life and responsibility of the dean. There are always opportunities to intervene in academic matters." At the other end of the spectrum are two presidents, one of whom acknowledges he has "a very hard time delegating the big issues in academic decision making to the provost." Another president explains, "The dean's position is more perceived as an administrative office flowing out of my office in which he handles for me academic matters in which he has considerable discretion, but he handles them in a sense as my agent. . . . I appoint [the dean] and in effect he is working with me and for me." In this case, the dean's job is to know the president's will and carry it out.

Most president-dean relationships in the study functioned somewhere between the dean having "free rein" and the dean serving as "the president's agent." More commonly, deans have responsibility for working with others, particularly with faculty, to shape an academic vision for the curriculum and programs that is consonant with the broader vision for the direction of the institution, articulated chiefly by the president. In this task, deans are neither working independently of the president, since cooperation is essential, nor are the deans simply implementing a vision they had little or no part in creating. Rather, they are engaged with the faculty, the president, and others to chart the course for the academic program. Not only are the most effective leadership practices communally based, but they are coordinated in all respects with broader institutional planning. That coordination is among the foremost practical challenges facing academic and executive officers.

One example from the study illustrates how formidable the task of achieving compatible understandings of leadership roles can be. The president and dean, both experienced administrators in the second year of their current positions, were consciously working to clarify and coordinate their leadership roles at the time of the site visit. The president, as a former faculty member and chief academic officer, maintained a lively interest in academic policy, program development, and faculty. While the president recognized that the dean "needs to be in some sense or another a strong academic leader," he also felt he could not do his own job with integrity

> without also having a very strong involvement in shaping the institution along the lines I think it should be shaped. And that means that the relationship between the president and the [dean] of this institution, whoever it is, has to be a very dynamic one, and it's going to be difficult to have the job descriptions that spell it out. . . . Some of it has to work out in terms of the evolving of the interpersonal relations—trust, really good communication, and basically *[a dean] who doesn't have a lot of vested interest in shaping the institution in light of an original vision that he has and thinks is the normative one for the whole institution.* (Italics mine)

As the president was struggling to sort out his own role in academic and institutional leadership, he also was concerned with the emergence of a rival or incompatible vision for the seminary. The president subsequently described the dean's role as a "mediating leadership," mediating between the high-level commitments of the president and their implementation in the concrete practices of the school. He saw the dean's role as mediating among the cultures of the disciplines, among the various schools of the seminary, and among faculty members and administrators to accomplish the president's vision. As the president explained, the dean is "not to be doing his own thing" in a way that operates outside the bounds the president would set.

The dean, on the other hand, was aware that their seminary was "an exception in choosing an academic as president." He concluded that, as a result, the roles of the executive and academic officers were going to blur. The dean also observed, "If you have two strong people as president and dean, trust and communication become very important because you don't have clear lines and you will not have clear lines." And again, "If you're dealing with persons with multiple gifts and/or interests, then you're not going to have segmentalized job descriptions and roles. I think that's an unrealistic expectation. Probably unwise." Because communication is key in this circumstance, the dean believed that more time was needed for shared planning. With their busy schedules, he noted, "the mutual shared dreaming, planning" necessary to a common vision "happens somewhere between less frequently than it should and infrequently. . . . It's clearly not where it has to be in my opinion."

This case raises several important issues. While research findings substantiate their claim that the president-dean relationship needs to be dynamic and flexible, their ready acceptance of a blurring of roles is problematic. Although trust and communication are indispensable and time for joint planning important, neither substitutes for an understanding and acceptance of their respective roles—how they are complementary and how they differ from one another. In the successful, long-term relationships found in the study, deans well understood how their presidents envisioned their own leadership and what they expected of them as dean. Deans, in turn, accepted that role and adapted their work accordingly.[14] Interviews did not reveal whether such understandings grew out of explicit conversations on the topic or simply emerged as they worked together over time. While some deans had considerable latitude in shaping their positions, the leadership role in all cases was defined in relation to the presidency.

In the example above, where the effort to find common ground and to reconcile differences was ultimately unsuccessful, the root cause of difficulty was the inability to reach a clear, mutually acceptable understanding of leadership roles. Nothing could be more fundamental. As the dean-president relationship plays out in the daily work of administration, other practices and attitudes become important as well. We turn now to practical strategies deans and presidents employ to coordinate their efforts and to work in partnership.

### *Communication*

When asked to describe the elements of an effective relationship, deans and presidents agreed, "Communication is the key." Communication on work-related issues occurs both in formal meetings, one-on-one or with other members of the president's administrative team or cabinet, and informally through spontaneous, unscheduled conversations almost any time and any place. On the survey, theological school deans estimated they spend an average of 2.2 hours per week in substantive conversation with their presidents, which is close to the 2.4 hours they consider optimal. In theological schools large and small, presidents and deans require regular opportunities to discuss issues, to deal with problems and crises, to share information, to plan, to receive and give counsel, and to coordinate their work.

At the sites visited for the study, there was wide variation in the balance between formal and informal modes of communication. Although most deans and presidents relied on a combination of the two, the predominance of the formal or the informal was generally a matter of the president's preferred working style and was influenced secondarily by such factors as institutional size and culture, the availability of the president, and the duration of their working relationship. These factors were evident both in one-on-one interactions of president and dean, as well as in the president's work with a senior administrative team or cabinet.

*Individual Meetings.* Most presidents and deans schedule weekly or biweekly meetings of an hour or more to discuss matters related to the academic area. At one seminary, the president tried to use a joint session of all vice presidents to deal with issues in their respective areas, but abandoned that approach when it became clear not all topics suited that format. Presidents and deans acknowledge that regularly scheduled meetings are invaluable for keeping each other well informed, up-to-date, and working cooperatively. The regularity of such meetings reveals little, however, about the actual frequency and the quality of their communication.

Several presidents and deans in the study did much of their work informally, through conversations in the hall, a quick stop by the office, telephone calls, or e-mail. Some administrators reported that the longer they worked together the more informal their communication became. Most deans and presidents depended on spontaneous, informal exchanges to conduct much of the business of both offices and to keep the lines of communication open. In one school, with a particularly strong oral tradition and a culture of informality, the executive and academic officers talked frequently but rarely scheduled formal meetings. In most schools, presidents and deans had informal exchanges on a weekly, even daily, basis, but they also set meetings to safeguard time in busy schedules and to insure they were never out of touch. While presidents and deans find their own optimal arrangements and no one pattern is suitable for all, research findings do suggest that frequent opportunities for conversation in a variety of formats is essential.

In addition to the frequency of conversations and the accessibility of both parties, deans and presidents also rely on the honesty, openness, and trustworthiness of these communications to make the relationship work. As in any relationship, these attributes often strengthen over time. One dean explained that he and the current president have "both been at the school a long time and know each other extremely well." Both run a very full schedule and, although they set meetings fairly regularly, they "do a lot of business on the fly. We have a lot of trust in each other because we've worked together so long." Presidents and deans also depend on each other to be open with information, forthright in their opinions, and able to keep confidences. When these principles are not followed, the integrity of the communication and ultimately of the relationship is threatened.

*Working in Administrative Teams.* Another forum in which presidents and deans routinely discuss administrative issues is in meetings of the president's council or cabinet, usually comprised of senior administrative officers, such as the vice presidents/directors of institutional advancement, finances, student affairs, formation, and the like. Presidents vary widely in their use of this group, and the frequency of their meetings generally is linked to the purpose the group serves. In schools where meetings are weekly or biweekly, the group tends to have one or more of the following purposes: to keep each other informed of developments in their respective areas, to obtain feedback on specific proposals, to discuss institutional problems or initiatives, to respond to crises, to undertake joint planning, or to make decisions.[15] In two schools where the administrative team was particularly strong, the chief academic officers confided that administrative council was the place "where decisions really get made."[16]

In most settings, the group of senior administrators served more of an advisory than a deliberative function. Presidents recognize that, beyond its contribution to institutional policy or planning, the group is valued for the regular communication and community building it affords to senior administrators working in separate spheres. As one president explained, "There is simply no substitute in my experience for sitting here with the whole administrative leadership on a regular basis . . . and tackling the problems together. I think that's the president's chief responsibility—to keep everybody talking and trying to solve problems together rather than everybody getting their own way working independently."

In schools where communications were more informal, the administrators met together "at the call of the president," which ranged from once monthly to once yearly. Groups meeting infrequently did so in response to crises or to deal with special projects. While some academic officers wished for more frequent meetings of senior administrators, most felt their informal communications with one another were adequate to handle routine administrative matters. Depending on the administrative structure and the particular distribution of duties, individual chief academic officers tended to work more closely with some administrators, such as the business manager or dean of students, than with others. Presidents who call few, if any, meetings of senior administrators have no assurance that communication is occurring in a uniform and timely way among them. Regular meetings would seem amply justified by their potential to afford senior administrators a broader view of the institution, to alert them to issues in other areas with consequences for their own, and to create a more cohesive leadership team.

In the cross section of theological schools reached by the survey, 91 percent of deans rated the relationships among major administrators "good" to "excellent," and 86 percent judged the quality of administrative teamwork as "good" to "excellent." Based on the small but representative sample of schools receiving site visits, these ratings would seem to reflect the ease of communication and cooperation among senior administrators rather than to indicate the nature or frequency of their formal group meetings. What site visits do make clear is that, in the hands of presidents who are effective team leaders, the group can offer multiple perspectives on issues and engage in the kind of joint, interactive thinking across administrative areas that one-on-one dialogue does not afford. This is one reason, as Bensimon and Neumann show in their study of teams and teamwork in higher education, that a group functioning as a team is more than the sum of its parts.[17]

*Working Styles*

How effectively individual deans and presidents work together can depend, in large part, on the compatibility of their working styles. This term is used broadly to refer to modes of thought, interaction, and communication that characterize how individuals conduct themselves in the workplace. Although the match or "fit" between president and dean can be assessed in a preliminary way at the time of hiring, initial impressions of compatibility may prove unfounded. Even in working relationships that prove to be effective, compatibility in working styles may be achieved gradually over time as deans and presidents work together.

In terms of working styles, the ten president-dean relationships examined in this study tend to cluster into three categories: first are those relationships in which the president and dean have similar and very compatible working styles; the second and largest group are relationships in which the president and dean have distinctly different, but complementary working styles; and third are those relationships in which the differences between the president and dean are problematic. Examining the varied forms such partnerships can take shows it is the match or fit between persons with different gifts, not their sameness in every detail, that is critical to success.

*Similar and Compatible Working Styles.* In two seminaries, the president and dean attributed their compatibility to the considerable similarity in their working styles. One dean described her relationship to the president by saying, "We work like hand in glove." In separate interviews, the president and dean of this school referred to the same shared characteristics: their task-orientation, their preference for quick turnaround, their ability to be direct with one another. After three years, both believed "they work well together," and faculty members observe, "They are a wonderful team." At the second school, the dean describes his relationship to the president as "superb," adding they both genuinely like each other, they both "live fast lifestyles," and they can talk frankly to one another. Although their areas of responsibility differ, their working styles and attitudes are similar. Since the beginning of their relationship, when they met two hours a week, they have kept each other well informed and have been able to talk openly about their concerns. According to the dean, both see the positive side of things and can work through difficult issues. The president cites their mutual respect for one another, their complementary skills, their friendship and humor.

*Different but Complementary Working Styles.* The most common pattern in the study was that of president and dean having notable differences in their working styles that, nonetheless, proved to be complementary. For example, one dean described himself as a short-range thinker, structured and organized, efficient in responding to requests, and willing to commit ideas to paper, whereas the president was a long-range thinker, inattentive to detail, slower to make decisions, and rarely given to explaining his ideas in writing. Both understood these differences, which were not insignificant, and achieved compatibility through clear and distinct job descriptions and good communication during their regular meetings.

Other examples are similar. One academic officer experienced initial frustration when he discovered that although he preferred to communicate important information by memo, the executive officer relied almost exclusively on oral communication. The dean eventually adapted. In another instance, the president's aversion to conflict meant that he preferred to deal with a sensitive issue, like racism, by speaking personally to those involved. As the dean explains, "The president is a great mediator who brings people together and tries to get them to resolve their differences. The president hears out both sides and prefers to have those involved find a resolution. He will determine the resolution only when he has to." The dean, on the other hand, felt the issue could best be dealt with in a public forum where the community was engaged and differing viewpoints could be expressed openly. At another seminary, the president was outgoing, the dean aloof; the president slow to act, the dean decisive. At yet another school, president and dean compared themselves on these same characteristics, which applied in reverse.

As these examples illustrate, differences in working styles often emanate from differences in personal habits and attitudes. Presidents and deans in this group sometimes were reassured to find in the other talents and skills they personally lacked. While almost any of the contrasting characteristics described above could become obstacles to a successful working relationship, presidents and deans who understood and respected their differences, who made accommodations where necessary, and who could utilize and balance their strengths were best able to achieve an effective partnership.

*Different and Problematic Working Styles.* While differences can be a source of strength for an administrative partnership, they also can be a liability. At one school, the president and dean both acknowledged that differences in their personalities and working styles had become a source of tension. The dean observed that personally the president was more an introvert and big-picture person, whereas he was an extrovert who focused on implementation and detail. His description continued:

> We are quite different, so we're working at that very hard at the moment. . . . He [the president] would like to have larger positional discussions and gets impatient when it moves to specifics; I get impatient if it doesn't move quickly enough. . . . I think [the president] is at times uncomfortable with my speaking before I think and my being out there with material prematurely. I'm uncomfortable with his overcaution and reticence in moving forward with 80 percent of the knowledge in order that you can get something done. So we work hard at respecting those differences, but those also create tensions or issues at times because of differences in style.

In addition to these stylistic differences, the president cited disagreement on specific issues and divergent understandings of the dean's role. The president was seeking a dean who had no interest in advancing an original vision for the institution. That was the president's job. The dean's role was to understand the president's vision and to implement it. The dean's self-described tendency to "be out there with material prematurely" was at odds with the president's preference to communicate his ideas directly to others without the mediation of the dean. Despite a conscious effort on both sides to bridge these differences, the relationship ended within the dean's first term.

In addition to the basic adjustments required of presidents and deans early in their partnership, difficulties can arise even after several years of working together. One president and dean in the study, who described themselves respectively as a visionary and a detail person, had worked well over time due largely to their mutual trust and good communication. Gradually, however, their conceptions of the dean's role diverged. The dean believed that his efficient management and ability to facilitate the work of the faculty was a strong complement to the president's own visionary leadership. The president, on the other hand, explained that "the dean wants to coordinate, but not invent. . . . He has no hunger for the job." The president wanted the dean to take more initiative, to exercise leadership in developing programs and faculty. While the president felt the problem was more a function of personality than of role, separate interviews with the president and the dean revealed their fundamentally different understandings of what constituted effectiveness in the dean's role. The president's prediction, that "his time as academic dean is drawing to a close," was prophetic.

These examples of the breakdown in the president-dean relationship illustrate how differences in working styles, coupled with different conceptions of the dean's role, can become problematic at various stages of the relationship. In the first example, the president and dean were conscious of the differences and tensions between them and made an effort to deal with them; in the second instance, whether the president had communicated his growing dissatisfaction to the dean or whether they had discussed their different views of the dean's role remained unclear. The latter case, in particular, underscores the need to have candid discussions of job expectations and performance on a regular basis.

Analysis of these three general types of relationships shows that differences in the working styles of president and dean can be complementary and a source of strength in one setting, but problematic and a source of tension in another. The ability to accommodate differences and to make the appropriate adaptations seems to depend, in large part, on a clear, shared understanding of their distinctive roles.[18] Without regular conversation about these matters, new and long-term relationships alike can be endangered.

### *Dealing with Conflict and Disagreement*

Even in successful dean-president relationships, disagreement is inevitable; skill in handling such differences, however, is not. Site visits revealed that differences of opinion on issues generally can be mediated or resolved through discussion. In response to the question, "How are difficulties resolved?" most presidents and deans simply said, "By talking about them." Depending on the nature of the disagreement, this may require lengthy, sometimes difficult discussions over a number of days. As one dean explained, she and the president "go toe-to-toe until they resolve it."

Given the complexity of administrative issues, however, not all disagreements admit of resolution.[19] Two examples from the study involved personnel decisions made while the president of one school and the dean of another were on sabbatical. Upon returning from sabbatical, neither approved of a decision made in their absence. Nothing could change the outcome, and both parties reached some accord only "by talking and the passage of time." In another example cited earlier, a president and dean differed on how to deal with a campus incident of racism: the president preferred to talk individually with the offenders; the dean preferred to schedule an open forum for community discussion. In this case, the differences were not mediated but allowed to stand; they were not resolved, but were managed as each dealt with the incident in his own way.[20]

When issues are both public and highly politicized, deans and presidents may find it difficult to resolve their differences privately and impossible to let them coexist. At a seminary committed to racial and gender diversity, a faculty search process created just such a dilemma. The campus was divided over the two finalists who represented differences of race, gender, and academic credentials. When the president responded to pressure from a faculty member and made the choice, the dean agreed with neither the process nor the outcome. The dean decided to capitulate, however, because avoiding further divisiveness and supporting the president was in the best interest of the school. As the dean explained, "The president is in charge"; the power of the presidency became the final arbiter when other strategies to reach agreement failed.

The ability of deans and presidents to work through their differences—to manage conflict, to resolve disagreements, and, on rare occasions, to agree to disagree—is critical to their relationship and to the effectiveness of both offices. Often deans and presidents use their private meetings to process issues so their public stance, whenever possible, can be unified and mutually supportive. Even on occasions when their differences on issues are expressed publicly and their mutual convincing is played out in a wider arena, deans still acknowledge the importance of being unified in their support of the final decision. While the issues that divide dean and president may be relatively few, the ability to reach some workable accommodation can test the true mettle of the relationship. At that juncture, other relational qualities, such as trust and support, are put to the test.

### *Other Qualities*

A seminary dean, who has worked with the same president for eight years, describes their relationship:

> We have a lot of trust in each other because we've worked together so long. . . . We have a great deal of trust in each other, we care for each other. I like him very much, and I think he likes me. We've been through some difficult things all the time we have been here, and I've always felt his support. . . . There is so much trust, and we can both be very honest with each other about what we

> think about issues. He's not wrong about very much around here, but when he is, I'm not afraid to say so.

This observation weaves together several of the characteristics deans and presidents identified as necessary for an effective relationship: trust grounded in honest communication, support in times of difficulty, and friendship.

*Trust.* Deans and presidents invariably found trust to be, as one dean put it, "the coin of the realm." As they work independently and together, deans and presidents count on one another to be persons of integrity, ability, and consistency. Trust affects all aspects of a working relationship. In communication, presidents and deans trust each other to be open and honest and, when necessary, to keep confidences. Presidents rely on deans to inform them in a forthright and timely way about issues and problems afloat in the community. As one dean noted, "Except for the board chair, the dean is the one person whose job is to tell the president the truth." Trust must also extend to other aspects of their work. "The president must respect my space and territory and responsibilities," one dean explained. "If [the president] can't trust the dean to make wise decisions, nothing will work out." At the heart of the dean-president relationships is their need to trust one another to be true to their word and to act accordingly.

*Mutual Support.* Trust and support are closely related, since deans and presidents depend on each other to stand by them and to support them in their role. While survey and interview findings revealed that most deans believe they serve with the full support of the president, crises and problems can arise that sorely test that support. One dean, for example, who described the president as "very affirming and helpful and supportive," discovered during a particularly difficult faculty hiring that the president and a board member made a private deal with a senior faculty member. Their deal, in effect, eliminated one of the two finalists and undermined the open and consultative search process the dean was directing. The president, who did not ordinarily involve himself in academic matters, made an "extra-process deal" with a faculty member and left the dean "swinging in the wind." However uncharacteristic, this incident showed a lack of support for the dean and resulted in a serious breach of trust.

More commonly, however, presidents and deans in the study were conscious of the need to coordinate their efforts and to avoid interference in each other's work. With few exceptions, deans and presidents sought to support each other in their roles and, even on points of disagreement, to deal with their differences in ways that did not undermine their work with other constituents. In some cases, deans and presidents work hard to protect one another. "My job is to buffer the president and caution him about landmines," a long-term dean explained. At one theological school, faculty were incensed over an administrative decision to seek the resignation of a venerated colleague. The dean stepped in and facilitated a heated faculty discussion of the issue, thereby avoiding the faculty's confrontation with the president. In the successful relationships, deans and presidents had respect for the differences in their roles and responsibilities, even while working in a coordinated fashion to fulfill them. These relationships achieved a workable balance between autonomy and interdependence.

However, in cases where either the president or dean has a protracted adversarial relationship with the faculty, the situation can be exceedingly difficult and complex. When presidents have a strained or hostile relationship with the faculty, the dean frequently is called upon to mediate and to interpret each to the other, while at the same time maintaining support for both parties. Conversely, as occurred in one instance in the study, the president may be required to step in and resolve misunderstandings between the chief academic officer and the faculty. In these situations, the mutual support of dean and president for one another is tested and ultimately must be balanced with their responsibilities to other constituent groups and to the welfare of the institution as a whole. If administrator-faculty breaches are severe and persistent, personnel changes may be in order; but if mediations prove successful, deans and presidents can enable one another to build more effective relationships.

*Friendship.* Presidents and deans expressed ambivalence about the desirability of developing a personal friendship. Many felt their working relationship was stronger and more effective because they connected on a personal level and genuinely liked each other. One seminary president compared the relationship to a marriage. Another observed, "It really is amazing how much of [the relationship] hangs on just how well you get along, how well you like each other, how much you can leave unspoken, and how much you have to articulate and constantly repeat." Deans and presidents alike recognized the value of their personal compatibility, which could range from consonant educational and theological values to a shared sense of humor. Some deans and presidents specifically planned social occasions outside of the regular work schedule to strengthen the bond between them.

Others, however, thought "it was easier if the dean and president were not good friends." As one dean explained, "The relationship can be myopic if the dean and president are too close. There is no way of critiquing each other." At times, the professional requirements of a job can strain close personal ties. As the dean's supervisor, presidents may be required to evaluate the dean's job performance or to make decisions contrary to the dean's wishes. Deans similarly may be called upon for their candid appraisal of the president's policies or may be expected to relay to the president unwelcome news. Presidents and deans walk a fine line. Professionally, they strive to achieve compatibility based on habits of effective communication and trust; at the same time, they need to preserve enough personal detachment to make honest responses and difficult decisions possible.

The preceding discussion of the dean-president relationship has examined the shared understandings and habits of interaction required to work together effectively. The many examples drawn from the Study of Chief Academic Officers offer less a blueprint for success than a collage of possible forms such relationships can take. Clearly, there are lessons to be learned. Research findings shed light on attitudes and behaviors worth cultivating, as well as pitfalls to be avoided. What is evident from site visits is the delicate balance in so many areas a sustained relationship requires. In the delineation of duties, deans and presidents must balance their cooperation and joint planning on the one hand, with the distinctness and independence of their roles on the other. In their professional interactions, they must balance their need for trust, support, and honest communication with a mutual respect for their personal and professional differences. As the long-term relationships in the study demonstrate, achieving and maintaining these balances is an ongoing task.

## Dual Allegiance

The interdependence of the offices of president and dean and the personal relationship that supports their administrative and leadership tasks are essential to understanding what the deanship is and how it functions in theological schools. But that is only part of the story. Chief academic officers also are empowered by the faculty to carry out the numerous responsibilities relating to the academic area and to serve as academic leader. The deanship has not one cornerstone, but two: the president and administration on the one hand and the faculty on the other. In the twofold allegiance their position requires, chief academic officers are challenged to balance the needs and demands of administrators and faculty, while serving as the link between these groups.

One dean in the study described the precariousness of this twofold allegiance:

> [M]ost deans function as the chief connector between faculty and administration. It is the dean who must relay information about faculty life and concerns to the president and board; it is also the dean who will interpret the decisions of the president and board to the faculty. In practice, this means that both faculty and president may expect the dean to be "their" colleague and confidante. Make no mistake about it: this can be a difficult balancing act.[21]

To understand how deans balance these requirements in their daily work, the survey, site visits, and focus groups conducted for this study asked deans to reflect on their dual allegiance. Although 92 percent of survey respondents agreed or strongly agreed with the statement, "At my institution faculty and administrators tend to cooperate effectively in making decisions," their responses to questions about where their primary allegiance would be if issues divided along faculty and administrative lines were considerably more mixed.[22]

On the survey, 59 percent of respondents agreed that "the primary allegiance of the dean should be with the faculty rather than with the administration."[23] Extended discussions during site visits, however, presented a different picture. Most deans felt the administration/faculty split was not common in their experience, and tension between the two groups tended to be more occasional than habitual. In some seminaries, the fact that many administrators were teaching members of the faculty and several faculty had administrative duties had a tendency to blur the conventional distinction. Although some deans more strongly identified with administration or with faculty, the majority felt their primary allegiance was to the institution and its mission. On this criterion, their alliances would vary with the issue and would not consistently favor any one group.[24] As one dean explained,

> I don't feel torn. I don't have any conscious first allegiance. . . . My primary allegiance would depend on the matter at issue and what I felt was the justice of the issue. . . . I really try to see the whole institution, the whole shebang. Thus far I've been able to do it. There may come a time when that is not quite possible, but I think it's part of the task, part of the responsibility.

In general, deans did not perceive their role as working *between* administrators and faculty but *with* both groups for the good of the whole.

In an essay written for this project, Russell E. Richey acknowledges that one's effectiveness as academic dean depends "on the success that you have in living credibly betwixt and between faculty and administration."[25] While serving as mediator between these (and other groups) can be a burden, Richey believes that "it can and should be also the fascination, excitement, pleasure, reward of the job." Addressing himself to a prospective dean, he continues: "You are the one who, by effectiveness in this mediation, makes the institution work. And because you are essential to this mediation, though you doubtless share it with others . . . , the school needs and respects your leadership. You make things happen."[26]

These comments underscore a significant finding of the study. Even in institutional cultures that minimize distinctions between administration and faculty, deans play a mediating role in maintaining communication, resolving differences, and building support. Deans in the study universally recognized the importance of this mediating function. As one dean explained, "The job *is* precisely to be in the middle."

While chief academic officers work in a constellation of relationships with various individuals and groups, the relationships with the president and the faculty are most fundamental to the dean's administration and leadership. Moving from analysis of the dean-president relationship, Chapter Four examines the dean's relationship to the faculty. The effectiveness of academic officers depends in large part on their ability to balance this dual allegiance and to maintain strong, vital relationships with both parties.

## Notes

[1] Kenneth A. Briggs, "The Costs of Money Trouble: Two Presidencies Done In by Financial Woe," *In Trust* (Summer 1994), 13–17. The case described is Andover Newton Theological School.

[2] Briggs, 13.

[3] See Chapter One, 16-19.

[4] While the exercise of leadership cannot, strictly speaking, be bifurcated in this way, the distinction between predominantly external and internal leadership roles does capture growing differences in the responsibilities of presidents and deans and in the way the two positions are perceived.

[5] "Describing the New Leader: What's Needed in a Theological School President Today. A Conversation," *In Trust* 8, no. 4 (Summer 1997), 20.

[6] These findings are amply confirmed in recent sources: Neely Dixon McCarter, *The President as Educator: A Study of the Seminary Presidency* (Atlanta, GA: Scholars Press, 1996), 25–27; Leon Pacala, "The Presidential Experience in Theological Education: A Study of Executive Leadership," *Theological Education* 29, no. 1 (Autumn 1992), 25; "Describing the New Leader," 20–23; *Theological Education.* The Study of the Seminary Presidency: Reflections of Seminary Leaders 32 (Supplement III 1996).

[7] Results of the survey of theological school deans indicate that 85 percent of respondents report to the chief executive officer of their school; 67 percent believe that the chief executive officer had the greatest influence on their hiring; and only 21 percent report that their appointment is determined, not by the president, but by vote of the faculty.

[8] Among the eleven sites visited for the study, only ten had both chief executive and chief academic officers. In one university divinity school, there was only one administrative position in which the executive and academic officer functions were combined.

[9] Analysis of responses on both topics indicates that ratings tended to be highest among new deans (0–2 yrs. in office) and lowest among midterm deans (3–6 yrs. in office). These differences, while notable, are not statistically significant.

[10] On the survey of theological school chief academic officers, 87 percent of respondents indicated that the primary responsibilities of their office were specified either in their contract/letter of appointment or in other institutional documents.

[11] The general profile of administrative responsibilities in Chapter One, Table 1, does suggest the principal components of the majority of chief academic officer positions in theological education.

[12] One of the few research-based studies of the deanship in higher education to discuss the president-dean relationship is reported in: John Wesley Gould, *The Academic Deanship* (New York: Teachers College Press, Columbia University, 1964), 52–61. While dated, this discussion offers interesting points of comparison with the dean-president relationship in theological schools.

[13] Mark Allyn Holman, *Presidential Search in Theological Schools: Process Makes a Difference,* distributed by agreement with The Association of Theological Schools in the United States and Canada (Oakland, CA: 1993), 5. Holman's report was part of the study of the seminary presidency, directed by Neely Dixon McCarter.

[14] This is not to suggest that mutual understanding and acceptance of roles are sufficient for a successful dean-president relationship. As the subsequent discussion shows, several other factors are critical as well.

[15] For an excellent analysis of the ways in which presidents can use their administrative teams, see Estela Mara Bensimon and Anna Neumann, *Redesigning Collegiate Leadership: Teams and Teamwork in Higher Education* (Baltimore, MD: The Johns Hopkins University Press, 1993), 32–53. Another concise, easily referenced guide to team building is: Madeleine F. Green and Sharon A. McDade, *Investing in Higher Education: A Handbook of Leadership Development* (Washington, DC: American Council on Education, 1991), 175–188.

[16] Both schools were described by their constituents as hierarchical, with a strong administrative presence. In one case, the large size of the school, its multiple administrative layers, and its history of top-down management enhanced its bureaucratic image; in the other case, the administrative practices of the school reflected a hierarchical church tradition.

[17] Bensimon and Neumann, 41–44, 54–79.

[18] Advisory committee member, Robert Birnbaum, has suggested that the converse also may apply: as deans and presidents make adaptations to one another, they come to a clearer understanding of their respective roles. This chicken-and-egg problem—whether the clarity regarding roles precedes or follows from the adaptation of their work—is difficult to determine in all cases and may differ for individual deans and presidents. Examples in this study generally illustrated problems in adapting to the role based on an insufficient understanding of it. Most important here is to recognize the need both for an understanding of roles and adaptation to them, in whatever sequence they may occur.

[19] A recent study entitled *Conflict Management in Higher Education* provides a helpful analysis of conflicts that typically occur among individuals and groups in academic settings. While the dean-president relationship is not addressed specifically, the general prescriptions for managing conflicts may have some applicability. See Susan A. Holton, "And Now . . . the Answers! How to Deal with Conflict in Higher Education," *Conflict Management in Higher Education,* New Directions for Higher Education No. 92 (San Francisco: Jossey-Bass, 1995), 79–89.

[20] Holton makes the helpful distinction between eliminating or resolving conflict, which is not always possible, and learning to manage it. The distinction turns on whether conflict is considered destructive or a necessary, even positive part of organizational life. Holton, 6–9.

[21] Elizabeth C. Nordbeck, "The Once and Future Dean: Reflections on Being a Chief Academic Officer," *Theological Education* 33 (Supplement Autumn 1996), 30.

[22] On a survey of theological school faculty, conducted in 1993 as part of the Auburn Center's Study of Theological School Faculty, responses to the statement, "Faculty and administrators tend to cooperate effectively in making decisions," were more guarded.

Faculty responses had a mean rating of 2.88 (4=strongly agree and 1=strongly disagree), compared to a mean of 3.45 on the deans' survey.

[23] On the survey of theological school faculty (see note 22), respondents were more definite in their view that "the primary allegiance of the academic dean should be with the faculty, rather than with the administration." On the faculty survey, the mean rating was 3.12, compared to a mean of 2.7 on the deans' survey.

[24] One dean acknowledged that her primary allegiance was to the institution, but "the institution has several different interests." This can be a complicating factor when deans must choose among competing interests.

[25] Russell E. Richey, "To a Candidate for Academic Leadership: A Letter," *Theological Education* 33 (Supplement Autumn 1996), 39.

[26] Richey, 39.

# 4 THE DEAN-FACULTY RELATIONSHIP

*"Clearly, my role is to make the faculty succeed. There is no other definition of the dean or provost."*

*Theological school dean*

When faculty reflect on what it takes to be a good dean, their list of necessary skills is impressive, often daunting. Four faculty members at one seminary considered the following characteristics desirable in a dean.

A good dean must be:

a visionary and a realist
a model of teaching and scholarship
personally strong and capable of being criticized
a consensus builder, able to deal with conflicts and with strong faculty members
decisive, but with appropriate consultation
available
collegial, assertive, and clear
flexible, but not ambiguous
an ombudsperson with students
a defender of the integrity of the program
good at interpersonal relationships
able to work effectively in the larger structure of the school, especially with the president
able to interpret the academic program to the church
deeply spiritual

This rich stew of attributes and competencies describes what just a few faculty members hope to find in their dean and typifies the lists drawn up by faculty at other theological schools in the study. If the other eighteen faculty members of this seminary had been polled, undoubtedly they would have added to the list. When another seminary began its search for a dean, faculty specified the qualifications they were seeking and, to the chagrin of the current dean, "their list covered a wall." Regardless of the size of their schools, chief academic officers confront numerous, diverse, sometimes contradictory expectations from individual faculty members. Taken together, their expectations seem to express the fond hope that deans, indeed, might "walk on water."

The number, variety, and character of faculty expectations reflect more than high hopes; they reflect the breadth of the dean's responsibilities in working with faculty and the range of skills these duties require. Presidents, deans, and faculty agree that the faculty is the dean's primary constituency, the focus of the managerial, leadership, and pastoral work of the office. Virtually all of the dean's administrative responsibilities discussed in Chapter One involve the faculty either directly or indirectly.[1] Deans work with faculty on matters ranging from curriculum and academic programs to faculty hiring, evaluation, and professional development, to accreditation and long-range planning. In these and other areas of administrative responsibility, deans are called upon to serve alternately (and often simultaneously) as managers who organize and facilitate academic operations, as leaders who guide the development and implementation of the corporate vision, and as pastors who attend to the personal, professional, and spiritual growth of faculty. While individual deans may not be gifted equally in all areas, such are the aptitudes and skills their broad responsibilities require.

The complexity of the dean-faculty relationship cannot be overestimated. In fulfilling their roles and responsibilities, deans work closely with faculty as individuals and as a group. This responsibility to particular persons and to the faculty collectively makes extraordinary demands on deans: they are expected to know the idiosyncracies of individual personalities, their behaviors, motivations, needs, and concerns, as well as to understand the dynamics of their interactions with one another and the character of the group as a whole. Even basic accomplishments, such as curriculum revision or a policy change, may depend on the dean's ability to work with faculty one-on-one, to mediate among various groups, and to deal effectively with the entire faculty.

The multifaceted nature of the dean-faculty relationship is the subject of this chapter. Drawing upon the research findings, we explore four related questions from the perspective of both deans and faculty:

- What is the character of the dean-faculty relationship? What are the mutual responsibilities and expectations of deans and faculty?

- What is required to establish and sustain an effective dean-faculty relationship?
- What strategies have deans found to be successful and unsuccessful in working with faculty?
- What is the dean's pastoral role in relation to faculty? Specifically, how do deans work to build the faculty, foster their professional growth and development, and create community?

While dean-faculty relationships undoubtedly differ in character across theological schools, this chapter focuses on common features of the relationship evident in findings from the survey of chief academic officers and interviews with deans and faculty members in the diverse schools visited for the study.

Since deans work closely with faculty in fulfilling their duties, the quality of the dean-faculty relationship has a direct bearing on the management of the academic area and on the dean's effectiveness as administrator and leader. Understanding how deans and faculty view the relationship and define its effectiveness, as well as understanding the concrete, practical strategies they use to weather difficulties and work productively together, is fundamental to academic governance and to the quality of community life. The relationship affords deans extraordinary opportunities for leadership and pastoral care in developing individual gifts of faculty, in nurturing their success, and in building community.

## The Character of the Relationship

The concept of the dean as servant is nowhere more clearly expressed than in the dean's relationship to faculty. Although theological school deans may conceive of their service more broadly in terms of the church and its ministry, many seek to realize it through administrative service to the seminary and, in particular, to the faculty. The opening quotation to this chapter in its full version explains the importance of the dean's service to faculty.

> The faculty are the heart of the school. Clearly, my role is to make the faculty succeed. There is no other definition of the dean or the provost. I believe that the students are best served as the faculty are satisfied, so it's not a student-run place, it's a faculty-run place. Faculty need administration with a certain kind of authority and power to facilitate them to lead, to give wider vision. . . . But at the core, the president and provost, particularly the provost, are there to serve the faculty. If they succeed, the rest of it works.

In this view, the role of administrators, particularly of academic officers, is to facilitate the work of the faculty and to help them succeed. This focus is warranted for two reasons: because "the faculty are the heart of the school" and because "the students are best served as the faculty are satisfied." The faculty are the heart of the school in several respects: as teacher/scholars, faculty are the bearers of the school's educational mission; while students and even administrators are transitory members of the academic community, the faculty collectively have a continuous presence, a permanence, that identifies them most closely with what the school is and may become. Through their teaching, scholarship, and service, faculty carry out the mission, establish the school's reputation, and, through curricular and hiring decisions, determine its future. If the faculty succeed, "the rest of it works." When chief academic officers facilitate the faculty's essential work, they also serve the students, the seminary, and the church in the process.

Each of the dean's principal roles underscores the service orientation of the office. As discussed in Chapter Two, the *managerial role* serves the seminary by tending to the nuts and bolts of daily operations and handling the administrative detail necessary to keep academic life organized and running smoothly. The dean's *leadership role,* particularly in cultures of shared governance, involves working collegially to develop a corporate vision, directing participatory decision-making processes, empowering faculty to exercise leadership, and securing broad ownership of academic decisions. In addition to these managerial and leadership roles, many deans also serve a *pastoral role* and tend to "the care and nurture of the faculty." Of the eleven deans interviewed during site visits, nine of them considered the task of facilitating the work of faculty and providing an environment in which their teaching and scholarship could flourish as foremost among their responsibilities.

The service orientation of theological school deans is further strengthened by the Judeo-Christian tradition of the seminaries which provides the foundation and inspiration for many of their personal and professional commitments. When academic officers in the study described their administrative work as a form of servant leadership, they did so mindful of the model of leader-as-servant found in Jesus Christ of the Gospels.[2] Deans frequently referred to Robert K. Greenleaf's theory of "servant leadership," which is articulated in the context of Christian values and aspirations, to explain the guiding principles of their own administrative work.[3]

*Mutual Responsibilities*

While faculty are understandably accepting of, even enthusiastic about, the dean's servant role, dean-faculty relationships are rarely, if ever, as straightforward and harmonious as this generalized description might suggest. Deans serve from a position of formal authority, and however limited the exercise of their authority and however collegial their practices, many deans find that simply occupying the office tends to set them apart. Several deans interviewed for the study found their relationship to faculty colleagues changed abruptly when they became administrators. As one dean explained, "There's something inevitable about occupying this office that puts a distance. I was just kind of 'Joe colleague' up on the third floor until I came down here, and I noticed immediately . . . some people treat you with reverence; some people are naturally antagonistic toward you." Another dean reported that students and teachers are on a first-name basis, but administrators are "set apart." Even in theological schools where administrator-faculty distinctions tend to blur as faculty take on a variety of administrative roles, the deanship can make even a familiar colleague an object of reverence or hostility. Such is the symbolic power of the office.

Certain of the deans' responsibilities create a distance between them and their faculty colleagues. For example, chief academic officers typically are involved not only in hiring faculty but in their subsequent evaluations and in promotion and tenure decisions. While such decisions never rest entirely with the dean but are arrived at jointly by departmental faculty, seminary committees, presidents, and boards, deans clearly are positioned to influence the outcome of these processes. Similarly, although the majority of deans do not have the primary administrative responsibility for faculty salaries, they often influence salary decisions.[4] Deans also recommend faculty members for important committees and special assignments, though presidents commonly consult in these matters and make the final appointments. As liaison between the faculty and other groups, deans may be the bearers of unwelcome news or may have to implement unpopular decisions. "They carry mail that's not always easy to read," as one dean put it. In rare instances, deans may be required to discipline or terminate a faculty member, though deans rarely, if ever, decide or act in such matters alone. Although the dean's decision-making power is shared, faculty often perceive the office and its incumbent as influencing decisions that have a direct impact on their lives.[5]

Faculty, in turn, usually play a role in evaluating the dean and, in a small number of theological schools, they decide on the dean's reappointment. On the survey, 46 percent of deans indicated that faculty participate in their performance review, and 79 percent agreed that the "continued appointment of the academic dean should be subject to faculty review."[6] However, in response to the statement, "My reappointment is determined by vote of the faculty," only 9 percent "strongly agreed" and 12 percent "somewhat agreed," indicating the infrequency of this practice.[7] In a case in 1990, a seminary faculty voted to deny the dean's re-election to a third term, an action that was unanticipated and undertaken for reasons not immediately apparent.[8] The seminary's board of trustees subsequently launched an inquiry into faculty views in order to understand their action and to solicit ideas on how to avoid such conflict in the future.

While faculty at relatively few seminaries decide on the dean's continued appointment so directly and decisively, the dean's ability to work effectively with the primary constituency of the office, the faculty, is almost always an important factor in decanal evaluations and reappointments. On the survey conducted for this study, deans indicated that "the ability to work well with faculty" was the most important criterion among the several used to evaluate their effectiveness.[9] While practices for evaluating deans will be discussed more fully in Chapter Seven, it is worth noting here that deans and faculty often evaluate one another and play an important role in deciding their respective futures. Some deans and faculty live comfortably with this fact, while others find it creates a distance and wariness between them.

### *Mutual Expectations*

Many factors of circumstance and personalities determine the expectations deans and faculty have of one another, but site visit interviews revealed that expectations tend to follow closely the primary requirements of their respective jobs. Faculty expectations of deans, for example, depended on how broadly or narrowly the dean's role was defined. At one seminary where the dean's role was perceived as strictly managerial, the competencies associated with leadership were notably absent from the faculty's list. Similarly, in theological schools that place high value on teaching and service, the dean's expectations of faculty were tailored to those institutional priorities.

When deans interviewed during site visits were asked to describe their expectations of faculty, their responses tended to focus on the quality of teaching and their work with students. "I expect the faculty to be first-class teachers" and "I want the faculty to operate in a professional and caring way with students and to be good teachers and to be responsible inside and outside of class" were typical responses. Another dean said he expected faculty "to develop a passion for learning among students." Although deans made somewhat fewer references to the need for faculty to strengthen their scholarship and service, this seemed attributable to the fact that one or the other was not an institutional priority or that faculty already were strong in these areas. A few deans mentioned the need for faculty to work collegially, to focus on institutional priorities, and to deal with issues in a more timely way. In general, however, deans' expectations focused on faculty fulfilling their basic responsibilities effectively.

By contrast, faculty expectations of deans went beyond the laundry list of qualities and competencies needed for deans to fulfill their administrative responsibilities. At several sites visited for this study, faculty expected the dean not only to have a good working relationship with them, but to know them personally, to understand their needs and desires, and to be their advocate to the president, the board, and other constituents. Faculty frequently referred to the need for deans to be good listeners, clearly important to knowing them and understanding their concerns. As faculty at one seminary explained, the dean must be "willing to take risks to champion faculty" and must "represent the faculty faithfully, even if he does not agree." The expectation among faculty in some schools that the dean is "on their side" harkens back to the difficult balancing act confronting deans who serve at the interface of faculty and administration, at once the representative and advocate for both groups.[10] As one dean suggested, the dean must encourage the faculty to take a larger view and see the dean's role as advocating for *both* faculty and administration. "There is some responsibility on the dean's part to facilitate that kind of understanding."

Faculty also expect their deans "to sort the wheat from the chaff," to conserve faculty time and energy by identifying the truly important issues that must concern them. Faculty at one seminary expected their dean "to sort out what's important" and to bring a range of solutions for their consideration. Another wanted the dean to "show the direction and then let go." Faculty expect the dean to focus their attention on critical issues and to involve them appropriately, while at the same time sparing them from frivolous or unimportant matters which, they are grateful, the dean is obliged to handle. While one aspect of the deans' service is doing the grunt work or, as one dean put it, having "the willingness and patience to attend all the meetings the faculty aren't interested in attending . . . and to take care of a lot of details," another aspect is identifying priorities and setting the academic agenda which, as we have seen, is a powerful form of the deans' leadership.

Closely related and necessary to this leadership role is the expectation that the dean will bring to faculty deliberations a broader institutional perspective and knowledge of the larger world of theological education. By virtue of the deans' position as senior administrator, faculty look to them for a comprehensive view of the curriculum and programs, "to know how the whole thing fits together," as one faculty member explained. Deans are expected to be aware of forces driving the institution from within and without and to bring this perspective to bear on academic decisions. Many deans, for example, are privy to financial information and enrollment data that may not be shared in detail with the faculty. This information may have consequences for what is possible in program expansion or faculty hiring. Deans also are expected to understand issues and trends at the forefront of theological education and to have a firm grasp of accrediting standards and other requirements that affect academic planning. Based on results of the study, faculty expect their deans to have this broader knowledge and to use it to frame discussions and to set directions for the academic area.

Thus, while deans' expectations of faculty tend to focus on their primary responsibilities as teachers and good citizens of the academic community, faculty expect deans not only to be competent academic administrators and to possess the infinite list of attributes and skills the work entails, but they also expect deans to know and understand them, to advocate for their interests, to protect them from administrative busy-work, and to focus their attention on important issues informed by broad institutional and theological education perspectives. Within the context of these mutual expectations, deans and faculty in the study identified the characteristics they consider essential to an effective working relationship.

## Effective Relationships

When asked what was required for a good relationship with faculty, one chief academic officer replied:

> You need to like faculty. You need to act from out of a faculty center. You need to have enough credibility from out of that center . . . and be considered fully a peer of the faculty (e.g. have tenure). . . . You need to be different than many

> of the faculty; the majority of the faculty don't think administratively, don't think holistically, that's not where they are.

This statement captures several prerequisites that deans bring to effective working relationships with faculty. First and most important is the need to like faculty, which, however obvious, cannot always be assumed. While deans readily acknowledge the unpleasantness of dealing with difficult personalities and contentious issues, those who work well with faculty operate from a foundation of positive regard and genuine concern for their success and well-being. As one seminary president put it, the dean must "have a gift for working with faculty."

Deans find that having the necessary qualifications and experience to be considered "fully a peer of the faculty" is important to their credibility and acceptance as administrators. At one seminary where the dean was not sufficiently credentialed to be viewed as a peer, faculty considered him more an office manager than a dean, and he regarded the students, not the faculty, as his primary constituency. However anomalous this situation, it underscores the value of the dean's faculty citizenship. The dean's academic standing can strengthen the dean's acceptance and credibility in the role of academic leader and, for many faculty, it portends the dean's ability "to act from out of a faculty center." Faculty confidence in such matters is critical to a successful working relationship.[11]

### *Trust and Respect*

When deans and faculty were asked what constitutes an effective relationship, "trust and respect" almost always were mentioned first and discussed together. While it is difficult to enumerate the many factors that foster trust and respect, professional competence, honest and open communication, fairness, and integrity are certainly among them. For an effective relationship, deans and faculty need to trust in each other's words and judgments and actions. Several deans described how they began as academic officers with a certain store of faculty trust and good will but, as one dean noted, "you can spend your capital in a hurry." Failure to achieve consistency between one's words and actions or to act fairly in dealing with people or to keep promises can erode that initial trust. As one dean observed about his own effectiveness: "All depends on faculty trust. The strength of the office is due to trust."

Mutual respect also has many sources and is closely allied to trust. Professionally, deans and faculty respect one another for the competence and skill they bring to their responsibilities; and personally, deans and faculty rely on honesty, openness, and integrity in their dealings with one another. Faculty further indicated their respect and trust of deans was enhanced by the dean's understanding of the challenges of faculty work. Deans who teach and advise students, who have experience balancing their scholarship, teaching, committee work, and other professional and church commitments, are more readily trusted to understand the issues important to faculty than deans without faculty experience. As one dean explained, "Faculty must trust the dean and be aware that the dean knows firsthand their pressures and responsibilities and understands them." Having been in the trenches can go a long way to establishing the dean's credibility and earning the respect and confidence of faculty.

Trust is so fundamental that, as one former dean explained, its loss can destroy relationships and undermine the functioning of the school. Although such extreme and irreparable consequences may be rarely observed, erosions of trust over time are more prevalent. He further noted that theological communities have the advantage of having at hand the resources of their religious traditions that can be invoked to understand and heal such breaches of faith. Joining together in worship and reflecting on Scripture and its implications for faithful practices can help in dealing with experiences of conflict and difficulty. In the recent book, *Practicing Our Faith: A Way of Life for a Searching People,* L. Gregory Jones discusses how the Christian faith informs the practice of forgiveness, which helps to restore communion with God and with one another.[12]

*Communication*

The truism that "good communication is a two-way street" was apparent in discussions with both deans and faculty. During site visit interviews, faculty frequently noted that effective deans convey necessary information in a timely manner and are straightforward and honest with faculty. Several deans described their own efforts to be open and above-board. This statement was typical: "I try to be honest and tell exactly what's on my mind. . . . I will tell concerns directly to them [the faculty] and expect and invite them to do that with me." Another dean, after twelve years in office, wanted faculty "to be forthright and communicative. Faculty should know they have a warrant to level with me." When faculty were asked during interviews what they contribute to an effective dean-faculty relationship, many were taken aback by the question and some admitted they had never considered the mutuality of the relationship and what it required of them. Upon reflection, faculty most frequently mentioned the contribution of their own openness and candor.

As most deans eventually discover, candid communications are not always tactful. While deans are expected to be attentive and sensitive to faculty concerns, they also must be sufficiently detached to withstand criticism and keep it in perspective. Deans in the study who had difficult dealings with faculty or who became lightning rods for faculty hostility and disappointment stressed the importance of being "thick-skinned, able to take insults and to depersonalize issues," as one dean put it. Two deans described the faculty as a "tough group" and had to learn "not to take confrontation personally." As one dean explained, she "diffuses criticism by not worrying about it or letting it throw her off course." Deans almost daily are challenged to remain open, to listen, and to respond constructively to what faculty are saying, while at the same time, they need enough resilience not to be undone or derailed by the harsh, impolitic remarks that can come with the territory. Clearly, efforts on the part of deans and faculty to maintain civil discourse and to create a culture of civility can be helpful to both parties.

Deans and faculty also noted the importance of the timeliness of their communications. If problems fester among the faculty and are only belatedly shared with the dean, the dean's ability to respond effectively may be compromised. If deans withhold important information from faculty or fail to communicate it in a timely way, faculty may become suspicious and distrustful. Even the promptness of a returned telephone call or e-mail can signal to faculty the dean's concern for them. As one dean explained, "When faculty contact my office, I get back to them promptly. I try not to die on too many hills regarding faculty." Another dean described such quick turnaround as "an act of faithfulness" to the managerial work of the office and to the faculty.

In reflecting on the work of the office, Elizabeth Nordbeck highlights the importance of recognizing the modes of communication endemic to one's own institutional culture. As she observes,

> Most seminaries are of an "in-between" size, that is, they may resemble either a family business, with informal, word of mouth patterns of communication, or a more structured, segmented business, where written communication is typical. At my first school, oral communication was the radical norm. . . . In that setting, written communication at best suggested pretentious formality; at worst

it hinted at a kind of veiled hostility. At my second school the reverse was true. There, hardly a communicable thought went unrecorded.[13]

Knowing *how* to communicate, as importantly as knowing *what* and *when*, can be essential to working effectively with faculty and other constituents. In particular, deans coming new to a school must be attentive to the patterns and preferred methods of communication and be prepared to adapt accordingly.

*Collegiality*

Although collegiality has many manifestations, it essentially involves individuals sharing collective responsibility for their common work. Faculty interviewed for the study often gauged the strength of their relationship to the dean by the collegiality evident in decision-making processes. As discussed in Chapter Two, deans play a significant role in determining the nature and extent of faculty participation in academic decisions. Particularly in areas where the dean has some discretion on whether to consult faculty and how extensively to include them in decisions, faculty can view the extent of their involvement as a barometer of the relationship itself. For example, a dean who usually worked closely with faculty bypassed a faculty committee and took a unilateral approach to the allocation of funds for computer purchases. This was a departure from the consultative processes the dean typically used, and the action strained the dean's relationship with some faculty who felt they were not treated inclusively and collegially in the process.

Deans also expect collegiality of the faculty, their willingness to work cooperatively with the dean and with one another and to assume responsibility for these activities. Faculty who resist working in good faith with the dean and other faculty can undermine progress on issues and erode the bonds that sustain community. During the decision-making process, for example, faculty members who absent themselves from important meetings and discussions only to raise strenuous objections late in the deliberative process can negatively affect the work of the entire group.

The quality of the dean-faculty relationship, as rated on separate surveys of theological school deans and faculty, was judged between "good" and "excellent" by both groups.[14] Among the theological school deans surveyed, 48 percent rated their relationship to faculty "excellent," and 46 percent rated it "good."[15] Site visits remind us, however, that dean-faculty relationships are never static. Even the most experienced and respected deans told stories of missteps with faculty and of difficult decisions that put a strain on their relationship. Faculty likewise acknowledged that their judgments were sometimes hasty and unfair. The strength of the dean-faculty relationship consists not in being trouble-free, an unrealistic expectation in even the smallest groups, but in the mutual understanding, resilience, even forgiveness practiced by both parties. These positive ratings of the dean-faculty relationship should be interpreted in this light.

## Strategies for Working with Faculty

With little or no preparation for academic administration, the majority of deans acquire administrative savvy through experience, learning from both their successes and failures what strategies are effective. As deans interviewed during site visits related the lessons from their own experience, it became clear there is no blueprint for success. Their advice reminds us that different settings require different approaches, and strategies that succeed famously in one school may be quite ineffective in another. Through these discussions, however, some basic principles emerged concerning knowing the faculty, consulting faculty, delegating to faculty, and dealing with faculty that seemed to cross institutional and denominational borders. They provide no "quick fix" but, rather, serve as occasions for reflection on working with faculty that might shed light on practices in individual settings.

### *Knowing the Faculty*

Knowing the faculty takes many forms. Several deans spoke of knowing the faculty politically, that is, knowing how they are likely to deal with issues, how they tend to divide and coalesce, and what it will take to mediate differences and achieve some measure of agreement among them. One particular dean modeled his own strategies on former president Lyndon Baines Johnson, who understood that "some people are dealt with more effectively one-on-one, some in small groups, and some in large groups." Having such knowledge about individual players in the decision-making process was an asset to deans in garnering faculty support for academic change.

Deans reported that they acquired such knowledge of individual and group dynamics through experience and through the many opportunities for informal interaction with faculty their work provides. As one faculty member stated, "The dean must be interactive, must be listening, and faculty must be heard." According to deans, much of this listening and hearing occurs in hallways and offices, over lunch, at faculty gatherings, during drop-in times at the dean's office, and at other social occasions. Several deans remarked on the necessity of these informal exchanges as a means of knowing faculty personally and professionally. At the eleven schools visited for this study, faculty were unfailingly appreciative of deans who extended themselves in these ways, whereas faculty were critical of those who tended to stay aloof or apart.

At two sites, faculty mentioned the importance of deans allowing themselves to be known, underscoring the necessity of mutuality in the dean-faculty relationship. Just as deans benefit from knowing who faculty are and how best to work with them, so too faculty members find it helpful to know how the dean approaches issues and what the priorities, values, strengths, and limitations of the dean might be. Recognizing that successful working relationships require such reciprocity, deans must gauge what is necessary and appropriate to reveal of themselves and when and how to do that most effectively.

Two characteristics of theological school communities foster the familiarity and concern among members helpful in establishing good working relationships. First, the relatively small size of theological schools enables administrators, faculty, staff, and students to know one another personally. What many described as the "family atmosphere" of their schools is likely to occur with greater ease than in larger, more formal settings. Second, the Judeo-Christian tradition foundational to these schools fosters an ethos of care and concern, and members typically place high value on being aware of others' needs and responding to them. These elements of the seminary ethos support deans, faculty, and others in their efforts to know and understand one another.

### *Consulting Faculty*

Deans who discussed their mistakes in working with faculty most often told of times when they failed to consult faculty sufficiently and to involve them appropriately in decisions.[16] Deans talked about these instances with regret, even while recognizing the benefit of the lessons learned. Interviewed during his sixth year in office, one dean reflected on his early years:

> One of the mistakes I made at first was I asserted my leadership too strongly. Looking back on it, I think that I'm . . . a very ambitious person, and I was very

> eager for change, and I was trying to initiate a lot of stuff from the top. . . . The constant thing I have to remind myself is not to force change from the office, but to consult way beyond the call of duty. You can never consult enough with committees or delegate enough to committees. There is an inefficiency in that process because it takes time to listen to all the voices. But I believe you cannot consult too much.

Another dean with a similar impatience for change revised the pay rate for summer courses to address an abuse of the system by an individual faculty member. Responses from faculty clearly indicated the need for more time and consultation regarding the decision. At another seminary, the dean recalled her tendency early on to do much of the work alone. In preparing the school's self-study for reaccreditation, she admits, "I should have consulted more broadly and had more writers involved in the process. I did too much of the work myself."

Rarely do faculty complain about being overconsulted. While faculty rely on the dean to handle administrative minutiae, they generally do expect to be consulted on decisions affecting their welfare and work. Even if faculty do not always see their counsel followed, participating in the deliberations and having their viewpoints considered can signify they are valued and respected as colleagues. If, at times, deans miscalculate which decisions warrant faculty involvement and which do not, most believe it best to err on the side of being too consultative. One dean in her first year found herself in a predicament at a faculty meeting: she had asked the faculty for their opinion on a minor regulation, and they simply sat in silence. She was surprised, but the experience helped her realize there were some (albeit few) administrative areas where she could take charge.

### *Delegating to Faculty*

Beyond consulting with faculty and soliciting their views, deans can delegate to faculty and give individuals and groups significant responsibility for specific projects. Delegating differs from consulting in the transfer of agency from the dean to other parties, signifying the dean's trust in the ability of the faculty member or committee to undertake and complete the project. Some deans routinely delegate to department chairs and program directors responsibility for the daily management of programs and faculty. Several deans visited for the study delegated to faculty committees such tasks as curriculum review and revision and directing faculty development programs, and they delegated to individuals an array of special projects. Other deans had difficulty with delegation, due perhaps to their perception that most tasks are not the kind that can be delegated or that no one else can be trusted to "do it right." Deans who delegate appropriately, like deans who consult frequently with faculty, express confidence in their faculty colleagues and respect for their work. While delegating may have its risks, deans who know their faculty and delegate wisely may be rewarded by what is gained through faculty participation and ownership.

Delegating to faculty is one of the principal means by which deans develop faculty leadership, a primary responsibility of the office.[17] One dean began the process when new faculty were hired. He believed that "if people have significant gifts they should be identified and encouraged." Most deans encouraged faculty by providing opportunities for them to develop their leadership skills, such as appointing them to chair departments or committees or tapping them for special assignments. "You need to keep trying to create ways to challenge people with potential effectiveness for leadership, to take some on and see where it goes," as one dean explained. During site visits, deans discussed several reasons for developing faculty leadership: they had a pastoral interest in nurturing individual gifts; they sought to utilize those gifts to address current community needs; and some had an eye on leadership succession in the dean's and president's offices. Whatever the short-term or long-term goals of particular deans, the majority recognized the importance of identifying and developing leadership talent among the faculty and empowering individuals to use their gifts for the good of the whole.

### *Dealing with Faculty*

An experienced university dean described his two most successful strategies in working with faculty: "communicating expectations in a low-key fashion, with humor, matter-of-factly, and without preaching or imperatives; and providing written information succinctly and up-front." Several deans noted the importance of humor and having a light touch in dealing with faculty. Even in tense situations, "losing one's temper is not productive," as both the dean and faculty confirmed. Punitive measures also can be counterproductive. One dean, who wanted to insure faculty would submit grades on time, withheld the paychecks of faculty whose grades were not in by the specified deadline. While this measure definitely got their attention, the price was anger and resentment on the part of some faculty. "Never back faculty into corners," another dean advised, and others echoed this wisdom.

The second issue of informing faculty can be more complex and context-specific. Some deans learn that many faculty do not regularly read their mail even if it is "succinct and up-front," though such notices do stand a better chance. One dean admitted he was least effective "when he presumed that new faculty would remember or old faculty would need no reminder." Another dean discovered the faculty relied on him to keep them informed of all policies, procedures, upcoming events, and important deadlines. Deans were guided in this process only by knowing their faculty sufficiently well to understand what information in what format would best serve their needs.

Most vexing to many deans is how to deal effectively with difficult faculty members who may be persistently negative or critical and whose attitudes may be demoralizing to other faculty. As noted previously, many deans had developed strategies for dealing with disagreements or conflicts on academic matters and some sought training and resources on managing conflict in higher education.[18] When deans confronted chronic difficulties of personality and temperament, however, they tended to develop strategies on an ad hoc basis and to rely on their own judgment or the advice and counsel available locally. Some deans mentioned that problems were solved fortuitously by well-timed leaves or early retirements. Although a large body of literature on dealing with difficult people exists in the popular press, academic officers seem to benefit most from confiding in trusted colleagues or gaining perspective from the firsthand, published accounts of other deans who may have dealt with similar problems. Appendix C contains several of these sources.

In some settings, academic officers also may confront what one dean called the problem of "managing the stars." This particular school had a faculty that included several well-published, noted senior scholars and a number of recent hires who joined the faculty fresh out of graduate school. The latter group tended to have full teaching loads, large numbers of advisees, and heavy committee assignments. These were the "worker bees," mostly untenured, who were involved, industrious, and committed to all faculty tasks. The dean's persistent dilemma was "managing the stars" in a way that would keep them productive, without unfairly exploiting the "worker bees" and denying them the time and opportunities to pursue their own scholarship. While many deans have other, less dramatic versions of this problem, virtually all confront the issue of dealing fairly and equitably with individual faculty members and being consistent when faced with their varied demands.

In schools with multiple expectations of faculty—that they be excellent teachers, published scholars, and actively involved in the seminary, professional societies, and the church—deans are challenged to find ways to recognize and support the diverse gifts of individual faculty members. Studies that broaden our understanding of what constitutes scholarship and that provide models for developing individual faculty work plans can be helpful.[19] For most deans, however, the challenge of being fair and consistent in supporting faculty comes almost daily in the numerous requests faculty make for additional resources, reduced teaching loads, and the like. At one university-related school, faculty expressed concern that their dean was "too soft" with demanding faculty when, for example, frequent conference-goers received a disproportionate amount of faculty travel funds. Some deans found that enlisting the help of the entire faculty to develop even-handed policies for the distribution of travel funds, faculty development support, and study leaves protected them from the pressure of individual lobbying in such matters. Fairness, which is so vital to an effective dean-faculty relationship, often was best achieved by faculty having a hand in creating policies for allocating the various discretionary forms of faculty support.

## The Dean's Pastoral Role

"Let faculty know you care about them." This advice from an experienced seminary dean goes to the heart of the dean's pastoral role in serving faculty. Caring for faculty takes many forms, including knowing them, communicating openly and honestly, involving them in projects by consulting and delegating, dealing with them fairly and with understanding of their difficulties and differences. When deans have administrative responsibilities for faculty hiring, evaluation, and professional development, their duties often go well beyond impersonal administration of programs to mentoring and counseling faculty, encouraging them in their teaching and scholarship, advocating for their needs, providing support, recognizing their accomplishments, and working to create community. The care and nurture of the faculty, in its many forms, is central to the dean's work.[20]

The majority of theological school deans come to their positions with ministerial experience, and many bring a strong personal sense of their pastoral role. Survey findings indicate that 84 percent of deans were ordained in their respective denominations, and 59 percent had done ministerial or pastoral work for the church prior to becoming deans, serving full-time in that capacity for an average of eight years. Only 6 percent of survey respondents, however, came to the deanship directly from the ministry. Among theological school deans, women were less likely than men to be ordained and to have ministerial experience.[21] While the pastoral role may be less well defined than the managerial and leadership roles, chief academic officers find it a significant and integral part of their administrative work.

How clearly the dean's pastoral duties are defined can vary widely among theological schools. Factors such as the traditional role of the dean within a school, expectations of the president and faculty, and the dean's own training and disposition can enhance or diminish the pastoral dimension of the dean's work. A rector of a Roman Catholic seminary, for example, clearly communicated to the dean at the time of hiring that his foremost responsibility was "to affirm, support, challenge, and move the faculty along; to meet regularly [with faculty] and encourage new directions." Other presidents, deans, and faculty frequently spoke of the dean's responsibility "to support and nurture the faculty." While this care for faculty may be implicit in many of the dean's duties, it is most evident as deans work to build the faculty, to foster their professional growth and vitality, and to create community. The seriousness and commitment with which deans approach these tasks determine their effectiveness in the pastoral role.

### *Building the Faculty*

Building the faculty, in this context, refers to the process of continuous planning for the composition of the faculty and the recruitment, hiring, and orientation of new faculty members. Survey results show that over 96 percent of theological school deans have the primary administrative responsibility for academic planning, and over 70 percent have responsibility for hiring academic personnel (faculty and staff). Interviews further reveal that deans with genuine concern for developing a quality faculty go well beyond announcing job openings and organizing search processes. They do considerable advanced planning to determine the types of positions and disciplinary areas in which faculty are needed; they are proactive in identifying and cultivating qualified candidates in those areas; and, once faculty are hired, they are intentional about orienting and integrating them into the institutional culture. Through these activities, deans play a critical role in building the faculty as a community of teacher/scholars through care in the selection and nurture of its newest members.

Site visits disclosed notable differences in how deans approach these tasks. Several deans clearly had worked with faculty and administrative colleagues to develop a vision for shaping the faculty in light of broader institutional goals. In these schools, decisions on faculty replacements and faculty searches were not ad hoc but undertaken in the context of a strategic plan that defined needs and priorities for the institution generally and for particular academic programs. Some schools were committed to globalization of the curriculum or to achieving greater gender and racial/ethnic diversity or to expanding specific programs. One dean, who had been particularly successful in developing the faculty, looked back upon her tenure in office with evident pride that the faculty had become international and truly ecumenical in its teaching and scholarship due to strategic hiring of faculty outside the Western tradition. This breadth brought the program distinction and, by all accounts, was achieved through the dean's leadership. By contrast, at another site the president lamented the dean's passive approach to faculty hiring. Faculty slots were filled routinely with little attention to reconfiguring positions or anticipating programmatic changes and without any effort on the dean's part to locate good candidates.[22]

Deans who were strongly committed to building the faculty took seriously the tasks of identifying promising candidates well in advance of job openings and of selecting them with care. An article on planning for pluralism in theological faculties described how deans can take an active role in faculty recruitment:

> The best work of a dean is accomplished by constantly working with department chairs years before faculty openings are available. The constant cultivation of potential candidates by phone, letter and informal/formal contacts at professional meetings is a primary prerequisite. Following bright young graduate students for a number of years during their studies with encouragement and advice is just as significant as courting the seasoned scholar who stands at the top of his/her field.[23]

In addition to taking initiative in cultivating promising candidates, deans also play a significant role internally in appointing search committee members and in determining how open, participatory, and thorough the hiring process will be. Several deans in the study believed in extensive campus interviews with prospective faculty to assess not only their professional competence but their ability to embrace the school's mission and values and their "fit" with the academic culture. One school interviewed candidates for three full days so faculty, administrators, students, and trustees could participate and contribute to such discernment. Implicit in such practices is the conviction that care in the search and selection process will pay off long-term in building a strong and committed faculty.

In addition to advanced planning and effective hiring practices, the cultural integration of newly hired faculty is critical to their relationship with colleagues and to their future development. The leadership deans provide in the orientation and mentoring of new members is an important part of their pastoral work. The deans' study suggests that, whereas most theological schools lack specific programs for integrating new faculty into the institutional culture, many have selective, informal approaches to this task.[24] Deans and/or presidents often meet with new faculty at the outset to discuss the terms of appointment and other expectations. Deans and faculty may provide various other kinds of orientation, ranging from showing new faculty where copy machines and supplies are located to informing them of rules and procedures to discussing subtler aspects of the institutional culture. Mentoring, on the other hand, is a more specialized relationship in which a colleague provides professional guidance to the new faculty member, such as counsel on course syllabi and teaching methods, discussion of research issues, and introduction to other professionals in the mentor's network. While schools may assign mentors to new faculty members, relationships usually flourish only if a natural affinity develops between the two parties.[25]

The success of individual faculty members and the strength of a school's faculty long-term depend on advanced planning for the shape and composition of the faculty, initiative in the cultivation and recruitment of able candidates, care in their selection, and active concern for the integration of new faculty into the academic community. The dean's leadership and pastoral care for faculty are critical at each stage of this process.

### *Supporting Faculty Growth and Renewal*

Although chief academic officers in most theological schools have the primary administrative responsibility for faculty development, many feel underprepared for this task. When deans were asked on the survey to identify areas in which they would like additional preparation and training, they placed "faculty development" at the top of the list. While most deans had considerable experience as faculty members prior to taking office, many lacked confidence in their ability to address the professional development needs of their colleagues.[26] Site visits revealed that some deans tended to underestimate their effectiveness because they lacked formal training for this work, while others had too traditional and limited a conception of what constituted faculty development.

If a dean's effectiveness in faculty development is measured solely by the amount of financial support available for sabbaticals, study leaves, computers, research assistance, travel, and the like, then deans in schools without ample resources may judge themselves deficient in meeting faculty needs.[27] If faculty development is conceived more broadly in terms of the various forms of support and encouragement that nurture faculty (only some of which require financial resources), then deans may be more effective than they realize in fulfilling this responsibility. While deans play a critical role in making the case for institutional resources for faculty development, funded programs are not the sole measure of the dean's or the institution's support. Findings of this study, along with an abundance of faculty development literature, confirm the importance of the many less tangible and costly forms of faculty support.

The dean's role in fostering faculty growth and renewal may include good stewardship of sabbatical and travel programs, highly personal forms of counsel and encouragement, and development of teamwork and collaboration among faculty. Through efforts such as these, many deans strive to create a positive climate in which faculty scholarship, teaching, service, and leadership can flourish. As deans in the study observed: "Setting the environment for faculty success is the dean's job; the dean is an enabler of the faculty."[28]

Five aspects of the dean's role in nurturing the professional development of faculty emerged from this study and are discussed briefly below. This discussion is intended to suggest, not exhaust, the various dimensions of the dean's work in fostering faculty growth and renewal. Readers interested in exploring other strategies for developing faculty that go beyond this research are encouraged to consult other publications on the subject.[29]

*1. By virtue of their office, deans have opportunities to know and understand individual faculty and to work with them to address their professional development needs.* An experienced theological school dean described how his work is largely defined by the care and nurture of faculty. Following are excerpts from his interview.

> Faculty need to believe that I care about them, their well-being, and their vocational success. If they believe that then I can make mistakes, a lot of things can go more slowly or quickly than they want and it works. I try to read what they write, congratulate them if something happens, and when they contact the office I get back to them promptly. I try to give financial support and have good ideas regarding faculty welfare and curriculum.
>
> The major shock in becoming a dean is that you have to deal with the dark side, the insecure side, the problematic side of a person. As a faculty person you can be a colleague, but part of being a colleague is that you're able to just walk away. It's their problem at some point so the friendships remain.
>
> The surprise as I talk to my colleagues who are deans is the percentage of time spent on personnel issues that are related to faculty insecurity, faculty problems, faculty special pleading that can be half or two-thirds of the job. So that you are just amazed at how your job is really shaped by the individual needs of the faculty and how you respond to them. And you succeed to the degree that you can do that well and help them succeed. So you really don't want to call yourself a personnel officer but that really is what you are. . . . That's the challenge, and I enjoy that very much.

As these passages suggest, deans come to know the personal problems and stresses of faculty in ways that other colleagues do not and are challenged to offer affirming and helpful responses. This dean believes, as do many of his peers, that his ultimate success as dean depends on his ability to address individual needs and to help faculty succeed. There are few clearer statements of the dean's pastoral role in serving faculty.

Deans in the study worked with individual faculty in a variety of ways. Deans generally had administrative oversight of faculty development funds for travel, study leaves, research assistants, and the like, and most had a small pool of discretionary funds for responding to faculty requests during the year. Utilizing these funds effectively, however, often depended on whether the dean had worked with individual faculty members to identify their needs and to develop plans for meeting them. One seminary, for example, has established a process for developing individual work plans, in which professional goals are translated into specific plans for the apportionment of time and workload.[30] These plans are reviewed by colleagues and considered in light of the seminary's overall needs and priorities. Knowing the long-term goals of individual members helps the seminary to anticipate the need for sabbaticals and other forms of professional development.

Most deans in the study relied on less formal methods for helping faculty to identify and address their needs. At one school, the dean met quarterly with faculty to review their course evaluations. During these individual consultations, he would discuss with them challenges they faced in the classroom and would encourage them to pursue scholarly work. These regular conversations enabled the dean to remain current with the diverse needs and concerns of individual faculty and to assist them in defining some specific ways to address them. Another dean attended to faculty more informally. He frequently conversed with faculty in offices and hallways and was alert to their mention of problems with teaching or obstacles to their research. This dean's approach was to steer faculty toward their strengths; if faculty members received bad reviews of their teaching, he would pair them with colleagues who could help them succeed. As a faculty member explained, the dean "has his fingers on everybody's pulse. He asks questions but does not give answers. Faculty come to him and feel affirmed."

Faculty development literature stresses the diversity of individual needs within any faculty body; not only do professional development requirements vary by discipline, but they change for persons at different stages of their professional lives. The types of opportunities sought by faculty in systematic theology and in pastoral care are likely to differ, and the support required by junior faculty in the early stages of their academic life may be quite unlike that needed by faculty at midcareer or nearing retirement.[31] Deans who recognize this diversity remain flexible in their responses to faculty needs and take multiple approaches to their nurture and support.

Evidence from this study suggests that deans who listen carefully to faculty, who are genuinely responsive to their concerns, who encourage their initiative and help them succeed are instrumental in creating a positive climate for faculty work. This pastoral care of individual faculty members, carried out almost daily through a variety of formal and informal means, is the centerpiece of the dean's work in developing the faculty.

2. *Deans can be instrumental in fostering teamwork and collaborative projects among faculty.* As solitary as scholarship and teaching traditionally have been in the academy, seminary faculties could function merely as a collection of individuals working independently under one roof. Deans play an important role in helping faculty to see their individual work as integral to the shared mission and part of a larger whole. Deans who can articulate that corporate identity and develop in individual faculty a sense of common purpose create

a positive climate for shared governance, collaborative research, team teaching, and countless other forms of cooperative work.

Deans take multiple approaches to developing these professional bonds among faculty. Several deans in the study hosted social occasions for faculty, such as late afternoon teas, weekly "TGIF" days, and occasional dinners at the dean's home. Although these events were primarily social, they were intended to build the personal relationships, the friendships, fundamental to cooperative and trusting professional relationships. To bring faculty together professionally, some deans sponsored faculty colloquies, brown-bag lunches, or discussion groups as occasions for faculty to give papers, to report on sabbatical or leave projects, or to discuss teaching and other areas of common concern. Through these sessions, faculty became acquainted with one another's work and sometimes discovered possibilities for joint research or team teaching. At several schools, deans organized events for public recognition of faculty accomplishments, gathering colleagues to celebrate publications and awards. By creating forums for social and professional interactions among faculty, deans serve as catalysts for developing their corporate identity and strengthening the bonds essential to community life.

*3. Many deans play an important role in securing and administering institutional funds for faculty development.* As senior academic administrators, deans often are expected not only to know what faculty need but to advocate for resources to address those needs. Whether institutional planning and budgeting are the work of the president or a senior administrative team, deans who are actively involved in these processes usually are expected to represent faculty interests and to help determine the priority professional development will have relative to other academic and institutional needs. The dean's judgment about how to utilize limited resources for the maximum benefit of faculty is especially crucial. For example, one dean felt strongly that he would "rather be extravagant with faculty development money than increase faculty salaries by 1 percent. The faculty are better served psychologically," he reasoned, "and you're better served by making them feel good about themselves." Deans play an important role in bringing their knowledge of faculty to bear on institutional policy decisions.

Deans also are instrumental in determining how faculty development funds, once secured, are used. Whether deans personally distribute funds or work with a faculty committee, they are influential in determining how flexibly and equitably funds are dispersed for faculty travel, sabbaticals, research assistance, and similar programs. A common problem is having numerous faculty requests for limited development resources. Some deans have enlisted the help of faculty in developing guidelines that establish priorities and deal fairly with faculty. Deans who involve faculty in thinking through such issues often strengthen the faculty's investment in their own professional development. Some deans also encourage colleagues to access outside funding sources to support both individual projects and larger academic initiatives.[32] As these examples illustrate, deans are critical players in establishing the priority of faculty development within the institution, in providing for the flexible and fair distribution of funds, and in encouraging efforts to seek financial support from outside sources.

*4. Deans can insure that other institutional practices are conducted in ways that support faculty growth and renewal.* The regular processes of curriculum revision and faculty evaluation, in particular, are rich with possibilities for faculty development. In the instance of curriculum review, changes in existing courses and requirements or the addition of new programs afford deans the opportunity to encourage faculty to pursue new scholarly interests, to develop courses in new areas and formats, and to work with colleagues in other departments. When deans see in curriculum review the potential for faculty to explore beyond their own disciplines and to develop new competencies, they give a positive dimension to a process that, too often, is marred by departmental turf wars and fear of change and loss. In a similar way, faculty evaluation can be a constructive stimulus for professional growth. Some deans use regular performance evaluation as an opportunity to direct faculty toward their strengths, as well as to address areas of weakness. By encouraging faculty to set professional development goals and helping them plan to meet those goals, deans utilize the development potential implicit in the evaluation process. Deans who give a constructive orientation to practices such as curriculum revision and evaluation can help the faculty realize their potential to support, affirm, and revitalize faculty work.

*5. Deans can foster faculty ownership of professional development programs by involving faculty directly in their design and implementation.* The responsiveness of faculty to professional development activities often depends on their involvement in planning and developing such programs. As in matters of governance, deans who empower faculty to participate in decisions concerning programs and activities are rewarded with the active support of faculty for development efforts. The dean's leadership in engaging faculty to think creatively about their professional growth and renewal and inviting their participation in meeting those needs is an important dimension of the dean's pastoral role. Explicit concern for who faculty members are and may become is central to the dean's pastoral work.

### *Creating Community*

Unquestionably, the dean is but one of many players in the task of creating community.[33] Leadership in this and other areas of academic life usually is distributed among those with and without formal leadership positions and is shared in complex and subtle ways by various members of the group.[34] Within academic institutions, however, the chief academic officer has distinctive opportunities to work with constituents, particularly with faculty, to provide leadership in creating community life. Much of the dean's work in developing the faculty and fostering collegial, participatory decision-making processes involves explicit efforts to nurture and sustain community.

Community refers to a group of individuals united by their commitment to shared beliefs, values, and purposes. In the theological school setting, these fundamental ideas and goals are commonly expressed in the institutional mission and most deeply and fully shared when embodied in academic and spiritual practices, such as teaching, learning, scholarship, spiritual formation, and worship. Community does not refer to superficial commonalities among persons nor to incidents of their cooperation. Community resides in the shared meaning and purposes that unify its members in their aspirations and their daily work.

Deans, as positional leaders, have opportunities to develop and nourish a sense of community, especially among the faculty. By virtue of their office, deans are able to convene colleagues, to invite them to come together for corporate reflection and conversation. Deans also are able, if not expected, to pose the questions and raise the issues that enable faculty to examine the core values and practices on which their community life depends. As in matters of governance, deans are influential in setting the academic agenda and defining the priority issues that command faculty time and attention. Taken together, the capacity to invite colleagues to join in discussion and to focus their attention on issues vital to their common life gives deans extraordinary opportunities to create and strengthen community.

In *The Courage to Teach,* Parker Palmer discusses the role of positional leaders in the task of creating a learning/teaching community.

> Community does not emerge spontaneously from some relational reflex, especially not in the complex and often conflicted institutions where most teachers work. If we are to have communities of discourse about teaching and learning—communities that are intentional about the topics to be pursued and the ground rules to be practiced—we need leaders who can call people toward that vision.
>
> Good talk about good teaching is unlikely to happen if presidents and principals, deans and department chairs, and others who have influence without position do not *expect* it and *invite* it into being. Those verbs are important because leaders who try to coerce conversation will fail. Conversation must be a free choice—but in the privatized academy, conversation begins only as leaders invite us out of our isolation into generative ways of using our freedom.[35]

Whether the talk focuses on teaching, as Palmer suggests, or on other topics, leaders are instrumental in expecting and inviting colleagues to participate. A leader's initiative to convene colleagues can convey the importance of the gathering to the group as a whole. Since such conversations do not happen naturally and spontaneously in most groups, leadership is required to raise issues that need to be examined, to encourage widespread, voluntary participation in discussions, and to direct the conversation in productive ways. Palmer's book is exceptionally helpful in offering practical suggestions for a process that will foster the open, constructive discourse necessary for "learning in community."[36]

The critical role of academic officers in inviting corporate reflection on fundamental issues was well illustrated some years ago when the Lilly Endowment invited a representative group of North American theological schools to participate in the Faculty Scholarship Development Grant Program.[37] The purpose of the program was to develop new institutional initiatives to increase the scholarly productivity of theological faculties and, at the same time, to encourage fundraising for the ongoing support of these efforts. Evaluation of the first round of grants revealed that deans who provided the most effective leadership used the grant as a catalyst for corporate reflection. Typically, they convened faculty, administrators, and trustees in a retreat setting for in-depth examination of the mission and foundational values of the seminary and fresh consideration of the meaning of scholarship within that context. Schools whose deans invited colleagues to explore such fundamental questions developed grant programs firmly grounded in the institutional mission and tailored to the group's shared understanding of the role of scholarship in their community. Their programs differed in quality, longevity, and effectiveness from those hastily assembled to meet a variety of short-term needs without the benefit of sustained corporate reflection on such basic issues.

While deans have the ability, even the responsibility, to invite participants to the table of community discourse and to raise questions that allow for in-depth exploration of their common life, the task can be formidable. Gathering together busy people with full and hectic schedules is rarely easy, and moving the conversation of academics from administrative detail to the deeper, more substantive issues of community life can require extraordinary patience and skill. Former seminary dean, Frederick Borsch, related a story of his own attempt to focus attention on matters of faith:

> I recall how, during a faculty gathering that was meant to be devoted to theological discourse, the conversation turned once again to curricular and administrative matters. "Why," I blurted out in frustration, "do we spend so little time talking about our faith in God or why we believe in the resurrection?" After a rather embarrassed silence, one of the older and wiser faculty said, "Fred, it's because we don't trust each other enough."
>
> At first I didn't want to admit he was right, but gradually I and others of us realized the truth in his response and began to make efforts to build our levels of trust and sharing.[38]

Clearly, changing the nature of the group's conversation involves more than introducing important topics; it requires deep levels of trust, built and nurtured over time, that make discussion of personal beliefs possible. Much has been learned about practical strategies for conducting conversations that will open participants to a deeply reflective process.[39] While all members are responsible for this work, deans often are looked to for leadership in beginning and sustaining such practices. Unless academic officers are intentional in their efforts to initiate and guide the conversations that build community, even the most richly endowed and promising collection of individuals may fail to discover the common ground of belief and action that unites them.

Theological schools have an advantage in the task of community building, since their members are connected in various ways to a rich tradition of religious values and practices. Even if differences exist among individuals within these traditions, as they inevitably do, where could there be more fertile ground for creating community than within schools dedicated to the study of these religious values and practices? In an essay entitled "Spirited Connections," authors D. Susan Wisely and Elizabeth M. Lynn call attention to "the resources of religious thought and language, as embodied in diverse religious traditions and texts," as fertile ground for community reflection.[40] They suggest that "traditional religious concepts like finitude, hope, forgiveness, sin, and grace address a depth of human experience untouched by modern social-scientific terminologies," and such concepts suggest perspectives and practices helpful in connecting individuals to a larger whole. The centrality of religious traditions and texts to the work of theological schools and the expertise of their members in mining such resources for their insight to contemporary problems can be a powerful focus for developing and deepening the experience of community.

In a recent essay, Larry Rasmussen illustrates how early forms of Jewish and Christian communities can inform our efforts to develop community in the present day.[41] When Rasmussen turns to the question of the steps required to shape communities, he finds the "rites, sacraments, and patterns of the gathered congregation provide a focus for thinking about how community is ordered among us." In particular, the eucharistic table raises issues essential to ordering all human communities:

> Do our practices welcome all to the table? Are the discriminating distinctions drawn between people in society of no account here, and how do we show that in the way we regulate our life together? Are the guests in turn called to be the hosts? Are means created and encouraged by which each participant can find gifts for meeting the hungers of the world? . . . Does the organization of community life—and not only the celebration of Eucharist—encourage leadership to emerge from the foot of the table? Do the ways we organize life together ask for participation that nurtures significant levels of personal commitment and responsibility, on a scale and in ways people can handle?[42]

When this example is applied to theological schools, one is struck by how many of the tasks of ordering the community are part of the work of the academic dean. In matters of academic governance and in other communal activities, the dean frequently decides who gets invited to the table, if guests in turn become hosts, if individual gifts are nourished, if leadership and participation are encouraged from the foot or the sides of the table, and, most importantly, how openly and democratically these very decisions about ordering community are made. Rasmussen finds that early Christian practices, such as the eucharistic table, provide a model of "community democracy" worthy of emulation in our contemporary efforts to build community.

In summary, the call of academic officers to lead and serve the faculty is a call both to nurture individual gifts and to create community. This most important and necessary work is possible only through an open, trusting relationship between dean and faculty. Deans play a significant role in fostering good communication, helping individuals manage conflict and disagreement, affirming and developing individual strengths, and encouraging conversations and practices among colleagues that nourish their common life. When deans succeed in these tasks, they are not only leading from the center of their institutions, but leading from the heart. Each day, deans have powerful means at their disposal to build or to erode the bonds that create community. Deans who find in their office its creative potential for good and who cultivate the leadership and pastoral skills needed to fulfill that potential make enormous contributions to the quality of community life in theological schools.

## Notes

[1] See Chapter One, Table 1.

[2] For reflection on Jesus Christ as servant-leader see: Henri J. M. Nouwen, *In the Name of Jesus: Reflections on Christian Leadership* (New York: The Crossroad Publishing Company, 1989).

[3] Robert K. Greenleaf, *Servant: Retrospect and Prospect* (Indianapolis, IN: The Robert K. Greenleaf Center, 1980, 1988), 4. "The idea of *servant* is deep in our Judeo-Christian heritage. The concordance to the Standard Revised Version of the Bible lists 1,300 references to *servant* (including serve and service)."

[4] Survey findings indicate that only 36.6 percent of deans have the primary administrative responsibility for faculty salaries. In estimating their influence in this area, deans rated their actual influence at 2.3 (mean), while they considered 2.7 (mean) to be optimal. (Rating scale for dean's influence: 4=decisive, 3=considerable, 2=some, 1=none.)

[5] In a conversation May 13, 1998, Craig Dykstra and Fred Hofheinz observed that if deans had greater responsibility for faculty salary and advancement decisions, their distinctive form of leadership, which depends on collegiality, might change. An increase in decanal responsibilities and authority could well exacerbate the dean's distance from the faculty that frequently occurs with the move to administration.

[6] The deans' responses to the statement concerning faculty review of their continued appointment had a mean rating of 3.17 (scale: 4=strongly agree – 1=strongly disagree). The same statement had a mean rating of 3.16 on the 1993 survey of theological faculties conducted by the Auburn Center. These and all subsequent statistical data from the faculty survey were provided by the Auburn Center. For a general description of the Auburn study and a report on other findings see: Barbara G. Wheeler, *True and False*. The First in a Series of Reports from a Study of Theological School Faculty, Auburn Studies, No. 4 (New York: Auburn Theological Seminary, 1996), and Barbara G. Wheeler and Mark N. Wilhelm, *Tending Talents*. The Second in a Series of Reports from a Study of Theological School Faculty, Auburn Studies, No. 5 (New York: Auburn Theological Seminary, 1997).

[7] Of the 9 percent of survey respondents who strongly agreed with the statement, there were no statistically significant differences among respondents by school size, type (university-related/independent), or denomination. However, the practice of determining the dean's reappointment by vote of the faculty was most prevalent in large (150–300 student FTE), independent, Protestant seminaries.

[8] "Changing Scenes," *In Trust* 2, no. 1 (Easter 1990), 27. These events reportedly occurred at Pacific School of Religion.

[9] Deans were asked on the survey to list the three characteristics most needed in an academic officer at their institutions. Seventy-one percent of respondents cited the "ability to work well with faculty," the highest percentage of deans on any single characteristic.

[10] See Chapter Three, pp. 100–102.

[11] In light of the importance of the dean's understanding of and credibility with faculty, the trend toward professionalization of academic administration is troubling. While other positions may be filled by professional administrators with administrative rather than academic preparations, this would be least appropriate to the deanship, which depends on an intimate connection with the faculty. This issue will be discussed more fully in Chapter Eight.

[12] L. Gregory Jones, "Forgiveness," in *Practicing Our Faith: A Way of Life for a Searching People,* Dorothy C. Bass, ed. (San Francisco: Jossey-Bass, 1997), 133–147.

[13] Elizabeth C. Nordbeck, "The Once and Future Dean: Reflections on Being a Chief Academic Officer," *Theological Education* 33 (Autumn 1996 Supplement), 29.

[14] The surveys cited here were both conducted in 1993: the survey of theological school chief academic officers as part of this study, and the faculty survey as part of the Auburn Center's Study of Theological School Faculty. When asked to rate the quality of the dean-faculty relationship at their schools, using the scale 4=excellent – 1=poor, respondents to the deans' survey had a mean rating of 3.47, and respondents to the faculty survey had a mean rating of 3.19. Administrators with faculty rank who completed the faculty survey had a mean rating of 3.35, whereas other faculty had a mean rating of 3.15.

[15] Only 2 percent of respondents (3 out of 164) rated their relationship to faculty "fair" or "poor." Four percent gave no answer or were undecided.

[16] Although consulting with faculty has been raised in other parts of the book, its critical role in the dean-faculty relationship warrants its reiteration.

[17] On the survey, 76 percent of deans indicated they had the primary administrative responsibility at their institution for "developing faculty leadership."

[18] See Chapter Two, pp. 70–73. Susan A. Holton, ed. *Conflict Management in Higher Education,* New Directions for Higher Education, no. 92 (San Francisco: Jossey-Bass, 1995), and Ann Lucas, "Managing Conflict," *Strengthening Departmental Leadership: A Team-Building Guide for Chairs in Colleges and Universities* (San Francisco: Jossey-Bass, 1994), 201–218.

[19] Deans may be assisted by the work of the Carnegie Foundation: Ernest L. Boyer's *Scholarship Reconsidered* (Princeton, NJ: The Carnegie Foundation for the Advancement of Teaching, 1990) and its follow-up, *Scholarship Assessed: Evaluation of the Professoriate,* by Charles E. Glassick, Mary Taylor Huber, and Gene I. Maeroff (San Francisco: Jossey-Bass, 1997). These works broaden the notion of what constitutes scholarship and provide guidance in assessing faculty work. Also helpful may be the annual conference on faculty roles and rewards sponsored by the American Association of Higher Education (AAHE).

A theological school model for weighting and balancing various duties through individualized work plans for faculty is discussed in: Barbara Brown Zikmund and William McKinney, "Choosing and Nurturing Faculty for an Unconventional Seminary," *Theological Education* 31, no. 2 (Spring 1995), 13–26.

[20] The dean's pastoral work is seldom limited to faculty, but may include students and other members of the seminary. Particularly with students, deans frequently offer advice and counsel on a range of personal and professional issues.

[21] On the deans' survey, only 22 percent of women respondents were ordained, compared to 93 percent of men; only 33 percent of women had ministerial or pastoral experience, compared to 63 percent of men. These gender differences were statistically significant.

[22] The 1993 study of theological school faculties by the Auburn Center has documented both the future need for seminary faculty by discipline and the supply of qualified candidates expected from doctoral programs. This type of data, unavailable until recently, offers an analysis of supply and demand that can inform the planning of individual institutions. Publications on this research include two reports cited earlier: Wheeler, *True and False,* and Wheeler and Wilhelm, *Tending Talents.*

[23] Walter C. Kaiser, Jr., "'Pluralism' as a Criterion for Excellence in Faculty Development," *Theological Education* 28, no.1 (Autumn 1991), 58.

[24] On the survey, theological school deans responded to the statement, "There are specific programs to integrate new faculty into the institutional culture," with a mean rating of 2.4 (scale 4=strongly agree – 1=strongly disagree), with only 7 percent "strongly agreeing" and 40 percent "somewhat agreeing" with this statement. Although many books and articles in the general area of faculty development discuss the integration and support of faculty during the first years of their appointment, two research-based studies are primarily concerned with these topics: within the theological school context is Wheeler's *Tending Talents,* 1–22; and Donald K. Jarvis, *Junior Faculty Development: A Handbook* (New York: The Modern Language Association of America, 1991). The dean's critical role in shaping faculty positions and selecting their occupants was further elaborated by Barbara Wheeler in an address entitled, "Shaping Theological Faculty for the Future: How Academic Deans Can Help," given at a Conference for Theological School Chief Academic Officers in Pittsburgh, PA, October 10, 1997.

[25] In a 1991 article, Max Stackhouse suggested that schools think of the faculty as a whole, not simply individual persons, as mentor and model. See Max L. Stackhouse, "The Faculty as Mentor and Model," *Theological Education* 28, no. 1 (Autumn 1991), 63–70.

[26] Eighty-three percent of survey respondents reported they were responsible for faculty development. Forty-two percent cited their need for additional preparation and training in faculty development, higher than for any other area of decanal responsibility.

[27] On the survey of theological school deans conducted for this study and the survey of theological school faculty conducted by the Auburn Center, deans and faculty both "somewhat agreed" with the statement, "My institution provides adequately for the professional development of faculty." On the scale 4=strongly agree – 1=strongly disagree, the mean rating for both deans and faculty was 2.8.

[28] James Hudnut-Beumler, "A New Dean Meets a New Day in Theological Education," *Theological Education* 33 (Supplement 1996), 19. In addition, the Auburn Center's study of theological faculty includes an inquiry into what makes theological schools good places to work. Their research indicates that schools with collegial and productive faculties have the following characteristics: a distinctive but open organizational culture, participatory leadership, organizational momentum, and faculty identification with the school's mission and culture. The deans' study corroborates these findings. See Wilhelm, "Good Places to Work," *Tending Talents,* 24–35.

[29] Issues relating to faculty development in theological education are the focus of the following publications: *Theological Education* 31, no. 2 (Spring 1995) on faculty development, evaluation, and advancement; *Theological Education* 27, no. 1 (Autumn 1991) on building theological faculties of the future; *Theological Education* 24, no. 1 (Autumn 1987) with articles on the dean's responsibility for faculty research. See also Wheeler and Wilhelm, *Tending Talents,* cited earlier, and John F. Canary, "The Spiritual Care of a Seminary Faculty," *Seminary Journal* 1, no. 3 (Winter 1995), 12–19.

The faculty development literature in higher education is vast. The following sources may provide a good starting point, since they discuss practical strategies for working with faculty and provide helpful reference to other works: Jack H. Schuster, Daniel W. Wheeler, and Associates, *Enhancing Faculty Careers: Strategies for Development and Renewal* (San Francisco: Jossey-Bass, 1990); Ann F. Lucas, *Strengthening Departmental Leadership: A Team-Building Guide for Chairs in Colleges and Universities* (San Francisco: Jossey-Bass, 1994); John W. Creswell and Associates, *The Academic Chairperson's Handbook* (Lincoln, NE: University of Nebraska Press, 1990).

[30] The Hartford Seminary model is explained in: Zikmund and McKinney, "Choosing and Nurturing Faculty," 13–26.

[31] A succinct discussion of the changing needs of faculty at different stages in their careers is presented in: Madeleine F. Green and Sharon A. McDade, *Investing in Higher Education: A Handbook of Leadership Development* (Washington, DC: American Council on Education, 1991), 159–163.

[32] The Association of Theological Schools in the United States and Canada (ATS) provides assistance to seminaries and to individual scholars seeking corporate and foundation funding. The Faculty Resource Center annually publishes a grants directory and sponsors several national and campus-based consultations to support theological schools in their fundraising efforts.

[33] When deans were asked on the survey who at their institutions had the primary responsibility for "building cooperation and trust, creating community," 48 percent of deans cited the president or chief executive, 31 percent the chief academic officer, 7 percent the faculty, and 6 percent other administrators. Unfortunately, the question did not probe the extent to which this responsibility was shared, though results show that community building can be located primarily with various individuals and groups.

[34] Theological school deans widely recognized community building as a form of leadership. On the survey, respondents judged "building cooperation and trust, creating community" as very important to effective leadership, with a mean rating of 3.84 (rating scale: 4=very important – 1=unimportant).

[35] Parker J. Palmer, *The Courage to Teach: Exploring the Inner Landscape of a Teacher's Life* (San Francisco: Jossey-Bass, 1998), 156.

[36] Particularly helpful is the chapter entitled, "Learning in Community: the Conversation of Colleagues," in Palmer, *The Courage to Teach,* 141–161.

[37] At the conclusion of the first round of the Faculty Scholarship Development Grant Program 1985–1989, I conducted an evaluation on behalf of the Lilly Endowment. Evaluation findings are contained in a written report to the Endowment, submitted June 1990.

[38] Frederick H. Borsch, "Faculty as Mentors and Models," *Theological Education* 28, no. 1 (Autumn 1991), 72.

[39] In addition to the Palmer text cited earlier, an essay on developing community at the Lilly Endowment and within Endowment-funded organizations offers several practical suggestions for initiating corporate reflection that translates readily to other settings. The authors frame these suggestions in thoughtful discussion of the value of community building. D. Susan Wisely and Elizabeth M. Lynn, "Spirited Connections," in *Spirit at Work: Discovering the Spirituality in Leadership,* by Jay A. Conger and Associates (San Francisco: Jossey-Bass, 1994), 100–131.

[40] Wisely and Lynn, "Spirited Connections," 121.

[41] Larry Rasmussen, "Shaping Communities," in *Practicing Our Faith: A Way of Life for a Searching People,* ed. Dorothy C. Bass (San Francisco: Jossey-Bass, 1997), 119–132.

[42] Rasmussen, 131.

# 5 THE DEAN'S WORK WITH SENIOR ADMINISTRATORS, BOARDS, AND CHURCH LEADERS

*"Often the point person for interfacing competing worlds and values is the dean."*
*James Hudnut-Beumler*

Virtually all activities and interests related to theological schools intersect in some way with the academic area. At this intersection, the chief academic officer works not only with the president and the faculty, but with other internal constituents and external publics of the school. In academic matters, the chief academic officer serves as a critical link between the academic program and faculty on the one hand and administrators, students, staff, board members, church leaders, denominational representatives, accrediting agencies, and academic organizations on the other.[1] While all are important to the academic life of a theological school, site visits revealed that three of these groups—senior administrative officers, board members, and church leaders—often had significant working relationships with the chief academic officer and were involved in shaping academic program, policy, and personnel decisions. The relationship of the chief academic officer to these groups and their influence on academic decision making and governance are the subject of this chapter.

The direct and critical connection of senior administrators, seminary boards, and church leaders to the academic life of theological schools is evident in these few examples taken from the study:

- To meet the needs of nontraditional students, the dean and faculty proposed reducing the weekday class schedule to four days and adding evening courses. The administrators in charge of auxiliary services objected, since fewer students on campus during regular hours would cause the cafeteria to lose money.
- Seminary trustees endorsed a high-profile leadership center for the school without faculty consultation. Subsequently, the dean was asked

to build faculty support for the center and to enlist faculty to develop and implement appropriate scholarly and educational programs.

- Denominational directives urged seminaries to establish a two-year pre-theology program for ministerial candidates who enter without sufficient academic preparation. When the faculty of one seminary developed a new curriculum to meet this requirement, area bishops expressed reluctance to utilize the program because of the time commitment.
- Following a particularly difficult faculty hiring process, the board of trustees returned to the faculty its final recommendation on a candidate, seeking greater consensus. When faculty failed to achieve consensus, the search ended with a provisional hire.
- The faculty of a denominational seminary voted to discontinue offering the Doctor of Ministry degree and to focus instead on their Ph.D. program. The church was angry and felt abandoned. The seminary responded by establishing a center for continuing education to serve the needs of pastors and church members.

Even these brief sketches show that senior administrators, boards, and church leaders can play a significant role in decisions affecting academic programs and personnel, many of which have long-term consequences for the life of the institution. Whether each of these groups is remote, intrusive, or able to work in partnership with the dean and the faculty often depends on the dean's ability to build bridges between academic and nonacademic areas of the seminary, between faculty and board governance, and between the academy and the church. This chapter examines the dean's role in forging relationships that make these vital connections possible.

Analysis of the dean's working relationship to senior administrators, board members, and church leaders must recognize that each is a primary constituency of the president. Theological school presidents supervise senior administrators and manage the administrative team, report directly to the governing board, and officially represent the school in dealing with denominational offices and local churches. Due to the primacy of the president's relationship to these groups, presidents decide whether senior administrators work together as a team or cabinet, and they typically determine how extensively individual administrators work with board members and church leaders. For example, some presidents may request that the dean attend certain meetings, make specific contacts, work closely with individuals on particular issues or deal with them in certain ways; other presidents may be less directive and give their deans latitude to work with seminary constituents as the issues warrant and as they see fit; still others may insist that the dean deal with the board and the denomination only through the president. The ability of presidents to set parameters for the dean's work accounts, in part, for the way individual deans relate to these groups.

Other factors also determine the nature and scope of the dean's working relationships. Institutional traditions and cultures may encourage close contact between the dean and the academic affairs committee of the board, for example, or foster distant relations with church officials who deal with the seminary only through the president. A dean's working relationship with a particular group also may change over time. For example, cooperation between the dean and an administrative colleague may intensify when they are called upon to handle an institutional crisis or to work together on a special project involving their respective areas. The dean's own interests and priorities also may determine the amount of time given to these relationships. A dean who focuses on strengthening ties between the seminary and the church may cultivate relationships with local pastors, whereas another dean whose interest is working with faculty on their classroom teaching may not. While the research reveals some general trends across theological schools concerning deans' relationships to constituents, such relationships can vary with differences in individual presidents and deans and with differences in institutional needs and traditions.

This chapter discusses, in turn, the chief academic officer's work with senior administrators, board members, and church leaders. Drawing upon survey data and personal interviews with deans and members of these groups, we examine the relationship of the chief academic officer and the academic area to these constituents and assess their role and influence in the academic life of theological schools. In addition to clarifying the distinctive contributions of these constituents, this discussion gives further evidence of the complexity and reach of the dean's work and the diverse relationships the office requires. It confirms that in their central and pivotal role, deans do more than facilitate communication and serve as intermediaries. Their larger task is to create the partnerships between academic personnel and other constituents that make possible their shared responsibility for academic leadership and governance.

## Senior Administrators

Senior administrators in theological schools typically include, in addition to the chief executive officer, the chief academic officer and the vice presidents or directors of institutional advancement, finance, student life or formation, and the like. The president usually appoints senior administrators, oversees their work in specific areas, coordinates their activities as an administrative team or cabinet, and consults them when dealing with institutional concerns. In cooperation with the president and with one another, senior administrators are responsible for the school's day-to-day operations and for coordination among the various units in the management and leadership of the seminary. The ability of senior administrators to work together effectively is critical to the cohesiveness and well-being of their institutions.

The general profile of theological school deans acquired through this study gives a clear sense of the importance of these administrative relationships. Survey respondents indicated that the "ability to work well with administrative colleagues" was among the top three criteria used to evaluate their effectiveness as chief academic officers.[2] These were closely followed by the "ability to be a team player," which applies broadly but includes their work with administrative colleagues. Deans responding to the survey estimated they spend an average of 3.6 hours per week in substantive conversation with administrators other than the president.[3] This exceeds the amount of time spent weekly with the president (average 2.2 hours) and with all other constituents except faculty and students. Given the centrality of the academic program and its interdependence with other administrative areas, the dean's relationship to senior administrators, individually and collectively, is critical to fulfilling the managerial and leadership responsibilities of the office. Quite simply, as one dean noted, "it is impossible to be a good dean without solid working relationships with other senior administrators."[4]

### *Individual Relationships*

During site visit interviews, deans were asked with which of their administrative colleagues, other than the president, they worked most closely. Their responses were remarkably varied. Several deans named the vice president for business affairs or finance; others mentioned the dean of students or vice rector for student formation; and still others cited the dean of admissions and the director of operations and personnel. Rarely were these alliances due simply to the nature of the dean's responsibilities. Interviews revealed that close working relationships with particular colleagues owed more to personal and ideological compatibilities than to specific requirements of the dean's office.

Theological school deans offered various explanations for the strength of these relationships. A provost was closest to the vice president for finance because he was committed to faculty and willing to listen, be flexible, and work as a team player. As the provost noted, "We like each other and know we depend on each other to succeed." Another dean explained his relationship to the vice president for business this way: "He sees himself as a servant of the church and the seminary"; when working together "we can disagree and argue, acknowledge our differing styles, and resolve our differences." Another dean was close to the associate dean of students because they are both "collegial, work well together, and are heading in the same direction." In these and similar cases, deans tended to develop close professional relationships with colleagues who shared their commitments to the institution and the faculty and whose personal styles were compatible with their own. As with other professional relationships, their success was attributable not to the absence of disagreement but to the ability of both parties to respect and manage such differences.

Not surprisingly, deans tended to have looser professional ties to administrators who were difficult to work with. The dean at one seminary had minimal dealings with the finance officer who, unlike the other administrators, was "not a colleague." Another dean was frequently at odds with the registrar due to differences in their interpretation of academic policies. While deans reported that some relationships were strengthened by intentional efforts to improve communication and cooperation, other incompatibilities proved more intractable. Faced with persistent tensions between the academic dean and dean of student life and between the finance and development officers, one seminary revised its organizational structure, reconfiguring one position and adding an executive vice president to oversee and mediate among the nonacademic areas. While such radical solutions appear to be rare, they underscore the importance of developing a group of senior administrators capable of working together effectively.

One seminary dean, new to his position, summarized well the basis for working cooperatively with other administrators. He found that the relationship with other administrators works better "on a personal level than it does on an organizational level." He continued,

> We don't act because we remember what the structure says. We act because we know one another and we appreciate the fact that each of us has a job to do, and if we don't do that job the institution won't function the way it ought to. We also recognize that each job is related to someone else's job, and if we assist them in doing what they are supposed to do, what we're supposed to do is enhanced as well.

In this view, cooperation among senior administrators is motivated less by the organizational chart than by the personal awareness that each area is related to every other and their mutual interdependence is necessary to the good of the whole.

### *Administrative Teams*

At sites visited for the study, presidents typically decided whether senior administrators met regularly as a group. Chapter Three discussed how these presidents differed in the frequency with which they convened senior administrators (ranging from once weekly to once yearly), in their ideas of the purposes the group served, and in their own efforts to build an administrative team.[5] Some presidents considered senior administrators as individuals working in separate spheres, and others viewed them as members of an administrative team whose deliberations and actions were undertaken jointly. Site visits revealed that, even in schools with good, informal patterns of communication, chief academic officers felt that regular, formal meetings with the administrative group as a whole were necessary and helpful. Deans expressed the greatest satisfaction with presidents who convened senior administrators not only for purposes of exchanging information but to work as a team in handling important institutional issues.

Several factors contribute to the dean's effectiveness in working with administrative colleagues as a group. Most important and often overlooked is the dean's "fit" with the prevailing administrative culture, which forms the context for dealings with the group as a whole. Site visits also revealed basic principles for working with administrative teams that enable deans to create partnerships with other administrators and enlist their support for the academic area.

*Administrative Cultures.* Two theological schools in the study had particularly well-defined administrative cultures with clear group norms and distinctive patterns of group interaction. In these cases, members who shared the predominant characteristics and practices of the group worked with colleagues more effectively than those who differed. In one seminary, a senior administrator felt hampered in working with administrative colleagues because she did not fit the group profile: she was not from the region, she was not a member of the school's denomination, she was not a graduate of the school, she was not male, and she was the only ordained woman among senior administrators. Her difference from other group members on these criteria often entailed differences from them on specific issues and the means she proposed to deal with them. After several years at the seminary, she acknowledged, "there is still a sense in which I feel like an outsider," a fact she felt could be a liability in working with administrative colleagues as a group.

At another seminary, the president "forcefully led" the administrative team which, as an extension of the president, was a powerful decision-making body. Within the group, discussions were lively, and team members were notably open and direct with one another. An exception was the academic dean whom colleagues described as "the least willing to be open," with the result that academic matters were discussed less frequently than issues in other areas and were considered subordinate to them. While the dean was articulate at meetings, his reticence became problematic. Administrative colleagues noted that, while he could be effective one-on-one, he lacked the personal assertiveness and directness characteristic of the administrative team. Members of the group attributed their insufficient attention to academic issues to the dean's uneasy fit with the group culture.

These examples underscore the power of administrative cultures and their importance in determining the effectiveness of individual members. Deans who felt that senior administrators at their schools worked successfully as a team often referred to the personal compatibility among their colleagues. Several attributed their success to good communication and the ability to discuss difficult issues openly, to rely on each other for advice and support, and, in the words of one dean, "to leave unified once decisions are made." Some deans attributed the ability to work in these mutually supportive ways to the fact that administrators had high regard for one another, understood each other's jobs without interfering, and had "confidence that each is capable in his or her own sphere." Deans frequently cited the trust and respect at the heart of their personal relationships as important factors in their ability to work well with other administrators.

*The Dean's Work with Administrative Teams.* Principles for working successfully with other administrators are illustrated by an example from one of the most experienced seminary deans in the study. According to a colleague's account, the dean presented the faculty's proposal for a revised curriculum to the administrative team. They discussed both the financial and facilities implications of the proposal and noted that, with fewer credit hours required, tuition revenues would certainly decrease. The vice president for business affairs, who had worked with the academic dean for several years, considered the business office a service to the academic area and a means of facilitating faculty work. Motivated to implement the curriculum the faculty had proposed, the administrative team accepted the business officer's recommendation to deal with the revenue shortage through gradual tuition increases. The dean's credibility with his administrative peers and their longstanding, mutually supportive relationships enhanced their willingness to restructure the institutional budget to enable adoption of the new curriculum.

In less collegial environments, administrators could decide that certain revenue losses presented an insurmountable obstacle and then require faculty to adjust the curriculum accordingly. When at another seminary the faculty recommended the hiring of a controversial New Testament scholar, some senior administrators advised the president not to approve the appointment, given its potential to offend several major donors and undermine fundraising efforts. Whether administrators support one another or are wary and slow to cooperate often depends on the personal levels of trust, respect, and acceptance among group members. Deans who work well with the senior administrative team tend to adapt to the group culture and develop good personal relationships with its members.

Effective deans also employ sound administrative practices, such as informing administrators in a timely way about important academic issues, soliciting their advice and counsel at appropriate stages in the decision-making process, working collegially to develop solutions to problems, negotiating among various interests, and securing their support and approval. Although decisions concerning academic programs, policy, and personnel often are the prerogative of the faculty, the support of senior administrators is important to their ultimate acceptance by the president and the board. The dean's ability to represent the faculty to the administration and the administration to the faculty, and to mediate differences between them, is a critical element in that process.

### *Administrative Influence on the Academic Area*

The working relationship between the chief academic officer and other senior administrators is critical, not only to the smooth operation of the institution, but to the successful adoption of academic policies and programs. While it is difficult to generalize about the influence senior administrators have on the academic area, evidence from site visits suggests that their primary concern is with the implementation of academic decisions and the practical consequences of these decisions for the nonacademic areas of the seminary. The research shows that senior administrators generally work in partnership with the chief academic officer and the faculty, and when questions and concerns arise, their usual response is not to scuttle a proposal but to remove obstacles and seek a workable solution. These findings are consistent with the survey results reported earlier, where deans gave positive ratings to "relationships among administrators" and to the quality of "administrative teamwork" at their schools.[6]

More difficult to discern is the degree to which senior administrators influence academic appointments or the substantive content of academic proposals. What complicates the issue in theological schools is the fact that senior administrators often hold faculty appointments and faculty rank. At one seminary in the study, all senior administrators, except the development officer, were members of the faculty and actively involved in faculty deliberations on academic matters. Since these administrators were vocal at faculty meetings and often of one mind, other faculty felt some decisions were railroaded due to the force of their collective influence. Because the blending of faculty and administrative appointments is commonplace in theological schools, separately assessing the influence of administrators as administrators becomes difficult. When senior administrators also function as members of the faculty, their influence on academic decisions may owe more to their involvement as faculty members than to their administrative function.

In addition, senior administrators usually serve one another and the president primarily in an advisory capacity, and their work together often takes the form of conversations and discussions rather than well-defined processes resulting in formal action. The effect these exchanges have on the final outcome of decisions can be difficult to trace. If a dean wants to create an endowment for faculty scholarship and the development officer declares it impossible given the donor pool, then the development officer may be readily identified as a principal cause of the idea's demise. However, with more complex issues that elicit a variety of responses over an extended period of time, the relative influence of the many participants in the dialogue may be more difficult to assess.

In their capacity as advisors to the president and sometimes as partners in making critical decisions, the senior administrative team may influence long-range institutional planning and various administrative and budgetary decisions that undoubtedly have consequences for the academic area. As we have seen, the involvement of senior administrators in such matters depends on the leadership style of individual presidents and can vary widely among theological schools. Among senior administrators, the chief academic officer plays a critical role in eliciting their support and cooperation on academic initiatives. The strength of the dean's relationship with administrative colleagues is an important factor in the success of these efforts.[7]

## Governing and Advisory Boards

In the vast literature on board governance, Barbara E. Taylor's 1987 book, *Working Effectively with Trustees,* deals with the relatively unexplored topic of the "mutual dependence" between an institution's board and its administrators and faculty. Its conclusion underscores a central finding of this research:

> *Boards cannot—and do not—govern alone.* . . . [B]oards should and do depend on administrators and faculty members for advice and recommendations. This relationship can be conceived as an exchange relationship in which the formal authority assigned to trustees in institutional charters is exchanged for the functional authority administrators possess by virtue of their expertise and full-time commitment to the institution.[8]

Based on analysis of "what boards actually do," Taylor argues that the formal or positional authority of the board depends for its efficacy on the expertise of administrators and faculty. Evidence from this study of theological schools confirms that senior administrators in large part determine the board's effectiveness in dealing with academic and other institutional matters. How chief academic officers work with boards and influence their performance, and how boards, in turn, influence academic decisions and the work of the faculty is the focus of this discussion.

### *Character of Seminary Boards*

To understand the relationship of chief academic officers to the board, we must first understand the basic structure and function of theological school boards. The eleven schools visited for this study had two different types of boards: most common, especially among independent, freestanding seminaries, were *governing boards* comprised of trustees who had ultimate authority and responsibility for the institution; other schools were served by *advisory boards* or boards of visitors, which lacked the formal authority of trustees but similarly functioned to advise and take action on proposals submitted by seminary administrators.[9] In seminaries with advisory boards, trustee responsibility for the institution was located either in a university governing board or with officials of the sponsoring religious organization. Despite differences in their formal authority, the two types of boards tended to be similar in structure and function and were utilized in comparable ways by seminary administrators.

Both advisory and governing boards typically operate through a system of standing committees that roughly parallels the administrative structure of the institution, with committees of academic and student affairs, institutional advancement, finances and budget, and the like.[10] In most seminaries, presidents delegate to senior administrators responsibility for staffing and working with the board committee most closely related to their administrative area. The chief academic officer, for example, staffs the academic or educational policy committee, which serves as the point of entry for the board's consideration of academic issues.[11] The chief academic officer's work with the committee is critical, since boards typically provide their most thorough review and discussion of issues at the committee level, and committee recommendations most often are supported by action of the full board.[12]

The chief academic officer and other senior administrators who staff board committees fulfill several related functions: as resource persons providing necessary information and background to committee members, as advisors to the committee chair in planning agendas, as representatives of constituents whose proposals come before the committee, and, most importantly, as the connecting link between the board and seminary personnel. In working with the board, senior administrators are more than conduits or go-betweens. As extensions of the president, their role is to develop and nurture the working relationship between the board and seminary constituents essential to effective governance. In the academic area, the chief academic officer maintains the relationship between the board and the faculty and fosters the communication, understanding, trust, and cooperation on which their joint responsibility for academic governance depends.

While the relationship between seminary boards and academic personnel is too complex to be treated exhaustively here, the survey and site visit data from the research enable us to sketch in broad outline some of its basic features.[13] Using examples of academic program and personnel decisions taken from the research, we examine briefly how boards and their academic committees deal with academic issues and how chief academic officers work with them on behalf of the faculty to arrive at mutually acceptable decisions. Exploring this relationship illuminates another facet of the dean's work and reveals the mutual dependence and influence between boards and the academic administrators and faculty of the schools.

*The Board's Role in Academic Affairs*

When theological school deans were asked on the survey to assess the leadership provided by various campus constituents, they rated the quality of board leadership as "good," trailing their ratings of executive, academic, and faculty leadership.[14] Some examples from site visits provide clues to the concerns underlying this assessment.

- According to one dean, the board's educational policies committee has "a high comfort level" with academic issues. In meetings, "the tone is usually affirming and supportive, not challenging." The president believes that in academic matters the board is "a rubber stamp." Board members so respect faculty prerogatives in the academic area that they do not question any proposals.
- Another dean claims that the board "has never helped my work and has never been a hindrance." The dean finds it "easy to manipulate trustees, i.e., to lead them in the direction I want them to go."
- A third dean describes his personal relationship to the board as "extremely positive" but believes "the board is almost too supportive." The general mood of the board is to go along with administrative recommendations and seldom to question or challenge what is presented. As the dean explains, "The relationship may be too positive. I would like more debate."

What is striking in these few examples is that each of the deans acknowledges a good working relationship with board members. Their disappointment lies in the fact that the board endorses proposals too readily, without the probing questions and critical review that could be helpful. Despite the ease of these relationships, deans were unanimous in their dissatisfaction with such reticence.

Academic officers were similarly dismayed by the opposite tendency of boards to exercise "top-down" decision making, which seemed to violate the spirit, if not the principle, of shared governance. For example, the faculty at one seminary led the process to revise and update the mission statement in response to a self-study recommendation. After consulting with the board and incorporating their suggestions, the faculty approved a revised statement that was forwarded to the board for final action. At their meeting, the board made further changes and approved a version different from the one the faculty submitted. As the dean explained, "I thought the process had gotten a bit reversed."

Even when board gestures are more positive, insufficient consultation with administrators and faculty can be damaging. At another seminary, the board decided to accept a substantial gift to establish a leadership institute without consulting the faculty, who were later expected to implement it. Faculty perceived this unilateral decision as evidence of the school's "top-down" management and felt the money could have been used more productively in other ways. While grateful for the board's creativity and initiative, the president acknowledged, "there wasn't a lot of process." The dean further noted that such events "create the ongoing suspicion" that faculty do not fully know what the presidents and senior administrators are up to. In this case, the dean became the point-person for building faculty support for the board's plan and improving the relationship between the two groups.

Not surprisingly, participants in the study found that effective boards operated between these two extremes: they neither abdicated their consultative role nor did they engage in "top-down" decision making without appropriate consultation of seminary personnel. A dean who described the governing board as "everything one could hope for" explained that "they understand the importance and independence of the academic area. They don't meddle." In a particular faculty hiring, for example, "they disagreed but accepted the decision." Another dean lauded the seminary board for achieving a good balance: "Board members ask questions but stay out of operations. They are not a rubber stamp, but they trust seminary personnel. They are helpful because they don't interfere."

Such general appraisals invite a closer look at how advisory and governing boards make substantive contributions to the academic life of their institutions without meddling or interfering with the work of administrators and faculty. Such concerns arise within the context of practices of shared governance, widely endorsed and adopted by theological schools and throughout American higher education.[15] Given that boards and faculty have distinct roles but joint responsibility for academic governance, how do boards work with the chief academic officer and the faculty to give shape and direction to the academic area? An overview of how boards function and influence the academic area and what determines their effectiveness in this work provides the context for understanding the significant role chief academic officers play in board development and governance.

*Board Function and Influence.* At the eleven theological schools visited for this study, boards and their academic committees performed three main functions. First, boards took initiative in generating proposals and in defining priorities for faculty attention. At three of the seminaries, the board committed their institutions explicitly to the goal of achieving greater gender and racial/ethnic diversity among faculty and held administrators and faculty accountable when making hiring decisions. Another seminary board took the lead in revising the school's mission statement as the basis for strategic planning. In this case, a board committee drafted the revised statement following consultation with faculty and other constituents. At another school, the board defined priority areas for the academic program. As one trustee explained, building the doctoral program was the priority in recent years, and "now the board is emphasizing training for ministry." Whether board initiatives involved clarifying the institutional mission or defining priorities and goals, they served to guide the work of administrators and faculty and to influence program, policy, and personnel decisions in the academic area.

Second, boards served a consultative function, responding to plans and proposals submitted by the dean and faculty. During curriculum revision processes, for example, deans frequently would inform the academic committee of the faculty's work in progress, soliciting ideas and inviting board members to raise questions and discuss the implications of curricular changes. One dean described the committee's function as "a sounding board" for testing different ideas and models as their work progressed. In interviews, both administrators and trustees noted that the outside perspective and breadth of experience board members bring to deliberations can be helpful to those fully immersed in the process. During a curriculum revision process at another seminary, board members with close ties to the church felt the proposed curriculum should give more attention to homiletics and field experience for prospective ministers. A trustee described how faculty were receptive to this suggestion and made the necessary changes to address the board's concern. While board counsel may not always be so readily accepted, this example shows that, in their consultative role, board members can raise questions and identify issues for consideration that ultimately shape the content of academic proposals.[16]

Third, by administrative request or institutional mandate, theological school boards regularly voted on recommendations forwarded by administrators and board committees. In governing boards, such formal actions served as the culmination of the decision-making process, and, in advisory boards, as the most critical stage in the progress toward final approval by the governing body. Theological schools differed somewhat on the academic issues their boards considered. Most boards discussed and formally approved academic program and curriculum changes, matters of academic policy, and faculty promotion and tenure decisions; but schools differed on whether their boards authorized faculty searches and approved hiring decisions, reviewed sabbatical proposals, or were involved in the hiring and evaluation of administrators other than the president. When boards acted on issues within their jurisdiction, they affected, in a direct and fundamental way, the academic life of their institutions.

In addition to shaping academic decisions in these three conventional ways, boards can play a quite different role in time of crisis. The most vivid illustration from the study concerned a faculty hiring process.[17] The school was firmly committed to the goal of increasing diversity in the gender and racial/ethnic make-up of the faculty. Following campus interviews for a tenure-track position, the faculty divided almost evenly between the two finalists, a man and a woman. The search committee was split. The students lined up on both sides. After much debate, the dean and president pressed for a decision and incurred the anger of faculty, who remained bitterly divided. When the president sent their decision to the board without consensus, the board sent it back for further discussion. The board conducted hearings for students and faculty in an effort to break the impasse. The search concluded in a compromise by hiring one of the two candidates on a temporary contract that would be reevaluated in three years.

In this instance, the board took the unusual action of returning a decision to the faculty, recognizing that a severe and persistent split among them remained unresolved. As the dean explained, when the board called for further discussion, their effort was to facilitate the process, not to coopt it. The concern was not to determine the final outcome but to deal with the destructive effects of the divisive and bitter disagreement that attended the search. As the dean explained, "They managed the conflict but did not resolve it. The board affirmed faculty in their role by returning the decision to them for further consideration." While this board worked with administrators and faculty beyond the strict parameters of their charter, their action served to expedite the decision-making process without abridging faculty rights and responsibilities. They contributed to academic governance by assuming a facilitative role.

*Board Effectiveness.* The board's ability to fulfill its role in academic governance—to provide leadership and good counsel, to make wise decisions, and to respond appropriately in time of crisis—depends on several factors.[18] Perhaps most obvious is the need for board members, individually and collectively, to understand their role, responsibility, and authority in governance and to have basic knowledge of the institution they serve. Board members at two seminaries in the study reported that the only directive they received upon joining the board was to attend meetings and participate, and their orientation consisted mainly of institutional documents for their personal review. Other expectations for their leadership, governance, and stewardship of the institution remained unspecified. Other seminaries in the study, some of which had participated in the Lilly Endowment's programs on trusteeship, recently had developed more extensive and formal board orientation programs and were committed to ongoing board education for new and continuing members.[19] Both deans and faculty report that the board's understanding of the institutional mission, academic programs, policies, and personnel are essential to its review and action on specific academic proposals.

The process and criteria for selecting board members also may affect the quality of their service. While most seminaries in the study had boards composed of church officials or representatives, clergy, and lay members, some had up to 80 percent of board members appointed by denominational offices. Often neither the sponsoring denominations nor the boards themselves seriously considered the special competencies of board appointees in areas other than finance and fundraising. As one trustee observed, members are selected for "their cash, clout, and connections." As a result, some deans reported being hampered in their work with the board's academic committee because members lacked the background and experience necessary for an informed response to curriculum, faculty hiring, and promotion and tenure recommendations. As one dean explained, "The board has least influence on academic and formation issues because they have no expertise in these areas." Both administrators and board members interviewed felt this explained, in part, the two opposing tendencies of seminary boards: to be reticent in engaging academic issues and to "rubber stamp" proposals from the faculty.

The third and perhaps most important factor affecting the quality of board service was the relationship between senior administrators and board members. While the president bears responsibility for establishing and sustaining a healthy relationship between the board and seminary personnel, other senior administrators play a significant role in assisting the president in this task and in fulfilling their specific responsibilities to board committees. Typically, both the president and chief academic officer work with the board on academic matters and negotiate the board-faculty relationship. The effectiveness of the academic committee, in particular, relies on the dean's understanding and support of its work. A closer look at the dean's responsibilities in serving the board shows how critical the dean is to the quality of board service.

### *The Dean's Work with the Board*

Theological school deans estimated they spend an average of just over two hours per month in substantive conversation with board members, less time than they spend with any other group.[20] This relatively small investment of the deans' time in direct contact with the board gives little indication of the importance of the dean-board relationship. The various ways in which deans support and facilitate the work of the board and foster communication and cooperation between the board and the faculty largely determine the quality of board deliberations and, ultimately, their effectiveness in governance. Based on this research, deans work with the board in three principal ways: providing board orientation and education in academic matters, serving as a resource to the board and its academic committee, and maintaining a vital, cooperative relationship between the board and the faculty.

*Board Education.* The task of orienting new members and providing for the board's continuing education generally is a shared responsibility of the board, the president, and senior administrators. Nowhere is such education more imperative than in the academic area. The board's informed review of academic proposals and ability to make final recommendations and decisions on academic matters requires, at minimum, an in-depth understanding of the institutional mission; knowledge of academic programs, their objectives, and their relation to the mission; familiarity with student backgrounds, aspirations, and needs; knowledge of faculty, individually and collectively, and an understanding of who they are, what they do as scholars, teachers, and student advisors, and how they serve the seminary and the church. Academic decisions that range from curriculum to degree requirements to faculty hiring, promotion, and tenure presume such basic knowledge of the inner workings of the school. Insuring that board members are well prepared for their role in governance requires intentional planning for board orientation and development. Chief academic officers often are most keenly aware of the need for board education in academic matters and best able to determine how those needs can be met most effectively.

Seminaries in the study took various approaches to board education. Some provided orientation for new members that included not only a portfolio of board and seminary documents but discussion of their import with selected board members and seminary administrators. Some new members were introduced to faculty and students when they gave presentations at board orientation sessions or during informal, social gatherings held for the board. Some seminaries explicitly invited new board members to tour the school and to attend classes and chapel services to get a firsthand glimpse of campus life. All of these activities afforded new members background on academic programs and an initial acquaintance with academic personnel.

Several schools in the study addressed the need for continuing board education at an annual board retreat or at an administrator-faculty retreat to which board members were invited. Retreats had the advantage of allowing an extended period of time for joint discussion of larger institutional issues. Retreats often provided the opportunity for presentations by the dean, faculty members, and students to inform the board of current academic programs, recent developments in faculty teaching or research, student concerns, and the like. While some seminaries included similar educational sessions as part of their regular board meetings, retreats proved more satisfactory in affording time for presentations and discussions without the press of a full business agenda. Retreats generally included social time that fostered personal relationships and increased understanding and good will among board members, administrators, and faculty.

Because chief academic officers are closest to the daily operations of the academic area, they usually have the most complete and detailed knowledge of academic matters and, quite possibly, the clearest sense of what others need to know. Consequently, deans in the study commonly served as resources to the full board: preparing information on academic proposals, providing periodic reports and presentations, and responding to questions that arose during discussions. In these ways, the chief academic officer supported the president in efforts to provide ongoing education of the board and to facilitate its work.

*Board Consultation and Decision Making.* When deans staff the board's academic committee, they often bear the primary responsibility for preparing its members to deal with the academic program, policy, and personnel decisions that come before them. When presenting proposals submitted by the faculty, the dean is called upon to provide the necessary background and context to enable the board's full and fair consideration of the changes proposed. Several board members acknowledged that the quality of board deliberations depends, in large part, on the completeness and accuracy of the information they have in hand. When presenting proposals for curricular change, for example, deans are expected to give a rationale for the proposed changes and to convey the substance of faculty debate on particular issues. Similarly, when board members are asked to approve faculty hiring recommendations, they often rely on the dean to explain the candidate's suitability and to address their concerns.

Two examples of hiring decisions offer insight into the board's dependence on the dean's assistance. One seminary board had difficulty approving the recommended candidates for three successive faculty positions. Trustees who discussed this problem proposed two solutions: first, the board needed clarification of its role in personnel matters; and second, board members needed to be more fully informed of the qualifications required for faculty positions as a context for the decisions they had to make. One trustee felt such measures would engender trust in faculty and administrators by more fully conveying the rationale for their recommendations. At another seminary, where the culture was "not to air concerns publicly," the dean received several calls from board members who thought the candidate proposed for a faculty position was "too extreme a fundamentalist." As the dean explained, "The matter was not raised publicly, but settled privately, and the candidate was hired because the board trusted the dean." In this case, the additional information the dean provided and his personal credibility both influenced the committee's decision.

A board's persistent difficulty in dealing with certain types of issues may signal the need for board education in a particular area. One dean in the study found that board members dealt effectively with most academic matters, but "tension occurred around tenure, because most members don't understand tenure." Since tenure is a practice foreign to corporate and business cultures and controversial even within academic circles, it is a prime topic for board education.[21] When deans are alert to issues the board finds problematic and develop strategies to address them, they do much to expedite the board's work.

Deans also enhance the quality of board deliberations by their timeliness in bringing academic matters to the board's attention. Several deans thought it advisable to inform the board of new initiatives and bring them to the committee for consultation well before they were asked to vote. This approach gave board members an opportunity to raise questions and offer input at a formative stage in the faculty's work, and it gave administrators and faculty time to respond to their suggestions. At a seminary where faculty were working on revision of one of their master's programs, the dean included the board in the very early stages of their project to get the benefit of their counsel and to pave the way for their final recommendation. Waiting to consult the board until a proposal is finalized has its risks. Serious concerns arising late in the process can delay or defeat even sound proposals at the board level. Once again, the dean's judgment about what information is needed and when can determine the board's effectiveness in dealing with academic issues.

Finally, deans bear significant responsibility for following up with the faculty on initiatives proposed by the board. If the board believes a serious curriculum review is in order, the dean is critical in conveying the board's urgency to the faculty and mobilizing them to act on that request. Deans or presidents who fail to respond in an appropriate and timely way to board initiatives may unwittingly diminish the board's participation and leadership.

*The Board-Faculty Relationship.* As the preceding discussion illustrates, deans represent the faculty and the board to one another and, therefore, play a pivotal role in the communication and cooperation between them. As representative and advocate for the faculty, the dean's task is to present proposals persuasively on their behalf, to convey to faculty the board's response, and to do both with accuracy, fairness, and sensitivity to each party. Once again, the dean is the nexus between two groups, fostering their relationship and promoting communication and cooperation between them. When issues become contentious, the dean's skills in diplomacy, negotiation, and mediation come into play. As in the administrator-faculty relationship, the dean serves as the connecting link between individuals and groups who have shared responsibility for the academic life of the institution.

When deans were asked on the survey to assess the quality of the board-faculty relationship at their schools, their mean rating was 2.5, midway between "good" and "fair," and the lowest rating among the seven constituent relationships they evaluated. While deans are not solely responsible for the quality of the board-faculty relationship, they work with the president, the faculty, and board members to insure its strength and vitality. Not only do deans formally represent faculty and board members to one another in matters of governance, but they help to determine the nature and extent of board-faculty interactions outside of regular meetings.

Most seminaries provided opportunities for board members and faculty to work together and to meet socially. In some seminaries, faculty representatives served on board committees, and board members served on search committees for faculty and administrative hirings. This enabled individual members of both groups to become personally acquainted and, most importantly, to communicate directly, to exchange ideas, and to work together on issues of mutual importance. As noted earlier, faculty members may be invited to make presentations at board meetings or at board orientation and development sessions, and schools frequently host an annual retreat for board members and faculty. One school took the further step of presenting board members with copies of books and articles published by the faculty so they would have a better appreciation of the range and quality of faculty scholarship.

Most seminaries also provided other occasions for board members and faculty to meet socially. Several schools held an annual or biannual dinner, where individuals could meet and discuss issues informally. Presidents and deans sometimes hosted luncheons for a small group of board members and invited a faculty member with interesting research to make a brief presentation. At some schools, the standing academic committees of the board and of the faculty met annually over lunch to discuss academic issues and to become better acquainted. Even when events were primarily social, they served to enhance understanding and communication between the two groups. As one trustee explained, interaction with the faculty "is more than just social. It's breaking down the barrier that starts to grow by nature between [the board and faculty] and reassures faculty that the board is not some group of ignorant business people or people from outside the institution who are coming to impose a bunch of policies." Similarly, board awareness of the dedication of the faculty, their deep, personal commitments to the seminary and the students, and the value of their research contributes to the mutual understanding and respect important to the board-faculty relationship.

To summarize, while governing boards have the ultimate responsibility and authority in academic matters, evidence suggests their most significant contributions may lie in their ability to focus attention on institutional mission and goals, to ask probing questions, and to offer constructive ideas and suggestions in response to faculty proposals. Based on this study, boards appear to influence academic decision making less through their formal authority, since administrative and faculty recommendations are rarely reversed, than through their ongoing dialogue with administrators and faculty about academic issues. Chief academic officers affect the quality of this dialogue by their responsiveness to the board's educational and development needs and by their skill in representing board members and seminary personnel to one another. Chief academic officers are directly involved in maintaining good communication and cooperation between the board and the faculty, and they bear considerable responsibility for creating opportunities for formal and informal interaction between the two groups. By developing and nurturing the board-faculty relationship, deans help to strengthen the bonds necessary for their collaboration in academic governance.

## Church Leaders

Among the most surprising findings of this research was the nature and extent of church influence on the academic life of the eleven theological schools visited for this study. Church officials were involved in academic decision making in three capacities: as members of advisory and governing boards; as bishops, pastors, and denominational representatives who had regular contact with the schools; and as direct participants in academic and administrative decisions concerning curriculum, faculty hiring, student admissions, and candidacy for ministry. This small but representative group of denominational and interdenominational seminaries affords perspective on the way church leaders work with seminary personnel on academic matters, their influence in the academic area, and the role of chief academic officers in the school's relationship with church leaders.

While our intent is not to examine the church-seminary relationship generally, a few preliminary observations set the context for our discussion. First, among ATS-related schools, relationships between seminaries and their sponsoring denominations can be complex and highly variable. Depending on the current denominational leadership and its focus, and depending on the priorities of seminary administrators, church-seminary relationships may vary in quality and intensity at different periods in a seminary's history. At the time of this study, many of the administrators, board members, and church leaders interviewed seemed keenly aware of the need to clarify and, in most cases, to strengthen the church-seminary relationship. Several schools had made explicit efforts to do so in recent years.

Second, while presidents typically had the primary responsibility for denominational relations and devoted up to 60 percent of their time to that task, they were supported in this work by senior administrators and faculty.[22] Since the foremost interest of sponsoring denominations is the seminary's preparation of ministers for the church, chief academic officers become involved with the larger church when issues arise regarding the academic preparation of students. Concern for the quality of ministerial candidates gives church leaders a vested interest in the quality of the faculty and academic programs, and the adequacy of both in meeting the church's need for well-trained clergy and lay ministers. On these issues, chief academic officers often are in contact with church leaders and become critical to the dialogue between the church and the seminary.

### *Church Influence on Academic Affairs*

Church leaders had direct and considerable influence on the academic life of the theological schools participating in this study. Only some of this influence came through seminary boards, where church officials and clergy figured prominently since many were appointed to represent their denominations.[23] As discussed above, board members had the capacity to be highly influential in academic and institutional matters: they shared responsibility for defining the mission and goals of the school and overseeing their implementation; in academic matters, they could initiate proposals, contribute substantively to faculty deliberations, and affect the outcome of academic decisions. Denominational influence was further evident when church officials chaired seminary boards, and when the sponsoring denomination had the final authority in governance. In these ways, the church could have considerable influence on seminary governance through the presence of its representatives at the board level.

Beyond board membership, church leaders had both formal and informal relationships to the seminary. Three seminaries in the study received directives from their denominational offices urging the schools to develop curricula to meet the needs of underprepared ministerial candidates entering the seminary and the continuing education needs of recent graduates serving as church pastors. Two other seminaries developed extension programs at specific sites in response to the church's request, and still others added courses to existing programs to address particular needs the church identified. In an effort to maintain communication and good relations with their denominations, two seminaries established offices on campus to develop educational programs for the churches, to serve students of the sponsoring denominations, and to coordinate seminary-church activities. Clearly, each of these schools was responsive to the expressed needs of the church, and churches had a direct impact on academic and administrative program development within the schools.[24]

Church leaders also influenced seminary practices in other ways. Several seminaries consulted church leaders during their curriculum revision process and encouraged their participation in faculty searches. Even when church representatives were not formally members of working committees, they had what a faculty member described as "indirect but identifiable influence" in faculty hiring and curriculum decisions. Much contact and conversation between church leaders and seminary personnel occurred outside of formal structures. Many seminary administrators and faculty were ordained and actively involved in the church, some serving as pastors or preaching regularly to local congregations, and some participating in denominational activities at the local and national levels.[25] Several seminaries employed pastors as adjunct professors and extended invitations to bishops and clergy to participate in important events at the seminary. Such occasions for interaction between church leaders and seminary personnel often fostered personal relationships that made an exchange of ideas on a variety of issues possible. Interviews revealed that church leaders and seminary administrators and faculty were rarely in doubt about each other's views. The church-seminary relationship played out in various settings, and members of both groups acknowledged the definite, if immeasurable, effect of their many conversations with one another.

Church leaders also expressed their approval or disapproval of seminaries by whether or not they sent ministerial candidates to study there. One dean of a Roman Catholic seminary described how bishops could educate priests for their dioceses at any number of seminaries. Effective recruitment often depended on maintaining a strong and positive image of the school and good relations with bishops and vocation directors. Given the general decline in denominational subsidies to seminaries in recent years, many schools have become increasingly tuition-dependent. Church leaders who essentially "vote with their feet" when referring students to a seminary can affect enrollment and, thereby, the total resources available to maintain the faculty and programs.

Finally, at two interdenominational seminaries in the study, representatives of the sponsoring denominations held administrative positions that made them full participants in curricular and hiring decisions. In both cases, the denominational representatives worked closely with the dean and served as members of the dean's cabinet or council; church representatives were voting members of the faculty and directly involved in faculty deliberations on a broad range of academic issues. At one school, denominational representatives also served on faculty search committees. Through these representatives, the churches had a voice and vote in all academic decisions and were present at meetings with the dean and faculty to express the needs and concerns of their denominations. At another seminary, denominational representatives served with faculty on a committee that approved candidates for the ministry, and the denomination was becoming increasingly involved in developing more stringent admission requirements. Each of these formal arrangements afforded denominations direct participation in academic decision making and considerable influence in academic matters, and they established an intimate connection between churches and their seminaries.

### *The Dean's Role in Church-Seminary Relations*

In an essay written for this project, James Hudnut-Beumler reflects on the relationship of the church to the academy and the dean's role within it.[26] Surprised by "how much disdain some church leaders have for the academic," Hudnut-Beumler likens his role as dean to that of a translator: "I explain the world view of the professors to the church constituency and interpret what the church is saying to the faculty."[27] In now familiar terms, he describes himself as a mediator whose work is to help both parties better understand one another. Like the president, the dean serves as a bridge between the seminary and the church and, particularly in academic matters, helps church leaders grow in comprehension and appreciation of faculty work. In a variety of settings, deans are called upon to explain academic practices, to respond to church needs and concerns relating to the academic area, and, generally, to assist the president in developing an effective church-seminary relationship.

Theological school deans responding to the survey rated the working relationship between school personnel and church leaders as "good," slightly higher than the board-faculty relationship.[28] While deans are not solely or primarily responsible for maintaining this relationship on behalf of the seminary, deans often work closely with church leaders as board members, as participants in seminary and church activities, and, in some instances, as administrative colleagues working within the seminary.[29] Deans also serve as contact persons for denominational representatives interested in the academic program and in admission for prospective students. One dean of a Roman Catholic seminary received frequent, often unscheduled visits from vocation directors who wanted to receive updates on current students from their diocese and to discuss future applicants. Similarly, the academic dean at a Lutheran seminary often met with denominational representatives about various academic program and policy issues.

Two other deans in the study were proactive in making contact with denominational officers. One dean estimated that he devoted one-sixth of his time to work at the denominational level. He was well known as pastor of a local church, and the denomination was receptive to his overtures on behalf of the seminary. At another seminary, both the president and dean "devoted considerable resources to relationship development and maintenance" with the sponsoring denomination. The dean regularly visited denominational offices to discuss the preparation of students for ministry and to nurture the church-seminary partnership. Although church relations were not an explicit part of the dean's role, both the president and the denomination welcomed the dean's initiatives.

Among the seminaries participating in the study, church leaders were extensively involved in institutional decision making and were influential through their work as board members, denominational officers, resident administrators, and clergy who had regular formal and informal contact with the schools. Chief academic officers, in turn, often worked directly with church leaders on academic policy, program, and personnel issues. Along with seminary presidents, deans served as representatives of their schools and their faculties at denominational meetings and relayed to academic personnel the needs of the church. As Russell Richey explained in his essay on the deanship: "The dean represents the church in the life of the school. The dean also represents the school in the life of the church."[30]

## Conclusion

This brief consideration of the dean's work with senior administrators, board members, and church leaders confirms the breadth of the dean's responsibilities and relationships and the dean's critical role in achieving cooperation among all constituent groups. Most difficult to convey in this account is the complexity inherent in the dean's work of representing the president, the faculty, the students, administrators, board members, and church leaders, each to the other, and forging from their diverse points of view a shared vision and direction for the academic area. Given the centrality of their positions, deans bear considerable responsibility for coordinating communication, negotiating differences, organizing decision making, and bringing individuals and groups to some measure of agreement. On a daily basis, the dean is a critical link in the community's continuing conversation about its academic life.

In serving these seminary constituents, deans often are expected to fulfill the multiple roles examined earlier in our discussion. They are expected to be managers, tending to the countless administrative details concerning the academic programs, policies, and personnel of the school; to be leaders, who work with all constituents to forge a shared vision for the academic area and to make it a reality through the academic decisions and practices for which they are jointly responsible; and to be pastors, who through these processes come to understand the needs and aspirations of many individuals and groups, who affirm individual gifts for the common good, and who develop among them a sense of community. These roles, discussed previously in some detail, assume even greater complexity in light of the expanding list of constituencies the dean serves. The dean's administrative responsibility for academic programs and personnel places the office at the intersection where diverse interests meet and where mutual understanding and cooperation among individuals become a practical necessity. The dean's essential work is to help develop the relationships that strengthen community and make collaborative decision making possible.

The remainder of this book turns our attention from the responsibilities, roles, and relationships of deans to their implicit demands on individual chief academic officers and the theological schools they serve. In light of the impressive challenges and opportunities of the job, we consider how individuals come to academic administration, what it requires of them personally and professionally, and how they assess its costs and rewards and discover its meaning and value. The following chapters also examine how theological schools conduct the hiring, evaluation, and professional development of academic officers, and how these practices become critical to effective administrative service.

## Notes

[1] Two of the university-related schools in the study and the Roman Catholic seminaries had advisory boards which, as their name implies, differed in their authority and responsibility from governing boards or boards of trustees. In schools with advisory boards, trustee responsibilities were held either by a university board of governors or by the head of the religious order or diocese that owned the seminary. Since presidents and senior administrators who worked with advisory boards and those who worked with governing boards related to them in comparable ways and gave similar weight to their recommendations, I sometimes use the term "governing board" to apply generally to all seminary boards in the study. The term "church leaders" is used to refer broadly to pastors, bishops, and other church officials in leadership positions at various levels of the ecclesial organization. In this list, "denominational representatives" refers to members holding ecclesial office (e.g., denominational committee members, vocation directors, and the like) who may not hold formal leadership positions.

[2] Deans rated the ability to work well with administrative colleagues "very important" in evaluating their effectiveness, with a mean rating of 3.8 (rating scale: 4=very important – 1=unimportant). There were no statistically significant differences among deans from different theological schools on this point. The other two of the top three criteria were: "ability to work well with the faculty" and "professional integrity (e.g., honesty, fairness)." The criteria for decanal evaluation will be discussed more fully in Chapter Seven.

[3] Deans in university-related theological schools reported spending more time with administrators than deans in freestanding schools: an estimated average of 4.5 hours per week for university deans, compared to 3.5 hours per week for deans in freestanding schools. When asked whether the amount of time spent was "too much" (3), "about right" (2), or "too little" (1), the university deans had a mean rating of 2.15, compared to a mean of 1.93 for deans in freestanding schools. These are statistically significant differences.

[4] James Hudnut-Beumler, "A New Dean Meets a New Day in Theological Education," *Theological Education* 33 (Autumn 1996 Supplement), 17–18.

[5] See Chapter Three, 91–92.

[6] See Chapter Three, 92. Survey respondents gave "relationships among major administrators" a mean rating of 3.44 and the "quality of administrative teamwork" a mean rating of 3.28 (rating scale: 4=excellent – 1=poor). Analysis reveals that "relationships among major administrators" were rated higher by men than by women, and higher by new deans (0–3 years in office) than by more experienced deans (6 years or more). "Administrative teamwork" was rated higher by deans in large seminaries (faculty FTE 31 or higher).

[7] Further study with a larger sample of institutions is needed to assess adequately the contribution of senior administrators to the academic area and to specific academic decisions.

[8] Barbara E. Taylor, *Working Effectively with Trustees: Building Cooperative Campus Leadership,* ASHE-ERIC Higher Education Report No. 2, (Washington, DC: Association for the Study of Higher Education, 1987), 99.

[9] Of the eleven seminaries visited for the study, eight worked directly with governing boards, and three had advisory boards. One of the advisory boards was a standing committee of a university governing board.

[10] Ideally, the board committee structure mirrors the administrative organization of the seminary, although there may be practical reasons why this is not always possible. For example, one board committee on internal affairs encompassed the seminary's two administrative areas of academic affairs and student formation. Such consolidation at the board level may be necessitated by the expertise and availability of board members and/or the number of issues likely to come before committees each year.

[11] F. Thomas Trotter, "Trustees and Academic Affairs," in *The Good Steward* (Washington, DC: Association of Governing Boards of Universities and Colleges, 1985), 94. Trotter observed, in 1985, that many seminary boards did not have active committee structures, "and among those that do, the priority committees are in the areas of finance, development, buildings and grounds." Based on the sample of theological schools in this study, the majority have taken steps to establish an academic affairs committee. Many still are not as strong as committees in other areas. Trotter offers a useful discussion of the board's role in academic affairs and the relationship between trustees and faculty.

[12] One exception was the academic committee that recommended to the full board a change in standardized tests required of future applicants. The board did not favor the change and sent it back to the committee, which eventually dropped the issue.

[13] Researchers recognize the diversity among theological schools in their use of boards and expect that data acquired from the eleven site visits, while having applicability beyond the participating schools, may not be universal.

[14] The quality of board leadership received a mean rating of 2.9 (scale: 4=excellent – 1=poor), compared to means of 3.3 for executive leadership, 3.2 for academic leadership, and 3.1 for faculty leadership. In a related question on the quality of board governance, the mean rating was 2.8, which ranked eighth among nine indicators of institutional well-being. Denominational differences on the latter question were statistically significant, with the quality of board governance rated highest by deans at Methodist seminaries (mean 3.3) and lowest by deans at Baptist seminaries (2.3).

[15] In 1966, the American Association of University Professors (AAUP), the American Council on Education (ACE), and the Association of Governing Boards of Universities and Colleges (AGB) adopted the "Statement on Government of Colleges and Universities," which called for "appropriately shared responsibility and cooperative action among the components of the academic institution." The statement differentiated the roles of governing board members, the president and administrators, faculty, and students in institutional governance, while establishing the necessity of their working jointly. In reference to the board-faculty relationship, the statement affirms: "The faculty has primary responsibility for such fundamental areas as curriculum, subject matter and methods of instruction, research, faculty status, and those aspects of student life which relate to the educational process. On these matters the power of review or final decision lodged in the governing board or delegated by it to the president should be exercised

adversely only in exceptional circumstances, and for reasons communicated to the faculty. It is desirable that the faculty should, following such communication, have opportunity for further consideration and further transmittal of its views to the president or board." While the governance statement was intended not as a blueprint but as a guide for colleges and universities, its basic principles have been adopted by the majority of higher education institutions.

[16] These examples further suggest that, in their consultative role, boards give attention not only to matters of institutional policy, commonly understood as their proper domain, but to the specifics of program implementation. As Barbara Taylor suggests, the conventional distinction between policy and operations rarely holds in actual practice. "While boards are advised to develop or at least participate in developing most important institutional policies, evidence suggests that they are more likely to involve themselves in the operating details of colleges and universities." Taylor, 52.

[17] This example was introduced in Chapter Two in the context of discussion of conflict in the decision-making process. See p. 73.

[18] For further ideas on board-faculty collaboration, see: Roger R. Kahle, "Learning to Work Together: Boards, Faculties, and the Benefits of Collaboration," *In Trust* 7, no. 4 (Summer 1996), 12–14.

[19] In the late 1980s and early 1990s, the Lilly Endowment sponsored various grant programs in Theological School Trusteeship, which supported board development projects, programs within individual seminaries, and mentoring partnerships between schools. Several schools in the study had participated in this grant program.

[20] Deans reported spending an average of .56 hours per week in substantive conversation with board members, which is less than the average of 1.2 hours/week with church leaders and 1.04 hours/week with peers at other schools. Further analysis revealed that deans in university-related schools and deans who had been in office 7–10 years spent more time with board members (.68 to .72 hours/week) than did other deans, and 38 percent of them thought it was "too little." These differences based on type of institution and length of service were statistically significant.

[21] The ambiguity and controversy surrounding tenure and academic freedom in theological education are evident in a published conversation among four theological school faculty members: "How Free Should Teachers Be? Academic Freedom, Tenure, and Keeping the Faith," *In Trust* 3, no. 3 (New Year 1992), 10–15. The American Association of Higher Education has undertaken the "New Pathways Project," a study of tenure practices in colleges and universities. At the time of this writing, their work was still in progress.

[22] This figure is taken from interviews with presidents for this research. In his study of the seminary presidency, Neely McCarter discusses the president's work with church leaders and the pressures that arise from the seminary's dual commitment to the church and the academy. Neely McCarter, *The President as Educator: A Study of the Seminary Presidency* (Atlanta, GA: Scholars Press, 1996), 105–109.

[23] Only one board among the eleven schools was composed entirely of individuals who were not serving as denominational representatives.

[24] The recent history of church-seminary relations also includes notable examples of denominational interference in seminary governance. Officials of the Roman Catholic Church were instrumental in the dismissal of two tenured professors: Charles Curran from the Catholic University of America in 1986, and Sister Carmel McEnroy from St. Meinrad Seminary in 1995. The conservative takeover of the Southern Baptist Convention in the mid-1990s subsequently led to the replacement of moderates on seminary boards and the firing of administrators and faculty from several Southern Baptist seminaries. These actions by church leaders raised serious concerns about due process, academic freedom and tenure, and faculty rights and responsibilities in academic matters. Among the many books and articles on these cases, two give a brief introduction to the principles at stake: "How Free Should Teachers Be?" 10–15; "Catholic and Baptist Faculty Fired," *In Trust* 6, no. 4 (Summer 1995), 24–25. Two excellent, detailed accounts of the Curran affair are: Charles E. Curran, *Faithful Dissent* (Kansas City, MO: Sheed and Ward, 1986), and Anne E. Patrick, *Liberating Conscience* (New York: Continuum, 1996). Two scholarly works discuss the divisions within the Southern Baptist Convention and their consequences for the seminaries and their faculty: Nancy T. Ammerman, *Baptist Battles: Social Change and Religious Conflict in the Southern Baptist Convention* (New Brunswick, NJ: Rutgers University Press, 1991), and Bill J. Leonard, *God's Last and Only Hope: The Fragmentation of the Southern Baptist Convention* (Grand Rapids, MI: Eerdmans, 1991).

[25] The survey of theological school deans showed that 85 percent were ordained, 59 percent had served as church ministers or pastors, and 17.7 percent had been administrators for their denominations or religious orders. Survey respondents estimated they spend approximately 7.5 percent of their time participating in church-related activities, which they considered "about right." A study of seminary presidents, conducted in 1992, reported that 96 percent of presidents were ordained, and 61 percent had served in parish ministry. See Mark Allyn Holman, *Presidential Search in Theological Schools: Process Makes a Difference* (Pittsburgh, PA: The Association of Theological Schools in the United States and Canada, 1993), 5.

[26] Hudnut-Beumler, "A New Dean Meets a New Day," 13–20. Hudnut-Beumler also acknowledges with gratitude his own pastoral experience and finds that "much of the dean's role is parallel to the pastor's" in this respect: "what gets done in each institution [the seminary and the church] depends not on fiat, or moralization, but on getting people to do what they want to do and have them want to do what they should."

[27] Hudnut-Beumler, 14–15.

[28] Survey respondents gave the relationship between school personnel and church leaders a mean rating of 2.85, compared to the mean rating of 2.5 for the board-faculty relationship (scale: 4=excellent – 1=poor).

[29] On the survey, deans reported spending an average of 1.2 hours per week in substantive conversation with church leaders, more than twice the time spent with board members (.56 hours per week). Since deans were asked to report separately on their time with senior administrators other than the president, board members, and church leaders, those church leaders who also served as board members or administrators most likely were not included in the "church leader" category.

[30] Russell E. Richey, "To a Candidate for Academic Leadership: A Letter," *Theological Education* 33 (Supplement Autumn 1996), 41.

# 6 Recruitment and Hiring of Chief Academic Officers

*"We don't know how to say to our young people that they ought to be aspiring to this type of position."*

*Theological school president*

Theological school communities bear considerable responsibility for the success or failure of their academic deans. The deans' ability to fulfill the roles and responsibilities described in the preceding chapters depends not only on individual competencies and skills but on the practices and policies of the schools concerning their hiring, evaluation, and professional development. How seriously theological schools cultivate potential candidates and conduct the selection process and how intentionally they guide and support academic officers once they are hired determine in large part the effectiveness of their administrative service. With the dean's work before us, we turn now to the organizational practices of theological schools so critical to the dean's success.

Hiring is the first and most important step toward an effective deanship. During the past decade, openings in the chief academic officer position have occurred in approximately 60 theological schools annually, or about 25 percent of the current membership of the Association of Theological Schools (ATS).[1] In filling these vacancies, theological schools vary considerably in their methods of identifying promising candidates and selecting their deans. Among the schools participating in this study, some deans arrived in office as the result of informal conversations and a presidential appointment, others were hired following a limited search, and still others were selected through extensive national searches with full participation of the campus community.

Our task in this chapter is to discuss the range of decanal hiring practices that presently exist in theological schools, to consider their rationale in particular settings, and to assess their relative merits. While there is no single formula for hiring chief academic officers that fits all schools or even fits the same institution at different times, much can be learned about the advantages and disadvantages of different approaches to hiring and their effect on the final outcome of the search.

Based on findings of the Study of Chief Academic Officers and on related research on administrative searches, we examine three principal stages in the recruitment and hiring process: planning the hiring process, conducting the hiring, and making the hiring decision. Our discussion concludes with analysis of the career paths of theological school deans and practical advice to those considering administrative service.[2] By examining current hiring practices, the chapter affords guidance both to schools anticipating changes in their chief academic officer position and to prospective candidates seeking to understand the sometimes mysterious path to academic administration.

## Planning the Hiring Process

Almost every decision at every stage of the hiring process has implications for the outcome of the search, as well as for community ownership and acceptance of the final decision. The planning phase is critical, since it determines how the hiring will be conducted, which candidates will be considered, and how inclusive the process will be. The hiring process typically begins when the president notifies the board and the academic community of the vacancy in the dean's office and receives the board's authorization to fill the position. Even in schools where presidents have considerable discretion in how they fill the vacancy, notification of constituents about an opening in senior administrative positions is standard practice. In only one instance in the study did the president replace the academic dean without announcing in advance his intention to do so. This unilateral approach to senior administrative appointments would not be acceptable in the majority of schools in the study.

The president or chief executive officer to whom the dean reports usually has the primary responsibility for planning for the dean's replacement. Unless institutional documents prescribe a process for administrative searches, which occurred principally among university-related schools in the study, presidents have considerable latitude in deciding how the dean will be chosen and how extensively the board, the faculty, and other constituents will be involved in the hiring process. As with other institutional decisions, presidents who allow constituents to participate, either personally or through their representatives, encourage community ownership and acceptance of the hiring decision and enable deans to come to their positions with a broad base of institutional support.[3]

Once the vacancy for the chief academic officer position is announced, theological schools face several tasks, including: assessing institutional needs, defining the qualifications and competencies the position requires, deciding whether or not to conduct a search, and determining how the process will be organized. In the absence of firm guidelines for administrative searches, presidents alone or in consultation with the faculty and/or the board usually decide how these preliminary tasks will be accomplished.

*Assessing Institutional Needs*

When an opening occurs in the chief academic officer position, theological schools may find themselves at different stages of clarity and agreement about the goals, needs, and priorities of the academic area. Hiring a senior academic administrator should not begin without explicit attention to these issues. Determining the qualifications, experiences, and competencies to be sought in a dean requires understanding and, ideally, agreement on the academic challenges facing the school at the particular time. Very different candidates will surface depending on whether the primary institutional need is for an organized and efficient manager to complement a visionary president, or an academic leader who can work with faculty to chart new directions, or an administrator adept at downsizing and financial planning, or a dean with pastoral gifts who can heal the rifts of the past and restore community, or some miraculous combination of these various skills. Asking the fundamental questions about where the institution is heading and what its priorities are is requisite to identifying the qualities most desirable, and necessary, in a dean or provost.[4]

Individual schools also may have other goals important to the search. An institutional commitment to increasing racial, ethnic, and gender diversity, for example, may affect the scope of the search and determine the final selection. As with hirings at other levels of the institution, those participating in the search and selection process must decide how these criteria will be weighed relative to other qualifications for the job. Failure to establish the relative importance of various qualifications can create problems. When the president at one seminary in the study convened faculty to discuss the qualities they were seeking in a dean, they compiled a list of attributes so vast and undifferentiated that their priorities were undetectable and the list was of little practical value in enabling them to distinguish among candidates. Without agreement on the most necessary and important characteristics of a prospective dean, searches may founder in their later stages and become seriously divisive.

Researchers often warn against circumventing this institutional needs assessment and making the assumption that deans who served in the past provide the blueprint for what is needed in the future. Institutions change. The qualities and skills required of institutional leaders change. An effective search is virtually impossible without a clear, shared understanding of current challenges facing the institution and the kind of academic officer needed to address them. Good searches require basic agreement among constituents about what they are looking for in a dean.

### *Defining Qualifications*

Among the four common errors in administrative searches listed in *The Search Committee Handbook,* the first two pertain to defining the qualifications for the job.

> The first error is that the [search] committee is looking for indefinable, even ineffable qualities in a person, which it needn't specify since "we'll know them when we see them." . . .
>
> The second error, captured in the delightful phrase of Rev. Timothy Healy of Georgetown University, is that the committee is "looking for God on a good day."[5]

Whether expectations are merely vague or wildly unrealistic, searches can founder without clarity, realism, and some measure of agreement on the qualities desired in a dean.

To gain perspective on the qualifications important to the office, theological school deans were asked on the survey to rate each of the items below. The following table lists qualifications in their order of importance to deans, indicating the respondents' mean rating for each item. (Rating scale: 4=very important – 1=unimportant).

**Table 4**
**Importance of Qualifications for the Dean's Position**

| | Mean Rating |
|---|---|
| Earned doctorate | 3.9 |
| Teaching experience in theological or higher education | 3.9 |
| Master of Divinity (M.Div.) degree | 3.4 |
| Pastoral or ministerial experience in the church | 3.2 |
| A record of scholarship | 3.2 |
| Prior administrative experience in theological or higher education | 3.1 |
| Ordination to the ministry/priesthood | 3.0 |
| Formal training in administration | 2.7 |

Most striking in this list is the relative importance given to academic, pastoral, and administrative experience and to formal training in each of these areas. Theological school deans considered prior administrative experience "somewhat important," and less important than experience in the academy and the church.[6] Similarly, formal training in administration was considerably less important than an earned doctorate, the M.Div. degree, and ordination. This is consistent with reports that fewer than half of theological school deans had administrative experience before becoming dean, and most had no formal preparation for administrative work.[7] The majority of theological school deans in the study learned principally on the job.

The importance attributed to an earned doctorate and teaching experience reflects the academic preparation, faculty status, and teaching responsibilities of the majority of deans, and both are among the qualifications needed to gain credibility with the faculty. An earned doctorate and teaching experience were rated "very important" by deans from a broad range of theological schools. In their ratings of ministerial training and experience, however, deans differed according to the denomination of their institutions, their gender, and length of service. The M.Div. degree and ordination were less important to deans in Roman Catholic seminaries than to deans in other schools.[8] Analysis of responses by gender showed that men, who were more likely to be ordained and to have served as pastors, rated the M.Div. degree, ordination, and pastoral experience as more important than did women deans.[9] Deans new to their positions (0–3 years in office) felt ordination was more important than did long-term deans (11 or more years in office).[10] These responses indicate that institutional context, individual background, and experience can influence one's perspective on the qualifications needed for the dean's work.

In an essay entitled "The Rules of the Game: The Unwritten Code of Career Mobility," authors Marlene Ross and Madeleine F. Green suggest that "the credentials one needs to *get* the job are not necessarily the same ones needed to *do* the job."[11] As they explain, "[A]n institution aspiring to greater 'excellence' may be tempted to look for a dean or president with impressive academic credentials, though the task at hand might really be raising money to fund good programs or building consensus among the faculty about needed reform."[12] Defining the necessary qualifications for the job requires careful consideration of what the daily work of academic administration actually demands.[13] Beyond the credentials and experiences listed above are qualities of character and personality, an array of managerial, leadership, and pastoral skills, and ideas and practices that gauge one's fit with the institutional culture and ability to address institutional needs. Candidates also must understand and be committed to the institutional mission, since they bear significant responsibility for its realization through academic program, policy, and personnel decisions.[14]

One president described the qualities sought in the academic vice president during a recent search: "We were looking for a person who had a long relationship with theological education, who had experience in academic leadership, who was known for attempting to be fair and open and evenhanded in the administration of that leadership, and a person who can get along with people." In any given search, various participants may have their own versions of the administrative and leadership practices important to the daily work of academic administration. Since no one candidate is likely to possess all the attributes desirable in a dean, reaching some consensus about the most necessary and important among them is crucial to selecting a dean appropriate to a particular school at a particular time. Successful hirings are founded on a clear and realistic sense of what the school is looking for, and successful deanships depend on a good match between individual abilities and the institutional needs and culture.

### *Deciding to Search*

Two decisions made during the planning phase can have a determinative effect on the outcome of the hiring process: the first is whether to conduct a formal search or simply to make an appointment, and, if conducting a search, the second decision is what type of search will it be: Will it be broad or narrow in scope? Will it be formal or informal in process?

The decision to search or not to search typically is made by the president in consultation with the faculty and, perhaps, with other constituent groups. Despite differences in their scope and formality, searches are distinguished by a process of seeking the application and nomination of eligible candidates. In the absence of a search, schools usually give serious consideration to known candidates, one of whom is appointed to the position. Each of these approaches, however, necessitates other important decisions. If the dean is to be appointed without a search, presidents must decide how extensively to consult the faculty and other constituents prior to making the appointment and what weight their input will have in the final decision. If schools decide to conduct a search, they must consider whether its scope will be international, national, regional, denominational, or limited to the school itself, and whether it will be organized formally with a search committee and a well-defined selection process or handled with a less prescriptive, more informal approach.

### *Organizing the Process*

When schools decide to conduct a search, they must address several issues relating to the search process: whether to establish a search committee and what its leadership, composition, and function will be; the budget for the search; the timeline and procedures for developing the job description, advertising the position, recruiting candidates and establishing a candidate pool, screening applications, conducting campus interviews, and making final recommendations to the appointing officer (typically, the president). Each stage of this process requires the further decision about which individuals and groups will be involved and what the nature of their participation will be. Fortunately, excellent guides are available to assist schools in organizing the principal stages of administrative searches. While several of these guides focus on presidential searches, the strategies they suggest are readily adaptable to other senior administrative positions.[15]

The planning required in advance of the search gives schools the opportunity to assess their needs and define their goals, to reflect on the qualities and skills most desirable in an academic leader, and to develop a hiring process appropriate for their particular institution. The broad participation of constituents in these tasks can determine the quality of the search process and, ultimately, its success in hiring a qualified dean with solid institutional support. Findings on the actual practices of theological schools in hiring chief academic officers reveal several approaches, each with its own rationale and implications for the final outcome of the search.

## Conducting the Hiring

### *To Search or to Appoint*

When theological school deans were asked on the survey about the process used at the time of their hiring, 43 percent reported their hiring occurred without a formal search process. In the majority of these cases, chief academic officers were selected from within the institution and appointed by the president, usually with consultation and approval of the faculty. This sizable percentage of academic officers appointed without a search may seem alarming until one considers the institutional factors affecting that decision.

Site visits revealed that some theological schools were unable to afford a full search, given the cost of advertising widely and bringing candidates in for campus interviews. In light of the relatively small size of theological schools (average 10 full-time faculty in 1993–1994), many find it difficult, if not impossible, to add entirely new personnel to the institutional budget and to absorb the ongoing cost of an administrative position that also may carry a tenured appointment to the faculty. Since the majority of deanships combine administrative and teaching duties, many schools find it preferable to look for administrative talent within and to make an appointment from current faculty or administrators. One seminary president, whose school could not afford to search externally, had his own solution. He deliberately sought to hire multitalented individuals for both faculty and administrative positions so he could call on them to fill administrative vacancies. "One of the most difficult jobs," he explains, is "getting good faculty who can serve as administrators, not hiring administrators directly."

The decision whether or not to do a search also may be influenced by the kind of academic administrator the school is seeking. Financial considerations aside, the president and/or faculty may determine either that a broad search is essential to locate the type of academic leader they need or that a search is unnecessary because they already know a well-qualified candidate who can fill the position. The location of that candidate within or outside the school may help to determine the breadth of the search or whether a search is conducted at all. The decision on the scope of the search also may depend on whether the president and/or faculty believe an inside or an outside candidate would be preferable at that particular time.

### *The Scope of the Search*

Among theological schools conducting a formal search for the chief academic officer, the scope of the searches differed widely. On the survey, 29 percent of deans indicated they were hired through a national search, and 19 percent were hired through limited searches, where the notice of vacancy was circulated outside the school but within a specific denomination or geographical region. Another 42 percent of deans reported that no announcement of vacancy was circulated outside the school. Within this group, some schools conducted an "internal search," soliciting applications and nominations from faculty and staff and screening and interviewing candidates, and others hired deans through informal consultations and a presidential appointment, but without a search process.

Among the eleven schools receiving site visits, five of the chief academic officers were hired through a national search, although the presidents and deans at nine schools expressed a preference for conducting national searches in the future.[16] Despite the preponderance of internal searches and appointments among theological schools, most recognize the advantage of searching widely to establish a broad applicant pool. When schools limit searches to the denomination or the region, they often are seeking someone within their faith tradition or well acquainted with the school. Only one of the schools visited for the study was mandated by university by-laws to conduct an international search for senior administrative positions. Schools at the two extremes—where broad searches are mandatory and where broad searches are financially impossible—are similarly prevented from responding flexibly at the time of the vacancy and tailoring the search to the current needs of the institution.

### *Internal vs. External Searches*

The findings of this study and the literature on administrative hiring amply confirm that internal and external searches each have their advantages and disadvantages, and that neither is appropriate for all schools or even for individual institutions at different times. In light of changing institutional conditions and needs, schools are well served by assessing the pros and cons of each approach when planning a specific search process.

*External Searches.* The arguments in favor of external searches are perhaps most obvious. The associate dean for academic affairs at a university divinity school explains the rationale for the national search that resulted in his hiring: looking externally "was advantageous at the time: the school was very stable, the dean (chief executive officer) was an insider, and an outsider was able to invigorate it with experience from elsewhere without the baggage insiders bring to the task." He added, "It helped there were no inside contenders for the job." Administrators and faculty interviewed at other seminaries most frequently noted the advantage of outside candidates bringing a fresh perspective and new ideas about curriculum, programs, and faculty. In the words of one dean, "If the dean's from inside, there's not enough creative mix, new blood, new ideas—not enough discontinuity." The president of another seminary similarly thought "an external search is preferable for the fresh approaches it can yield. I believe that sometimes schools can become incestuous, and they don't take on new and visionary directions."

While outside deans lack experience within the community, they arrive unencumbered by the baggage of accumulated slights, debts, and other liabilities. Outsiders also avoid the awkwardness of moving suddenly from faculty to administration. As one dean discovered, "It is easier to be from outside than to suddenly be raised above one's peers." Some schools specifically sought a dean from the outside to achieve a balance with an inside president and with senior administrators elevated from within. The need for balance also can apply in reverse. One president, who came from outside the seminary, felt it advantageous to have a chief academic officer from inside the school who was well acquainted with the institution and the faculty. Some schools searched externally for the simple reason that no qualified insiders were available or interested in the position.

In addition to the fact that some schools cannot afford to conduct an external search, others believe there are disadvantages to hiring a dean from outside the school. One dean, who came to his current position from a faculty/administrative post at another seminary, noted that "the downside is that you do come ignorant." An outsider requires time to understand the ethos of the institution and to learn about its people, its practices of communication and decision making, its politics, traditions, needs, and challenges for the future. The learning curve can differ depending on individuals and the institutions. Some of the faculty and administrators interviewed for the study estimated it would take from two to four years for new deans "to learn the ropes," a luxury that some schools cannot afford. One president thought this disadvantage could be overcome "if she/he comes to a swift understanding of the institutional culture, if she/he can be evaluated for fit with the institution by responses to hypothetical questions and through reference checks."

A school's past experience with an outside hire, positive or negative, also can be a factor. Faculty at one university divinity school told of a dean from the outside who proposed changes that were inappropriate, and potentially damaging, in light of the school's denominational affiliations and place within the university. This vivid institutional memory caused several constituents to prefer inside candidates for the continuity in leadership and their understanding of "how things work."

*Internal Searches.* The arguments in favor of internal searches are compelling to many theological schools in light of their relatively small size and strong cultural identities. Given the distinctive mission and ethos of many theological schools and the familial character of their communities, seminaries often find it difficult to weigh the advantages of "new blood" and a "fresh perspective" over against the risk involved in hiring an outsider who takes time to learn about the institution and, ultimately, may not fit in. One president noted, "An insider brings continuity, an appreciation for tradition, and institutional loyalty." On a practical level, an insider comes to the position with established contacts and firsthand knowledge of the institution and its practices. One dean, who had come into office from the faculty, explained, "You know all the problems and personalities and egos and do not have to spend time learning this. You can hit the ground running. You know who you can trust and whose positions you value."

In addition to negative factors, such as financial limitations that discourage adding new positions, and positive factors, such as the availability of a desirable internal candidate, seminary personnel most often cite as the reason for looking within the school the importance of the fit between the prospective dean and the values and practices of the community. Some prefer an insider precisely because they want continuity and stability, and they fear an outsider might "shake things up." Schools clearly have different needs at different times. One seminary president explained the school's preference for an inside candidate: "There was a lot of uneasiness about an outsider coming in, and an insider had not been selected for the longest time. We were more comfortable going with [the inside candidate]."

Although survey data shows that 58 percent of theological school deans in 1993–1994 came from within their institutions, this widespread preference for inside candidates can have its costs. When the data on hiring practices were analyzed according to the gender and racial/ethnic characteristics of deans, results clearly showed that internal searches favored the hiring of white male candidates, whereas national searches favored the hiring of women and racial/ethnic minorities. Searches conducted internally with no announcement of vacancy outside the school resulted in the hiring of 44 percent of white deans, compared to 13 percent of deans of other racial groups. When searches were external and vacancies were nationally advertised, 75 percent of minority deans and 27 percent of white deans were hired, and 50 percent of women deans and 27 percent of men deans were hired.[17] These data strongly suggest that theological schools seeking to strengthen the gender and racial/ethnic diversity of their senior administrators are best served by a national search and the broader candidate pool it provides.

Studies on hiring women and minorities in colleges and universities suggest that innovative, proactive strategies generally are required to broaden the applicant pool.[18] While many factors influence an institution's success in recruiting, hiring, and retaining minority members, the passive approach of publishing ads and waiting for applications to arrive is clearly insufficient. Rather, the strategy must be to "go out and find the talent," to be on the lookout for women and minority scholars enrolled in doctoral programs, to provide visiting-scholar opportunities or postdoctoral fellowships at the school, to establish ties with predominantly minority colleges, universities, and theological schools, to be attentive to prospective candidates at professional meetings, and the like.[19] Theological schools seeking to strengthen the diversity of their faculty and administration must recognize that recruitment and hiring practices can be an important factor in their success.

### *Search Committees*

In the 57 percent of theological schools conducting a formal search for the chief academic officer, presidents typically appointed a search committee to manage the principal stages of the search process: to advertise the job opening, to solicit applications and nominations, to screen applicants and develop a candidate pool, to conduct interviews, and to make final recommendations.[20] Several of these stages may have auxiliary tasks, such as checking references or doing telephone interviews, and the committee's charge may vary from recommending one candidate to narrowing the field to two or three finalists for final selection by the president and/or faculty. At each stage, the search committee must decide how to involve other constituents in the search, how to utilize their input, and how to communicate with them throughout the process. While variations exist in the duties of search committees and their methods of fulfilling them, those developing a broad and inclusive search process bring the perspectives of various constituents to bear on the hiring decision and are able to assess community acceptance and support of the prospective dean.

The composition of the search committee can be a critical factor in achieving broad constituent representation in the hiring process. As noted in a manual on administrative searches, the use of broadly representative search committees reflects

> the common-sense notion that in judging talent, several heads can be better than one. By bringing a wide spectrum of minds (faculty minds especially) to bear on administrative appointments, wiser, more broadly acceptable choices become possible. Indeed, a search committee legitimates an appointment as no other method can.[21]

On the survey of theological school deans, those whose schools utilized search committees in their hiring were asked about the composition of the committee. The table below indicates the percentage of these search committees with representatives from each group.

**Table 5**
**Composition of Search Committees for Chief Academic Officers**

| Committee members | % of search committees |
|---|---|
| Faculty | 96 |
| Chief executive officer | 82 |
| Senior administrators | 75 |
| Members of board of trustees | 70 |
| Students | 63 |
| Denominational leaders | 22 |

The strong representation of faculty, presidents, and senior administrators on the committee reflects their close working relationship with the chief academic officer and the importance of their direct involvement in the search process. While the majority of chief executive officers were members of the search committee, others, particularly in university-related schools, charged the committee with handling much of the search and requested a recommendation of one or more finalists at the end of the process.[22] In most cases, presidents made the hiring decision, pending the formal approval of the governing board.

Most striking in this data is that 70 percent of dean search committees included board members and 22 percent included denominational leaders not serving on the board.[23] As discussed in Chapter Five, chief academic officers have significant working relationships with these groups, which is formally acknowledged by their presence on the search committee. Further, the involvement of board members and church leaders in assessing the current challenges facing the academic area and the kind of academic leadership needed for the institution can be an invaluable means of enhancing communication among seminary constituents and developing a shared understanding of these critical issues. Search committee deliberations also serve an educational purpose for board members and church leaders who have few opportunities for serious, in-depth discussion of academic matters with faculty, administrators, or students.

The effective organization and functioning of a search committee can be more difficult than may at first appear. One seminary's story of an unsuccessful search illustrates that point. As part of a national search for the academic dean, the president appointed a search committee composed of five faculty, one student, and one alumnus. The committee saw its role as receiving and screening applications, and the committee felt the final recommendation should come from the faculty. After the committee selected three finalists and brought them to campus for interviews, the faculty recommended a candidate the president could not accept. Since the president and faculty could not agree, the search ended without a hire. The president subsequently appointed an interim dean from the faculty to serve for two years, when another search would be conducted.

In retrospect, the relation of the president to the search committee and the committee's composition and function all contributed to the failure of the process. The president acknowledges that he selected an inappropriate chair for the committee and had not been sufficiently clear about his charge to the committee or about his expectations for the dean. The committee proceeded without clarity or agreement about the qualities they were seeking and about the roles of the president and the faculty in selecting the dean. As the process unfolded, the president was involved only in interviewing candidates but was not included in subsequent discussions of the merits of particular candidates. These unfortunate oversights resulted in an impasse between the president and faculty and faculty resentment that the president did not accept "their candidate."

The second search, with a stronger candidate pool and the previous errors corrected, ended successfully. This time the president not only was careful to appoint an effective chair and to clarify his expectations for the dean and his charge to the committee, but the president sat on the committee and participated in discussions. These strategies strengthened communication among the president, the faculty, and other constituents at every stage of the process. This example illustrates that successful searches depend, in large part, on the effectiveness of the search committee and on the strength of communication between the president and the committee on both substantive and procedural matters relating to the search.

### *Recruitment and Selection of Candidates*

Theological schools committed to searching for chief academic officers outside their own institution employ a variety of recruitment strategies, ranging from placing advertisements of the job opening in national, denominational, and regional publications to hiring search consultants or a search firm to making personal contacts with prospective candidates. Survey findings reveal that, among chief academic officers serving in 1993–1994, 52 percent were identified through personal contact by denominational and/or school personnel. Beyond the passive measure of publishing an ad and waiting for applications to come in, some schools were proactive in their efforts to locate and make personal contact with promising candidates. Many believe, as one senior administrator stated, "The best candidates surface by word of mouth and networking." This can be particularly effective in the close-knit circles of denominations and theological schools.

When presidents and/or search committees screen applications to establish the candidate pool, they often contact personal references and arrange to interview the top candidates.[24] Site visits revealed some interesting variations on the usual practice of bringing the finalists to campus for interviews with the president, the search committee, and other constituent groups. In the case of one school conducting a national search, the search committee narrowed the field to five or six viable candidates; the president then visited and interviewed each of them and selected three candidates to invite to campus for consideration by the seminary community. At another school, the pool of candidates for the provost position was established by recent searches at the dean level. The president wanted the provost in place immediately, so he chose from among the candidates a person he knew well and brought only the one candidate to campus for interviews and verification.

Over three-quarters of the chief academic officers responding to the survey reported that personal interviews were part of the hiring process.[25] As expected, the deans most extensively interviewed were from outside the institution, and those receiving no personal interviews or interviewed only by the president were hired from within the school and without a formal search process. The table below shows the percentage of theological school deans interviewed by each group.

**Table 6**
**Personal Interviews**

| | % of deans interviewed |
|---|---|
| Chief executive officers | 68 |
| Faculty | 54 |
| Major administrators | 42 |
| Board of trustees | 40 |
| Students | 35 |
| Denominational leaders | 7 |

Analysis of these data shows a strong correlation between the individuals and groups conducting the interviews and those represented on the search committee. Since the survey did not ask for the number of persons interviewing from each group, it is difficult to estimate how extensively various constituents were involved. The participation of chief executive officers, faculty, and senior administrators showed little variation among theological schools of different sizes, types, and denominations; however, some differences among schools did arise in the participation of the other constituent groups.[26]

Guidelines to administrative hiring stress the difficulty of conducting effective personal interviews: the need to have clear objectives, sound interviewing techniques, well-formulated questions, and an ability to assess candidate performance and balance it with other information acquired during the search process.[27] Interviews and campus visits, when conducted well, can prove mutually beneficial for the candidate and the school. Candidates have an opportunity to learn both the requirements and unwritten expectations of the job, to assess its challenges and opportunities, and to gauge their compatibility with prospective colleagues. Schools gain insight into the candidate's views on critical issues, working style, communication and interpersonal skills, interest in the job, and a wide range of personal qualities, attitudes, and beliefs. Most importantly, interviews are an opportunity to assess the candidate's fit and personal chemistry with other campus constituents. Search manuals warn, however, that "you are not looking for the 'most liked' candidate; you are looking for abilities matched to a post. . . . [T]he issue isn't, Who fits best? (i.e., 'is most like us'), but, Is this candidate sufficiently in tune with the culture here to garner support and be able to work effectively?"[28]

At every stage of the process, then, theological school communities face several critical decisions, each of which has consequences for the outcome of the search: Should hiring the chief academic officer be accomplished through a search or an appointment? If searching, should the search be internal or external, broad or limited in scope? If a search committee is appointed, who will serve and what will their function be? Will recruitment efforts be passive or proactive? How open and participatory will the process be? How extensively will constituents be involved in candidate interviews and making the final recommendation? The answer to these questions can determine the quality and breadth of the candidate pool and the degree of community ownership for the hiring decision. How the search is conducted can determine whether a school succeeds in hiring an appropriately qualified dean who can work effectively with colleagues and provide the kind of leadership needed for the academic area.

## Making the Hiring Decision

Once campus visits are completed, the search committee typically solicits from constituents responses to the campus interviews and makes recommendations to the president based on this and other information obtained throughout the search process. In schools without a search committee, the president may receive input directly prior to making the hiring decision. As the appointing officer, the president or chief executive officer typically makes the final selection, pending the approval of the governing board.

### *Influence on the Hiring Decision*

Theological school deans were asked on the survey how much influence various individuals and groups should have in selecting the chief academic officer. Their responses confirmed site visit findings that most deans believe the president and faculty should have considerable influence and other constituents moderate influence. Their mean ratings were as follows: (Rating scale: 3=considerable influence, 2=moderate influence, 1=little or no influence)

**Table 7**
**Influence in Selecting the Chief Academic Officer**

| | Mean Ratings |
|---|---|
| Chief executive officer | 2.9 |
| Faculty | 2.8 |
| Senior administrators | 2.2 |
| Members of board of trustees | 2.1 |
| Students | 1.9 |
| Denominational leaders other than trustees | 1.4 |

These responses suggest that, whereas all constituents should participate in selecting the chief academic officer, the president and faculty with whom the dean has the closest ties should have the greatest influence.[29] When deans were asked the further question about who should have the *decisive* influence in hiring the chief academic officer, 60 percent indicated the president and 20 percent indicated the faculty; fewer than 8 percent of deans cited any of the other constituents.

Typically, presidents make the hiring decision and negotiate the terms of appointment with the incoming dean. Site visit interviews clearly indicated that most presidents actively seek faculty approval for the chosen candidate and would not appoint a chief academic officer without it.[30] This process recognizes the president and the faculty as the dean's primary constituents and the dean's pivotal role in serving them both. While faculty often have considerable influence in selecting a new dean and deans subsequently are evaluated on their ability to work with faculty, survey results indicate that the practice of determining the dean's reappointment by faculty vote is relatively rare.[31]

### *Terms of Appointment*

At the time of appointment, deans have an opportunity to discuss, and perhaps negotiate, such critical issues as their academic standing, workload, compensation, and other conditions of employment. Particularly, deans coming to their positions from outside the institution must reach agreement on academic rank and tenure. Even deans hired from within the institution must clarify the specific responsibilities of office, their role in relation to the president, faculty, and other constituents, as well as both the explicit and implicit expectations of these groups.[32] While understanding the role and responsibilities of office may develop as the work proceeds, achieving as much clarity and agreement as possible at the outset can prevent misunderstandings down the road. Similarly helpful is consideration upfront of salary, benefits, and other terms of the job.[33]

Chief academic officers, unlike other senior administrators, often are required or expected to teach and remain active in their scholarship while performing their administrative duties. Given the fact that 93 percent of theological school deans teach, and 43 percent are either expected or required to do scholarly work, it becomes important for deans to clarify the amount of teaching and scholarship expected and to negotiate a fair and reasonable balance between academic and administrative tasks.[34] Several deans in the study, for example, arranged to spend one day each week out of the office to devote to their academic work or to deal with larger projects that require uninterrupted time. Others received commitments for study leaves or sabbaticals. The time of hiring presents an occasion for deans to clarify expectations and to reach agreement on workload and other conditions of the job.

### *Orientation*

A final and often overlooked stage of the hiring process is the orientation of the new academic officer to the institution and the work of the office. Even deans coming into the office from another position within the school may be unfamiliar with administrative procedures and the rhythm and specific duties of the dean's office. Someone knowledgeable about the work of the dean's office, such as the outgoing dean or an administrative assistant, can be an invaluable resource to the new dean needing to learn the ropes. Also essential are conversations with the president, other administrators, and perhaps a senior member of the faculty who can provide background on current issues and a sense of the social/political dynamics of the institution. One dean in the study noted how helpful the president had been to him from the very beginning, when he could talk candidly about his frustrations and concerns. Whether deans come from within or outside the institution, those new to the position benefit immeasurably from orientation to the work of the office by trusted colleagues.

To summarize, while there is no blueprint for a successful search and no single profile of the successful dean, steps can be taken during the planning, search, and hiring processes to locate a candidate whose qualifications and skills are a good match for the institution. How the search and hiring are conducted can affect community acceptance and support for the incoming dean and, in turn, the dean's ability to serve effectively in the role. As the appointing officer, the president bears responsibility for clarifying the duties and expectations of the office, for establishing a reasonable workload, and for providing the orientation and support necessary for a strong beginning.

## Sources of Theological School Deans

The preceding discussion of hiring practices would be incomplete without an understanding of where theological school deans come from. Survey data from the Study of Chief Academic Officers reveal the sources of deans who served theological schools in 1993–1994. Survey respondents were asked to specify their primary occupation immediately prior to their present position.[35]

**Table 8**
**Sources of Chief Academic Officers**

| | % of deans |
|---|---|
| Faculty at present institution | 47.0 |
| Faculty in another theological school | 12.8 |
| Faculty in a college or university | 5.5 |
| Total faculty | 65.3 |
| Administrator at present institution | 11.0 |
| Administrator in another theological school | 7.3 |
| Administrator in a college or university | 3.0 |
| Administrator for denomination, diocese, or religious order | 4.3 |
| Total administration | 25.6 |
| Ministerial or pastoral work for the church | 6.1 |
| Work in the corporate or business world | .6 |
| Other | 2.4 |

As these data indicate, 65 percent of deans came directly from the faculty, and just over 21 percent came from administrative posts in an academic setting.[36] Approximately 78 percent were from theological schools and, as reported earlier, 58 percent were from within their own institutions. Data analysis showed no statistically significant differences among theological schools in the sources of their deans.[37]

The adjustment involved in moving from the faculty to an administrative position, even within the same institution, should not be underestimated. A faculty member with firsthand knowledge of the academic life and the challenges of the classroom may be quite unfamiliar with the administrative complexity of the academic area and of the institution as a whole. During site visit interviews, several deans noted how little they understood the dean's job prior to taking office, even though they had considerable experience working with deans over the years. Although 44 percent of theological school deans had some type of previous administrative experience, only 21 percent held administrative posts within the schools they presently served. Consequently, the majority of chief academic officers, whether from within or outside the school, require orientation to the administrative operations and culture of which they now are an integral part. Presidents and senior administrators, in particular, play a critical role in providing information and support to incoming chief academic officers lacking senior administrative experience at their institutions.

## A Note to Prospective Deans

While theological schools are responsible for employing effective hiring practices and selecting deans wisely, candidates for the office also have the responsibility to assess their personal readiness for administrative service and the requirements and expectations of the position. Survey findings indicate the majority of theological school deans accepted their positions without adequately addressing these issues. Approximately 70 percent of survey respondents found that their original expectations of the job differed from the actual experience of doing it. Specifically, the deans reported they had not fully realized what the job entailed, the skills it required, the effect it would have on other relationships, and its overwhelming time constraints. Only about 25 percent of deans were sufficiently informed about their positions so that the job matched their expectations.

Candidates for chief academic officer positions can narrow the gap between expectations and reality by careful preparation and active participation in the hiring process. First, prospective candidates need to acquire as much information as possible about the institution and the position. In addition to requesting school publications, using informal channels to contact colleagues who may know the culture and climate of the school, its recent history, its strengths, weaknesses, and challenges can be exceptionally helpful. Even prospective candidates from within the institution can benefit from conversations with colleagues about the challenges and needs of the academic area. Interviews with the president, search committee, and other campus constituents present an opportunity not only for school personnel to learn about the candidate, but for the candidate to ask probing questions about the institution, its people, and the requirements of the job. Interviews are an occasion for mutual assessment, and even deans hired informally from within the institution should have candid conversations with the president and other colleagues about what the job will require.

Second, candidates have a responsibility to themselves and to their prospective employers to assess honestly their own aptitude for administrative work. Clearly, this task is impossible without an understanding of what the job entails, what its stresses and challenges will be. The earlier observation about the difference between the credentials one needs to *get* the job and the skills one needs to *do* the job is crucial. Prospective deans must appraise their abilities, needs, and interests not against the criteria required of a successful applicant but against the criteria for a successful dean. The questions must focus on the configuration of competencies and attributes required to perform the daily work of the office in a particular setting. The perspective of personal and professional associates can be helpful to candidates assessing their readiness for academic administration and, where appropriate, their fit with a specific institution.

Finally, candidates who eventually accept positions as chief academic officers must be mindful of the conditions of employment requisite to fulfilling the myriad duties of the office: the time required to meet the administrative responsibilities and challenges of the position, the amount of teaching and scholarship possible in combination with administrative tasks, and the provisions for study days, leaves, sabbaticals, and vacations. At the time of appointment, deans and presidents should undertake a preliminary assessment of the total workload of the office and agree on the conditions of employment that will make the job manageable. Incoming deans also should be candid with their presidents about the skills they bring to the job and areas where they need additional preparation and training. Raising the need for ongoing professional development at the time of hiring not only indicates the dean's awareness of the challenges ahead, but initiates the practice of planning jointly with the president about ways to develop and strengthen one's administrative skills. As we will discuss more fully in Chapter Seven, addressing the professional development needs of chief academic officers not only can have practical benefits for the current officeholder, but can be a powerful indicator of institutional support for the academic area and its leadership.

## Notes

[1] See Introduction, note 1. Data of the Association indicated 233 member schools in 1996. Jonathan Strom and Daniel Aleshire, eds., *Fact Book on Theological Education 1996–1997* (Pittsburgh, PA: The Association of Theological Schools in the United States and Canada, 1997), 2.

[2] Selected findings of the Study of Chief Academic Officers regarding decanal hiring practices in theological education were discussed in an earlier publication for this project: Mary Abdul-Rahman, *Career Paths and Hiring Practices of Chief Academic Officers in Theological Schools,* Monograph Series on Academic Leadership, vol. 3 (St. Paul, MN: University of St. Thomas, 1996), 1–15.

[3] In 1981, the American Association of University Professors (AAUP) approved a revised and expanded statement concerning "Faculty Participation in the Selection, Evaluation, and Retention of Administrators." "[T]he 'Statement' asserts the expectation that faculty members will have a significant role in the selection of academic administrators, including the president, academic deans, department heads, and chairmen." "Faculty Participation in the Selection, Evaluation, and Retention of Administrators," *Academe* (October 1981), 323.

[4] As project advisory committee member, Robert Birnbaum, suggests, just as goals drive searches, searches also can lead to goals.

[5] Theodore J. Marchese and Jane Fiori Lawrence, *The Search Committee Handbook: A Guide to Recruiting Administrators* (Washington, DC: American Association for Higher Education, 1988), 19.

[6] In a related question, survey respondents were asked to indicate their agreement or disagreement with the following statement: "It is more important for an academic dean to have proven administrative ability than a distinguished record of scholarship and teaching." The mean rating was 2.7, indicating they "somewhat agreed" with this statement. (Rating scale: 4=strongly agree – 1=strongly disagree.) Examining this statement in light of Table 4 suggests that experience as a teacher/scholar and experience as an administrator both are more important than a record of academic distinction.

[7] On the survey, 44 percent of deans indicated they had academic administrative experience prior to their current position. In terms of formal preparation for administrative work, only 1.8 percent of the deans surveyed held a doctorate in education, and none of the deans interviewed during site visits had formal training for administrative work.

[8] The M.Div. degree was rated most important by deans at mainline Protestant seminaries (mean 3.8) and least important by deans at Roman Catholic seminaries (mean 2.8). Similarly, ordination was most important in Protestant seminaries (mean 3.0 to 3.2) and least important in Roman Catholic and interdenominational/nondenominational seminaries (mean 2.7 to 2.9). Denominational differences regarding ordination were significant at the .07 level.

[9] Men and women deans differed on the importance of these factors as follows: M.Div. degree (men 3.5, women 2.7); ordination (men 3.1, women 1.8); pastoral or ministerial experience (men 3.3, women 2.9). Gender differences on the last item were statistically significant at the .07 level.

[10] New deans (0–3 years in office) rated ordination "somewhat important" (mean 3.2), compared to long-term deans (11 or more years in office) who rated it between "somewhat" and "not very important" (mean 2.5).

[11] Marlene Ross and Madeleine F. Green, "The Rules of the Game: The Unwritten Code of Career Mobility," in *Administrative Careers and the Marketplace,* Kathryn M. Moore and Susan B. Twombly, eds. New Directions for Higher Education, no. 72 (San Francisco: Jossey-Bass, 1990), 71.

[12] Ross and Green, 71.

[13] Even job descriptions may not be reliable indicators of the daily work of the office. As noted in Chapter One, job descriptions often do not keep pace with changes in job requirements.

[14] Richard Kaplowitz reports on a 1982 study of deans of education where both the chairs of dean search committees and the deans hired in those searches were surveyed regarding the qualities they considered most important for success on the job. As Kaplowitz states, "Seven key factors appeared on both groups' lists of their ten most important criteria. Leadership and decision-making skills were the two top factors on each list. The other five criteria common to both the committees' and deans' lists were: sensitivity to faculty needs, program development skills, faculty relations skills, communications skills, and a vision for education." The study also noted discrepancies between published criteria and those actually considered important. Richard A. Kaplowitz, *Selecting College and University Personnel: The Quest and the Questions.* ASHE-ERIC Higher Education Report No. 8 (Washington, DC: Association for the Study of Higher Education, 1986), 59.

[15] Among the most helpful guides to administrative searches are the following: Marchese and Lawrence, *The Search Committee Handbook,* 1988; Mark Allyn Holman, *Presidential Search in Theological Schools: Process Makes a Difference.* Oakland, CA: 1993, distributed by agreement with the Association of Theological Schools in the United States and Canada (ATS); Kaplowitz, *Selecting College and University Personnel,* 1986; John W. Nason, *Presidential Search: A Guide to the Process of Selecting and Appointing College and University Presidents.* Washington, DC: The Association of Governing Boards of Universities and Colleges, 1980, 1984; James M. Unglaube, "Searching for Senior Administrators," in A. J. Falender and J. C. Merson, eds., *Management Techniques for Small and Specialized Institutions.* New Directions for Higher Education, no. 42. San Francisco: Jossey-Bass, 1983.

[16] The remaining two of the eleven schools preferred to be flexible and determine the nature of the search depending on institutional needs at the time of vacancy.

[17] Research published in 1988 on administrative mobility and gender in four-year colleges and universities offers some interesting comparative data. The study analyzed position changes among administrators between 1969 and 1980 in academic, student, and administrative affairs. While the study concluded that "women were promoted at a

slightly higher rate than men within institutions," women in academic affairs "were more successful in gaining access to positions from outside institutions than their female counterparts in other administrative specialties." Mary Ann Sagaria, "Administrative Mobility and Gender: Patterns and Processes in Higher Education," *The Journal of Higher Education* 59, no. 3 (May/June 1988), 322–324.

[18] Marian J. Swoboda, "Hiring Women and Minorities," in *The Art of Hiring in America's Colleges and Universities,* Ronald H. Stein and Stephen Joel Trachtenberg, eds. (Buffalo, NY: Prometheus Books, 1993), 123–136; Kaplowitz, *Selecting College and University Personnel,* 47–51.

[19] Swoboda, 131–133.

[20] Data on the percentage of theological schools conducting formal searches and utilizing search committees are acquired from the 1993 survey of chief academic officers in which respondents reported on practices used in their own hiring. Approximately 13.6 percent of survey respondents did not answer questions about the existence and composition of the search committee. The data on searches, therefore, are approximate since some deans did not recall or did not know the practices used by their seminaries when they were hired.

[21] Marchese and Lawrence, 3.

[22] Chief executive officers served on 85 percent of the search committees in freestanding theological schools but only on 57 percent of the search committees in university-related schools.

[23] The actual percentage of denominational leaders on search committees may be somewhat higher since some also may be serving as representatives of the board.

[24] Among survey respondents, 40 percent indicated the school contacted their personal references.

[25] Survey results on the personal interviews conducted at the time of hiring are difficult to interpret: 21 percent of survey respondents did not answer the question and another 34 percent answered it only partially. Analysis of the responses received shows that 2 percent of deans had no personal interviews at the time of hiring, and, among the 77 percent of deans interviewed, 13 percent were interviewed only by the president.

[26] Survey results indicate that trustee interviews were least common in large schools and in Roman Catholic seminaries. Analysis based on institutional size shows that trustees interviewed in 45 percent of small schools (1–75 student FTE), compared to 31 percent of mid-sized schools (76–150 student FTE), and 23 percent of large schools (151–300 student FTE). Denominational analysis shows that only 33 percent of trustees in Roman Catholic schools conducted interviews, compared to 68 or 69 percent in other theological schools.

Student interviews of dean candidates were least common in large theological schools: students participated in interviews in 41 percent of small schools, 36 percent of mid-sized schools, and only 23 percent of large schools.

Denominational leaders conducted interviews more frequently in university-related theological schools (44 percent) than in freestanding/independent schools (9 percent).

[27] Marchese and Lawrence offer a concise introduction to effective interviewing and its role in the hiring process. They estimate that you can learn 80 percent of what you need to learn about a candidate *prior* to the campus interview. Marchese and Lawrence, 37–47.

[28] Marchese and Lawrence, 44–45.

[29] The deans' perspective on how much influence the chief executive officer should have differed according to the type of seminary: 92 percent of deans in freestanding/independent seminaries, compared to 75 percent of deans in university-related schools, thought the president should have "considerable influence" on the selection of the chief academic officer. However, 25 percent of deans in university-related schools thought denominational leaders should have "considerable influence," compared to 5 percent in freestanding schools. On the issue of the influence of senior administrators, 51 percent of deans in Roman Catholic seminaries thought senior administrators should have "considerable influence" in the dean selection, compared to 28–29 percent of deans in other seminaries.

[30] On a 1993 survey of theological school faculty conducted by the Auburn Center, respondents gave the statement, "Faculty should play a determinative role in hiring the CAO/academic dean," a mean rating of 3.51 (rating scale: 4=strongly agree – 1=strongly disagree).

[31] In response to the statement on the deans' survey, "My reappointment is determined by vote of the faculty," only 9 percent of respondents strongly agreed, 12 percent somewhat agreed, 17 percent somewhat disagreed, and 55 percent strongly disagreed. The mean rating was 1.7 on the scale: 4=strongly agreed – 1=strongly disagreed.

[32] On the survey, 47 percent of deans indicated their administrative duties were specified in their contract, whereas 87 percent noted they were specified either in a contract or in other institutional documents.

[33] In response to survey questions regarding their financial compensations, 77 percent of deans considered their compensation satisfactory, and 71 percent indicated there were different salary schedules for faculty and administrators at their schools.

[34] As reported in Chapter One, teaching is required of 38 percent of deans and expected of 38 percent of deans; scholarship is required of only 3 percent of deans, but expected of 40 percent.

[35] In addition to the question about the deans' position immediately prior to the deanship, survey respondents were asked about their previous professional experience. Findings on their previous experience are reported in Chapter Eight.

[36] Data on academic deans' careers in four-year colleges and universities shows that "[a] faculty position is also the typical entry point for deans. However, relatively few individuals move from faculty to department chair, to assistant or associate dean, to dean. . . . [P]rofessional school deans often skip intermediate positions and jump directly from faculty positions to deanships." Susan B. Twombly, "Career Maps and Institutional Highways," in *Administrative Careers and the Marketplace,* Kathryn M. Moore and Susan B. Twombly, eds. New Directions for Higher Education, no. 72 (San Francisco: Jossey-Bass, 1990), 10–11.

[37] A 1992 report on sources of executive leadership in theological education affords an interesting comparison to the sources of academic leadership. Leon Pacala, "The Presidential Experience in Theological Education: A Study of Executive Leadership," *Theological Education* 29, no. 1 (Autumn 1992), 13. The report indicates 55 percent of presidents are appointed from positions in theological schools and 53 percent come from within the institution they serve. Further, 35 percent come from faculty positions and 35 percent from administrative positions in theological or higher education; 14 percent come from denominational/judicatory offices and 12 percent from the pastorate.

# 7 Evaluation and Professional Development

*"As dean, you're out there by yourself. You need to get perspective."*
*Theological school dean*

A passage from Peter Seldin's book, *Evaluating and Developing Administrative Performance,* sets the theme of this chapter:

> Much too often, academics look upon appraisal of performance and professional development as unrelated processes. The fact is, they are a single process and make most sense as such. True, administrative evaluation can be helpful in making personnel decisions and in responding to external and internal pressures. But its core purpose is to locate areas of needed or desired improvement and to point the way to personal and professional development. . . .[1]

Administrative evaluation and professional development, as Seldin states, are a single process. Performance evaluation is widely considered "the entry point for professional development."[2] Evaluation identifies areas of strength and areas where growth and revitalization are needed; professional development provides opportunities for addressing those needs and responding to the insights the evaluation offers. A fair, balanced appraisal of administrative work provides the stimulus and direction for professional development.

The majority of theological school deans welcome evaluation of their administrative work and seek increased institutional support for their professional development. Findings of the Study of Chief Academic Officers disprove the common assumptions that many administrators fear evaluation and are somewhat indifferent to professional development. On the contrary, survey results indicate that 87 percent of deans believe that regular evaluation can help them perform their jobs more effectively, whereas only 10 percent think that performance evaluation of administrators is a waste of time.[3] Of the eleven deans interviewed during site visits, all spoke positively about the benefits of evaluation and seven explicitly sought from their presidents more regular and more formal evaluation. Deans were similarly emphatic about their need for professional development. Survey responses indicate that deans consider sabbaticals and leaves, study time, travel to conferences and workshops, and the like important to their professional growth and vitality (See Table 11). However, more than half of the theological school deans surveyed (55 percent) do not believe their institutions provide adequately for their professional development.

Given the deans' clearly articulated need for stronger, more effective evaluation and professional development programs, this chapter examines the current practices of theological schools in both areas. We begin by considering several reasons for conducting administrative evaluation and the roadblocks to evaluation discovered in the course of this research. Analysis of current practices for evaluation of chief academic officers includes discussion of evaluation methods and criteria and the role of the president, faculty, and other constituents in the process. Since a primary goal of evaluation is to support and strengthen academic officers in their work, evaluation is incomplete without practical strategies for responding to the needs identified. Whether a dean or provost needs training in finances or accreditation procedures or wishes to learn more about leading a curriculum revision or simply needs time away from the job for personal renewal, such evaluation findings are valuable only if they are taken seriously and lead to specific plans for how the identified needs will be addressed. In short, effective evaluation requires professional development.

Our discussion of professional development turns on a paradox: although professional development opportunities are widely available to chief academic officers in theological schools, the majority consider institutional support for administrative development inadequate. To understand this apparent contradiction, we begin by examining current administrative development practices in theological schools, including the opportunities available to deans and the deans' perceptions of their importance. However, not until we consider what effective professional development requires do we gain insight into the deans' dissatisfaction. As we shall see, the success of development programs depends not only on the availability of development opportunities but on the larger framework of institutional practices needed to support them. At the present time, few theological schools have the infrastructure of coordinated practices necessary for effective administrative development.[4]

## Evaluation

*Why Evaluate?*

The first and most fundamental question is "Why evaluate administrative performance?" The standard reasons given for evaluating administrators in higher education underscore the importance, indeed the necessity, of personnel evaluation generally.[5] First, evaluation is a means of improving *individual* job performance and satisfaction. Evaluation enables individuals to learn their personal strengths and weaknesses, to identify areas where they are successful and where additional preparation and training are needed. Evaluation also gives administrators an opportunity to assess the requirements and expectations of the job and to determine what organizational and/or personal changes are needed to enhance their effectiveness and job satisfaction.

Second, evaluation of individual administrators can improve *institutional* performance by increasing understanding among constituents and by addressing the evaluation issues such as communication, teamwork, management and leadership skills. Administrative evaluations also help the president and board stay apprised of the kind of support needed to strengthen the operation and leadership of the institution.

In addition to these formative or developmental purposes, evaluation also can be summative in nature and useful in making fair and informed personnel decisions. A third reason to do administrative evaluation is to obtain comparative data helpful in determining retention, promotion, salary, and other employment decisions. While some try to separate performance from the reward structure, theorists like Seldin say, "Why try?" In discussing guidelines for successful evaluation programs, Seldin argues that the "evaluation system must avoid the trap of trying to separate performance evaluation from the reward structure in an effort to avoid the 'taint' of money issues from the assessment and feedback counseling process. The two are so naturally intertwined as to defy separation."[6] This issue of separation did not arise, however, in the sites visited for this study.

Fourth, personnel evaluation can help the institution respond to requests by accrediting agencies and other external organizations for evaluative data. In its newly revised guidelines for accreditation, the Association of Theological Schools in the United States and Canada (ATS) explicitly mandates that member institutions "shall develop and implement ongoing evaluation procedures for employees, students, educational programs, and all institutional activities." The guidelines explain that a "comprehensive evaluation process is the primary resource an institution uses to determine the extent to which it is accomplishing its purpose."[7] At a time of increasing public accountability, institutions are expected to assess how effectively their personnel and programs are accomplishing the stated purpose of the organization. Evaluation of administrators is one component of a comprehensive institutional assessment.

The fifth and perhaps most compelling reason is offered by the theological school deans interviewed for this study. Quite simply, without formal evaluation they do not have a balanced and accurate sense of how they are doing. While most deans receive feedback from faculty and administrative colleagues, few believe that random, informal comments provide a reliable assessment of their work. The dean of a university divinity school considered the lack of formal evaluation "terrible." Not having such evaluation is "a handicap in improving performance. . . . When it's always only informal, you cannot be sure if you're reading the signs right." Another dean similarly observed, "I get feedback all the time, but I'm not sure it's accurate." The majority of chief academic officers in the study thought evaluation by their administrative colleagues and constituents was important to understanding and improving their job performance.

### *Roadblocks to Evaluation*

Despite the obvious benefits of regular performance review, several presidents interviewed during site visits acknowledged their discomfort with administrative evaluation. One president felt that broad-based evaluation might expose the dean to unfair criticism; another was hesitant "to take an aggressive approach to evaluation" because he did not want to alienate those who took their administrative posts at his request and without additional compensation. Developing an evaluation that is balanced, fair, and constructive for the individual also can be time-consuming and may require specialized knowledge of evaluation methods and instruments.[8] In small institutions like theological schools, familiarity and frequent informal conversation among faculty, administrators, and other personnel may seem to obviate the need for a formal evaluation process. For these reasons, most presidents at schools visited for this study evaluated their chief academic officers informally, if at all. Although presidents generally recognized the benefit of some type of formal evaluation for administrators, only four of the eleven schools visited had such programs in place. In several cases, evaluation occurred only at the dean's insistence.

Evaluation of senior administrators also is influenced by the culture of evaluation within the institution as a whole. The quality and regularity of other evaluation practices can create a favorable or unfavorable climate for administrative evaluation. If the board of trustees takes seriously its responsibility to evaluate the president, if the school has sound, well-defined processes for evaluation of faculty and staff, if the faculty are up-to-date on methods for assessing student learning, then evaluating senior administrators may be a welcome addition to other established practices. On the other hand, evaluation of senior administrators would be difficult to institute in schools that traditionally have been indifferent or uncomfortable with evaluation and lax in its practice. Clearly, leadership from the board and the president is needed to assert the importance of quality assessment for the institution and to encourage and support the development of effective evaluation practices. The care with which the board evaluates the president and the president evaluates senior administrators can serve as a model for personnel evaluation at other levels of the institution.

### *Evaluation Practices in Theological Schools*

To understand current practices for evaluating theological school deans, we will analyze survey and site visit data for what they reveal about: 1) the methods of evaluation, both formal and informal; 2) the criteria or standards employed in judging performance; and 3) the role the faculty and other constituents play in the evaluation process.

*Evaluation Methods.* The process for evaluating the chief academic officer can be either informal or formal. *Informal evaluations* usually are conducted annually and consist of a meeting with the president or immediate supervisor to discuss the dean's success in achieving goals and in fulfilling the responsibilities of office. Sometimes deans are required to submit an annual report or self-evaluation in which they review the past year and set goals for the future. Formal evaluation, by contrast, has a defined process through which other constituents participate in the dean's evaluation. Usually undertaken in the second or third year or at the time of reappointment, formal evaluations are conducted by the president, the president's representative, or an evaluation committee and may include a written self-evaluation or portfolio prepared by the dean, an evaluation form distributed to faculty and a sampling of other constituents, selected interviews with constituent representatives, and a written summary of evaluation findings prepared by the director of the process and presented to the dean. Regardless of who oversees the evaluation, the president usually meets with the dean to discuss the results and to identify areas where improvement or new skills are needed. Depending on the nature of the process, the dean may have an opportunity to respond to the findings in writing, and the president may give a general report to the campus community and/or to those who participated in the evaluation process.

Findings of the Study of Chief Academic Officers revealed that, while informal evaluation is most commonly practiced in theological schools, it is far from universal. On the survey, approximately 60 percent of chief academic officers indicated that they met annually with their immediate supervisor for a performance evaluation and received regular feedback from colleagues on how well they were doing their job.[9] Site visits were consistent with these data. In seven of the eleven schools visited for the study, deans met annually or biennially with the president to review and discuss their job performance. Some of these meetings were "conversational, informal, and relatively low-key," as one dean put it. In only two instances were deans required to do a self-evaluation in preparation for the meeting. Even deans who had annual, informal evaluations with the president requested that these sessions be supplemented by periodic formal evaluations of their work.

*Formal evaluations* of chief academic officers were conducted in fewer schools and occurred less frequently. In only four of the eleven schools receiving site visits did the dean's evaluation include a questionnaire distributed to the faculty and selected members of other groups. On the survey of theological school deans, 46 percent of respondents reported that faculty participate in their performance review, but it was unclear whether they were consulted informally or polled in a more systematic way. Only 25 percent of deans indicated that they received a written appraisal of their job performance.

As further testimony to the importance of formal evaluation, seven of the eleven deans visited for the study specifically requested that a broad-based formal evaluation be established to give them feedback from senior administrators, faculty, and students. After four years in office, one dean insisted on a formal evaluation that included faculty, staff, and students, as well as colleagues from other theological schools. The dean, in the end, found it "tough, but helpful." Two other deans in their second year in office requested formal evaluation, but only one succeeded in getting an evaluation in place. The dean who succeeded felt strongly that she could not expect faculty to participate in pre-tenure and post-tenure review without herself being evaluated on a regular basis.

Evidence from this research strongly suggests that most deans require and actively seek feedback not only from the president, but from the faculty and other constituents with whom they work. While informal evaluations are most common in theological schools and deans generally regard them as helpful, they are not sufficient. Given the deans' broad responsibilities and close working relationship with various constituent groups, the direct involvement of these groups in the evaluation is necessary to give deans a comprehensive and balanced assessment of their job performance. Without the participation of faculty, students, senior administrators, board members, and possibly church leaders, deans lack appraisal of significant portions of their daily work and the distinctive perspective each of these groups can bring. Such broad-based assessment also tends to correct the bias of a single evaluator and to create a more complete profile of the dean's work.[10]

*Evaluation Criteria.* Effective evaluation is impossible without clear and appropriate criteria for determining job success. Ideally, at the time of hiring, the president and chief academic officer would reach mutual understanding and agreement on the responsibilities of office, expectations for their fulfillment, and standards for performance evaluation. As we have seen, lack of clarity about the dean's role and responsibilities can lead to different, even conflicting expectations of the dean and disagreement about what constitutes effectiveness in the position. To avoid such confusion, some academic officers are not only informed, but consulted, about the criteria used in their evaluation. On the survey, 74 percent of theological school deans indicated they had input in determining the evaluation criteria for their job, a practice most common among deans with seven or more years in office.[11] Somewhat fewer deans, 69 percent, reported that evaluation criteria had been clearly explained to them, orally or in writing.[12] Thus, the majority of chief academic officers were informed of the standards for effective job performance and had input in determining what those standards would be.

In a related survey question, deans were offered a list of evaluation criteria and were asked to indicate their importance to those who evaluate their job performance. The following table lists the nine items (of seventeen total items) that received a mean rating of 3.5 or higher on the rating scale: 4=very important – 1=unimportant.

**Table 9**
**Criteria for Evaluating Chief Academic Officers**
**(Deans' estimate of their importance**
**to those who evaluate their job performance)**

| | Mean Ratings |
|---|---|
| Ability to work well with the faculty | 3.9 |
| Professional integrity (e.g., honesty, fairness) | 3.9 |
| Ability to work well with administrative colleagues | 3.8 |
| Ability to be a team player | 3.7 |
| Sound administrative and managerial skills | 3.7 |
| Capacity for strong leadership | 3.6 |
| Ability to mediate conflict and disagreement | 3.6 |
| Ability to keep things running smoothly | 3.6 |
| Ability to advocate effectively for the academic area | 3.5 |

Several of the items most highly rated focus on the dean's ability to work effectively with colleagues, underscoring the fundamentally relational character of the office and the importance of working collegially. While data analysis revealed little variation among deans in different settings, "working as a team player" was perceived as "very important" by 76 percent of deans in freestanding seminaries, compared to 45 percent of deans in university-related schools.[13] Also significant in this listing is the expectation that deans not only manage the academic area and keep things running smoothly but that they exercise leadership and advocate effectively for the academic area. These results indicate that most theological school deans are aware that leadership is an expectation of their position and an important criterion for determining their administrative effectiveness.[14]

*The Role of the Faculty and Other Constituents.* The president, as immediate supervisor of the chief academic officer, is responsible for organizing and conducting the performance evaluation. As with hiring, presidents generally determine the type of evaluation to be used and how inclusive the process will be. While there is no single model of evaluation appropriate to deans in all settings, findings of this study suggest that a process that fosters broad constituent participation generally tends to be most satisfying and helpful to deans, in part because it takes into account the scope of their work and affords appraisal of its multiple dimensions. A process that solicits direct feedback from various constituents most adequately reflects the range and complexity of the dean's role. Presidents who periodically utilize an inclusive evaluation process signal to the senior administrators, faculty, board members, and other participants that their perspectives are valued and their input concerning the academic leadership of the institution truly matters.[15]

As the dean's primary constituency, faculty play a critical role in evaluating the dean's work. Even presidents who conduct informal evaluations are remiss if they fail to elicit the appraisal of the faculty. In a formal process, selected faculty may serve as members of the evaluation committee or may participate in personal interviews or focus groups, whereas all faculty usually are polled through a brief questionnaire. Despite the importance of faculty assessment, only 46 percent of theological school deans surveyed indicated that faculty participated in their performance evaluation. However, 79 percent of deans agreed with the statement, "The continued appointment of the academic dean should be subject to faculty review." Theological school faculty, responding to this statement in a separate survey, concurred.[16] Although the majority of deans favor the active participation of faculty in their performance evaluations, the actual practices of theological schools are lagging in this regard.

While faculty appraisal is an important component of the dean's evaluation and a factor in the dean's reappointment, faculty rarely decide on the dean's continuation in office. Only 21 percent of deans reported their reappointment was determined by vote of the faculty.[17] While presidents may consult faculty and other constituents prior to the dean's reappointment, the final decision usually rests with the president.

In summary, performance evaluation of administrators, as Seldin suggests, must be "firmly rooted in the traditions, purposes, and academic culture" of the institution.[18] Evidence from this research shows that, within theological schools, evaluation of chief academic officers tends to be informal, if conducted at all. Several of the deans interviewed strongly indicated the necessity of periodic formal evaluation that would solicit input from various constituent groups and provide a balanced, comprehensive assessment of their work.

Clearly, institutional leadership is required to address this need. Board members, presidents, and senior administrators must recognize the multiple benefits of evaluation both for individuals and their institutions and must work cooperatively to develop reliable and appropriate methods of assessment at various levels of the organization. Evaluation is most effective not when it is hastily developed to meet a crisis, but when it becomes a regular and ongoing part of institutional life. Evaluation is the basic component of a system of institutional support that identifies the strengths, needs, challenges, and satisfactions of individual members and, through professional development, seeks to address them. Performance evaluation and professional development go hand in hand. Both have the potential to promote the growth and vitality of individuals and, in doing so, to strengthen the community as a whole.

## Professional Development

Professional development in theological schools reflects the general trend in higher education. As Madeleine Green observes, "The academy has been quicker to recognize the need to nurture faculty vitality than to foster the continued growth of its administrators."[19] Theological school deans in this study share that perception: only 40 percent of deans surveyed believe their schools provided adequately for the professional development of administrators, whereas 69 percent consider provisions for faculty development adequate.[20] Further, the deans' dissatisfaction with institutional support for administrative development is curiously at odds with their reports that significant development opportunities are available. Making sense of this apparent contradiction is an aim of this discussion.

We begin with an overview of the professional development opportunities available to theological school deans and their assessment of their importance. The questions is: What does it take for these opportunities to become effective means of professional growth and renewal? If administrative development is viewed not as an isolated set of programs and activities but as an integral part of the larger fabric of organizational and individual life, then other institutional practices, including evaluation, are required for them to be truly beneficial. Consideration of these practices sheds light on our initial paradox and shows what is necessary to utilize existing opportunities effectively. Our discussion of various resources for professional development leads to a holistic model that urges attention not only to the acquisition of administrative competencies but also to personal development and the quality of intellectual and spiritual life. The chapter concludes with recommendations on practical strategies for the development and renewal of academic leaders.

### *Development Programs in Theological Schools*

Chief academic officers were asked on the survey to identify the professional development opportunities provided by their institutions, whether or not they personally took advantage of them. The development activities listed were of three basic types: those that support travel and participation in off-campus programs for professional enrichment, those that provide time through sabbaticals and leaves to do scholarly work, and professional consultations. The table below shows the percentage of theological school deans who have support from their schools for these activities.

**Table 10**
**Professional Development Opportunities Available to Theological School Deans**

| % of Deans with Opportunities Available | |
|---|---|
| 88% | Travel to conferences and workshops in my academic discipline |
| 88% | Travel to conferences and workshops in theological education or administration |
| 79% | A sabbatical (at least once every seven years) |
| 75% | Opportunities for consulting outside the institution |
| 63% | Support for seminars and training sessions to update and strengthen my administrative skills |
| 48% | Regular study time during the academic year |
| 24% | Short-term leaves for professional reading, writing, scholarship |

Survey data shows that more than three-quarters of all respondents received support for travel to conferences and workshops in their academic fields and in theological education and regular sabbaticals, and nearly two-thirds were supported to attend seminars for administrative development. Data analysis reveals that support for seminars to update and strengthen administrative skills was more available to deans in freestanding seminaries than in university-related schools, and consulting opportunities were more available to women deans than to men.[21] In general, the majority of theological schools afford their academic officers many of the traditional forms of professional development support.

In a related question, deans were asked to rate the importance of each of these opportunities to their own professional growth and development. The following table lists items in the order of their importance to deans. Ratings scale: 4=very important – 1=unimportant.

**Table 11**
**Importance of Opportunities to Professional Growth and Development**

| Mean Rating | |
|---|---|
| 3.7 | A sabbatical (at least once every seven years) |
| 3.6 | Travel to conferences and workshops in my academic discipline |
| 3.6 | Regular study time during the academic year |
| 3.5 | Travel to conferences and workshops in theological education or administration |
| 3.2 | Short-term leaves for professional reading, writing, scholarship |
| 3.1 | Support for seminars and training sessions to update and strengthen my administrative skills |
| 2.9 | Opportunities for consulting outside the institution |

When Tables 10 and 11 are compared, over 60 percent of survey respondents indicated their institutions support the professional development activities they consider important. Among the four items that the deans judged "very important" (3.5–4.0), only "regular study time during the academic year" was not widely available. Short-term leaves for scholarly work, rated "somewhat important" (3.2), were available to only 24 percent of respondents.[22] Analysis further showed that deans who had the opportunities available were more likely to consider them important, whereas deans who did not have opportunities available tended to rate them lower in importance.

Also noteworthy is the fact that several of the most highly rated development opportunities relate to the dean's academic and scholarly life, rather than to specifically administrative concerns.[23] As a seminary president explained, "The lack of attention to scholarship can be a source of tension for a dean. The previous dean left the position because if he did another term, he'd be totally out of touch with his field." Whether motivated by institutional requirements, professional necessity, or personal enrichment, many deans seek to remain active as scholars throughout the period of their administrative service. Site visit interviews revealed that deans who had regular study time or short-term leaves for scholarly work usually made specific, formal arrangements for these activities as part of their contract. If such time was not prearranged and protected at the outset, the press of administrative duties made it difficult, if not impossible, to capture once the year was underway. These provisions were especially important to deans who sought to maintain some level of scholarly productivity during their administrative tenure. Thus, support for scholarly work can be an important source of administrative development.

This largely favorable picture of the professional development opportunities available to academic officers is curiously at odds with the finding that over half the deans surveyed disagreed with the statement, "My institution provides adequately for the professional development of administrators." While this judgment is partially explained by respondents whose schools either lack or offer minimal support for development, it also suggests that the availability of such opportunities does not, in itself, satisfy an individual's professional development needs. What, then, are the factors that contribute to successful professional development for academic administrators? How can the existing opportunities for learning, growth, and revitalization that deans consider important to their work be utilized more effectively?

### *Elements of Effective Professional Development*

Research shows that professional development is most effective when explicitly linked to institutional mission and goals and to the distinctive needs of individual administrators.[24] Even with financial resources and the best of intentions, development activities may have little long-term impact unless the following conditions are met: 1) individual needs are clearly defined at the time of hiring and on an ongoing basis; 2) professional development is supported by other institutional practices; and 3) development needs are addressed in a timely manner with activities tailored to the individual, the requirements of the position, and the goals of the institution. These fundamental principles focus not on the development opportunities themselves but on the conditions of their utilization. They describe institutional practices that encourage a planned, rather than an ad hoc, approach to professional development. Meeting these conditions ultimately determines the value and benefit of development efforts.

*Identifying Professional Development Needs.* Effective professional development begins at the time of hiring and occurs continuously throughout one's professional life. While the needs of new and experienced deans may differ and while the requirements of particular positions and institutions vary, professional development remains essential to the growth and renewal of individual administrators. Identifying the needs of individuals at various stages of their administrative service is the first and most important step in planning to address those needs.

*New Deans.* Professional development planning is especially critical for new deans. Research findings on the career paths of chief academic officers in theological schools shed considerable light on their development needs during their first years in office. As noted previously, 65 percent of deans come to their positions directly from the faculty. Although 44 percent have had some previous administrative experience, only 11 percent have served as academic officers. While deans readily acknowledge that faculty experience is indispensable to their administrative work, they also recognize that the job requires managerial and leadership skills for which they have little or no formal training and for which they may not be well prepared.

Despite the fact that many theological school deans accepted their positions because "they felt they had the skills," 40 percent found "that the job differed a great deal from what they expected, and there was much they did not anticipate."[25] Once in office, deans generally found they needed to acquire organizational and time-management skills, broader and more detailed knowledge of academic policy and governance procedures, and special training in areas such as accreditation, personnel matters, and finances. When deans were asked during site visit interviews what would have been most helpful to them during their first years in office, all mentioned training in specific areas where they lacked experience and skills.

At the outset, presidents, who are responsible for hiring deans and overseeing their work, are uniquely positioned to know the dean's background, preparation, and aptitude for administration and to understand the specific requirements of the job. Early in the dean's first year, the president and dean should identify the specific areas where additional preparation and skills are needed and then develop a plan to access resources on and off campus to begin to address those needs. The president also has knowledge of institutional planning and priorities and can anticipate what will be needed in the future. As G. Melvin Hipps observes, it is impossible to discuss "the development of faculty and administrators until it has been determined *what they are being developed to do.*"[26] Presidents can bring the broader institutional perspective to the discussion of individual professional development.

This assessment of needs in consultation with the president or supervisor gives new deans assurance of concern and support for their growth in office and can begin to establish a pattern of regular discussion of their professional development. While annual performance reviews and periodic formal evaluation are needed to identify needs more specifically, early and ongoing conversations about the requirements of the job and the skills needed to meet them are essential. Valuable time is lost if presidents wait a year or more to assess the dean's needs and to plan effective ways to address them.

Some presidents in the study offered their deans financial support for professional development but left it to them to define their own needs. As one president stated during a site visit interview, "There are sufficient funds for professional development, and the dean has carte blanche in selecting professional development options for himself." This approach assumes that the dean has a clear sense of what the job entails, what resources are available, and which of them would be most helpful. These judgments may be especially difficult early in the dean's term, and time and money may be poorly invested without adequate consultation and efforts to locate development opportunities appropriate to individual and institutional needs.

*Experienced Deans.* As research in adult development amply demonstrates, the need for professional growth and enrichment does not end with the mastery of basic knowledge and skills; it simply changes with different stages of one's professional life.[27] Even experienced administrators find that developing leadership skills is an ongoing process, and new managerial skills may be needed as job requirements change. Some deans may be asked to take on additional administrative responsibilities as their presidents devote more time to external constituents and resource development. When a school experiences low enrollment and economic hardship, the dean may be expected to have detailed knowledge of institutional finances and to participate in fundraising activities. In response to such organizational changes, academic officers may be called upon to acquire administrative expertise in a broader range of areas. However, even in the absence of dramatic changes in the job, most deans experience the need to update their knowledge, to sharpen their skills, and to seek revitalization and renewal.

To gain perspective on the professional development needs of theological school deans, the survey asked them to indicate areas in which they felt most prepared and least prepared for their work. Not surprisingly, deans reported they felt "most prepared and effective" in the areas of curriculum and academic programs, and academic priorities and planning, both of which are closely associated with faculty experience. They felt "least prepared" in areas such as fundraising, academic budgets, and faculty development, which are more managerial in nature and less likely to be part of faculty work.[28]

Further, the survey asked deans to identify those areas in which they would like to receive additional preparation and training. The following table lists the top six areas and the percentage of survey respondents with an interest in each. Except for fundraising, all are areas in which academic officers have the primary administrative responsibility at their institutions.

**Table 12**
**Professional Development Needs of Theological School Deans**

| % of Deans | |
|---|---|
| 42% | Faculty development |
| 32% | Fundraising for academic programs |
| 32% | Faculty evaluation |
| 32% | Academic budgets |
| 28% | Academic priorities and planning |
| 20% | Preparing for accreditation |

These data show that approximately one-third of deans would like further training in several areas of their administrative responsibility. These responses were quite consistent for academic officers from different types and sizes of schools. However, deans in their first three years of service identified the largest number of areas where they need further preparation and training. Although only 10 percent of all respondents had responsibility for "fundraising for academic programs," 32 percent would like further training in this area. Fundraising clearly is a significant interest for deans, and this finding may anticipate their increasing involvement in this area.

While this profile of theological school deans undoubtedly is helpful in planning professional development conferences and workshops, guiding individual deans to the appropriate offerings is a more complex task. Administrative development depends for its effectiveness on the regular conduct and coordination of other institutional practices.

*Related Institutional Practices.* As we have seen, the chief executive officer responsible for hiring and supervising the chief academic officer has the primary responsibility for initiating discussion of the responsibilities of office and the individual's capacity to meet them. At the time of the initial appointment and throughout the dean's tenure, the president has numerous opportunities to address these issues with the dean and to assist in planning for the dean's professional development. The president's active and continuing interest in the welfare of the dean is critical. Unless presidents encourage their deans to reflect on the challenges of the job and support the dean's efforts to develop administrative skills, individuals may lack the incentive or the guidance needed to do so. Presidents who explicitly attend to the professional growth and well-being of their deans signal the importance of their administrative work and provide an indispensable form of mentoring and pastoral care.

Beyond these informal methods of assessing needs and attending to professional development, periodic formal evaluation of the dean's job performance can give specificity and dimension to professional development planning. As we have seen, an evaluation of the dean's work with broad constituent participation affords insight to multiple dimensions of the job from persons most directly acquainted with them. Such broad-based assessment provides a fuller, clearer picture of the dean's strengths and areas where additional skills and development are needed. This information can assist deans in focusing their professional development efforts.

The evaluation and professional development literature also suggests that administrators develop "growth contracts" to link defined needs to specific, practical strategies for addressing them. A fully developed growth contract includes the following:

> [A growth contract] is a detailed written plan of future progress, prepared by the administrator [e.g., the dean] and approved by the supervisor, that contains a description of the administrator's present duties and responsibilities, a self-assessment, a succinct enumeration of performance goals and a timetable for their achievement, a learning and development scheme linked to each goal, a discussion of the means of measuring each goal's achievement, and an enumeration of budgetary and other needed support.[29]

A growth contract formalizes professional development planning and insures coordination among its various stages of assessing needs, setting goals, locating development opportunities, and estimating the financial and other forms of support they require. While this general formula for growth contracts may be adapted for use in particular settings, the model is a sound and useful one. Growth contracts are a means of translating the ongoing discussion of development needs into concrete and specific plans, which are linked to the requirements of the job and undertaken in consultation with the president.[30]

Another important component of professional development is reward for administrators who strengthen their job performance and meet their specified goals. Unlike faculty whose professional growth typically is recognized through promotion and tenure, administrators have few, if any, formal means of acknowledging their progress. As Seldin observes, "If administrators are denied reward after improving their skills, they will tend to lose interest in the development program."[31] Whether rewards take the form of a salary increase, time from routine tasks to pursue other interests, or recognition within the seminary community, such rewards tend to acknowledge the administrator's effort to improve and to fulfill or exceed job expectations. Rewards, in whatever form, offer institutional recognition of these accomplishments and encourage continued efforts for professional growth.

Presidents play a significant role in making evaluation and professional development a priority, both in personal dealings with individual administrators and through other institutional policies and practices. Presidential leadership is critical to establishing effective, consistent evaluation procedures and to dedicating the necessary time and resources to the development, renewal, and recognition of academic administrators.

*The Timing and Appropriateness of Development Activities.* Since needs change as individuals and circumstances change, ongoing and regular needs assessment is essential if professional development is to be timely, appropriate, and ultimately beneficial. Research nationally on administrative development confirms the importance of selecting the right program at the right time. As Sharon McDade states,

> There is both a right time and a wrong time for certain types of professional development. The benefits of a program can be completely lost if the administrator is not in the right career and experience stage. . . . Professional development experiences should be chosen not only for their content but for the match of program goals and format to the maturation stage of the administrator.[32]

New deans, whose familiarity with available resources may be somewhat limited, may find it particularly difficult to select the programs and activities best suited to their job requirements and professional needs. Several deans who had attended management workshops at later stages of their deanships wished they could have had those opportunities during the first years when the learning curve was steep and help was most needed. Formal and informal evaluations and consultations with the president, peer administrators, and other colleagues help to gauge the type of development activities most appropriate to the individual at a particular time and place.

Our initial puzzlement that deans with significant opportunities available nonetheless considered administrative development inadequate at their institutions is largely resolved. The availability of financial support for conferences, seminars, and sabbaticals, while essential, is not enough. Choosing the right activities at the right time requires an intentional and regular process of assessing individual and institutional needs. Through collegial consultations, performance evaluation, and professional development planning, deans come to understand their needs and to devise specific and appropriate ways to address them. In the absence of these institutional practices and the guidance they provide, academic officers may find their professional development less than satisfactory, and theological schools may receive little payback for their investment.

Once development needs are identified, administrators still face the challenge of finding programs and opportunities that will address them effectively. Below is a brief guide to national resources for academic administrators and other strategies for personal and professional renewal recommended by theological school deans.

### *Resources and Development Strategies for Theological School Deans*

Given the distinctiveness of individual administrators and their institutions, no one model of professional development fits all theological schools or all chief academic officers. From a range of options, administrators must select the development activities that best meet their needs and are feasible in terms of available time and funding. Selected development opportunities for academic officers are discussed below under the following headings: 1) national resources for academic administrators; 2) peer and mentor relationships; and 3) forms of personal renewal. Along with a brief description of these activities is a discussion of their potential benefit to theological school deans.

*National Resources for Academic Administrators.* Foremost among traditional development opportunities are conferences, workshops, seminars, and institutes. Usually these events are sponsored by national organizations and are designed to convene administrators from various schools who have similar needs and interests. Appendix C offers a selected list of professional development programs of particular interest to chief academic officers. They are organized in three basic categories: those sponsored by the Association of Theological Schools in the United States and Canada (ATS) for theological school deans and their colleagues; those for academic officers in higher education generally; and those for leadership development of senior administrators and others related to higher education. While this list describes only a few of the many available resources, it serves to indicate the basic content and format characteristic of administrative development programs.[33]

Since any given program can have "diverse effects for different people at distinct points in their lives," the immediate and long-term gains from development programs are difficult to evaluate.[34] What is most critical, however, is that individuals clearly identify the specific skills or knowledge they desire and then research available programs to find one that best matches their needs. As researchers note, "Although there is no real substitute for on-the-job learning, professional development programs provide an excellent alternative and 'can be far more efficient in delivering a concentrated dose of needed information and skills.'"[35] Those seeking the acquisition of specific management skills or sustained attention to leadership development may be well served by the longer, more intensive summer institutes or a workshop focused on a specific area of interest. Others wishing to update their knowledge on a variety of topics may prefer national conferences that explore a broad array of issues. Most important is to select the development opportunity that, in format and content, will be responsive to one's professional needs.

Among the benefits of joining colleagues from other institutions to address issues of common interest are the obvious ones: making contacts and developing networks with peers, updating one's knowledge, acquiring new ideas and skills, and gaining fresh perspective on one's job and institution. Research shows that participants who choose programs that are directly applicable to their jobs and are able to utilize what they have learned immediately or in the near future reap the greatest benefit.[36] Workshops and conferences that encourage participation by institutional teams enable members to acquire a common frame of reference and frequently to develop projects on which they continue to work after they return to campus. Even when administrators attend workshops alone, benefits can be extended by a follow-up report to colleagues on the valuable and applicable content of the program. This combination of careful program selection and feedback to the institution upon return tends to maximize the usefulness of development programs.[37]

*Peer and Mentor Relationships.* Chief academic officers interviewed for the study cited contact with administrative peers from other theological schools as one of the most important and necessary forms of professional development. Deans find that meeting with colleagues enables them to discuss issues of common concern, to share experiences, and to learn from others who face similar challenges. One dean, who had served two years at a rural seminary, wondered if the role as she conceived it was characteristic of "what deans do." Since chief academic officers tend to be one-of-a-kind on their campuses, it may be difficult to find anyone who has firsthand knowledge of the job. As deans settle into their positions, many find it increasingly necessary to establish a wider network of administrative colleagues and to have regular contact with other theological school deans.

One of the principal means by which academic officers make contact with their peers is through national conferences and workshops, such as those discussed above. Research on professional development shows that ". . . participants in professional development programs attended by administrators of similar types, levels, and responsibilities tend to develop and then maintain stronger networks for trading information, providing support, serving as another source of endorsements for jobs, and supplying professional assistance."[38] Contact with other theological school deans, particularly from similar types of institutions, is most likely to foster ongoing professional relationships. While many of the programs for deans from a cross section of higher education institutions may be useful for skill development, comparable programs for theological school deans have the added benefit of convening peers with a broader range of common experiences and interests. The Association of Theological Schools is exploring the possibility of establishing a permanent professional organization for deans to address this need. Deans who had served on ATS accrediting teams also found the experience valuable for the comprehensive and in-depth perspective it gave on other theological schools.

Several deans interviewed for the study further suggested that travel to another theological school to work with the dean or an extended visit from the dean of another school to their campus would be most beneficial. Such visits by a trusted and respected colleague afford an opportunity to elicit advice and counsel and to gain an outside view of one's own situation. Visits of at least two days' duration enable an in-depth exploration of issues and afford familiarity with the organizational culture in which the issues arise. A visit by an experienced colleague or an opportunity to observe another dean at work can have the advantage of addressing one's situation and needs in a direct and personal way. The cost of visits is relatively modest, and the benefits may be considerable. In addition to their practical value, such visits reduce the isolation of individual deans and strengthen their professional ties with their colleagues in the theological education community. As one dean suggested, chief academic officers, as members of this community, have an obligation to provide this support and counsel to one another.

Among the many collegial relationships of deans are those described in the literature as mentor relationships. In *Leaders for a New Era: Strategies for Higher Education,* Madeleine Green observes that "mentoring relationships can take on many different forms—from an intense personal relationship between a senior person and a junior one, in which the mentor has an important influence on the career of the protégé, to a less intimate mentoring model in which the mentor serves as a coach, sponsor, or role model."[39] While "mentor-protégé relationships are frequently spontaneous and informal rather than deliberate parts of a development program," at least one national association has a voluntary program that pairs new deans with more experienced colleagues, and another, the ACE Fellows Program, formally designates a mentor for each participant in the year-long administrative internship program.[40] Because the success of mentor relationships depends in large part on the chemistry between the parties, results can be highly variable, and relationships that develop spontaneously are often most effective.

Mentor-protégé relationships provide the new administrator with opportunities for learning and feedback, guidance in career planning, greater visibility, and increased contact with colleagues in the mentor's network.[41] While mentors may be found among colleagues in other theological schools, they just as readily may be present within one's own institution among faculty or administrative colleagues, particularly the president/rector. Deans in the study who had ready access to the president and who were explicitly encouraged to ask questions and confide on difficult matters felt less isolated and more supported in their role. Survey findings further showed that 82 percent of theological school deans felt they were able to discuss their needs and plans with their supervisor. By virtue of their office, presidents are well positioned to serve a mentor role. For the academic dean, the mentor-protégé relationship may be a significant and highly effective source of professional development.

*Forms of Personal Renewal.* In an essay entitled "Academic Administration as an Inner Journey," Gordon T. Smith notes that beyond the competencies and skills required of deans, there is an inner journey that may be far more crucial to their long-term effectiveness. According to Smith, this inner journey "involves my emotional development, my journey as a person of prayer, the integrity of my working relationships, and the quality of my intimate relationships."[42] Several deans interviewed during site visits spoke, in particular, of the need to remain vital intellectually and spiritually and to maintain a balance between their personal and professional lives. Deans felt that taking time to pursue scholarly interests and to be involved in practices that nurture them spiritually were critical to their effectiveness as administrators. As Smith succinctly states, "[P]ersonal development is a professional issue."[43]

This holistic view that personal and professional development are inextricably linked has some important, practical consequences for administrative development. In this view, professional development is not exclusively a matter of acquiring job-related competencies and skills (although this is critical), but it also must support activities that foster the growth and renewal of the whole person. As previously noted, many theological school deans, who were actively engaged in scholarship and teaching prior to taking on their administrative role, find they are personally energized by maintaining these activities at some level. This explains, in part, why 93 percent of deans teach, even though only 38 percent are required to do so. When academic officers rated the importance of professional development opportunities, they gave the highest ranking to activities, such as sabbaticals and professional meetings, that support their scholarly work.[44] (See Table 11.) In the same rating, the two items that focus specifically on developing administrative skills were ranked fourth and sixth (out of seven) in order of importance. Given the availability of financial support to travel to conferences or to dedicate time to special projects, many deans choose to pursue their academic rather than administrative interests. These findings indicate that most deans seek opportunities to remain vital academically and consider such activities important to their growth and development.

Several academic officers interviewed for the study also affirmed the necessity of attending to their spiritual development. When one dean with twelve years in office was asked what he would include in a development program for long-term deans, he replied: "training in management skills and communication, *time with an academic discipline, work on spirituality and one's own soul,* and contact with administrators in higher education." (Italics mine.) This list recognizes that intellectual and spiritual development are on equal footing with the cultivation of administrative competencies and relationships.

While personal development in its many forms is essential to administrative effectiveness, spiritual development may have the most direct impact on the quality of leadership and one's influence on the academic community. In an essay on the relationship of spirituality and leadership, Parker Palmer discusses the power of a leader

> to project on other people his or her shadow, or his or her light. A leader is a person who has an unusual degree of power to create the conditions under which other people must live and move and have their being, conditions that can either be as illuminating as heaven or as shadowy as hell.[45]

Palmer goes on to identify several "shadows" that positional leaders may unwittingly cast upon their communities: insecurity about their own identity and worth, the view of life as a battleground, "functional atheism" whereby they see themselves as ultimately responsible for everything, fear of chaos, and fear of negative evaluation and failure.[46] In Palmer's view, the consequence of the leaders' inability to deal with their own inner lives is that they create "conditions of real misery for lots and lots of folks and unfulfilled missions for lots and lots of institutions."[47]

Gordon Smith similarly recognizes the deep spiritual roots of effective leadership. Focusing on the role of the chief academic officer, Smith states that "we must come to our work with a clear sense of who we are, what we are called to do within the institution, when and where we can make a difference. . . ." Clarity on such fundamental issues, Smith believes, "only comes from a well-defined and nurtured spiritual center. To achieve this there is no substitute for the regular practice of prayer and solitude, providing the time and space for reflection and contemplation. It is in solitude that our vocations are nurtured and clarified. . . ."[48]

Recent writings on the spirituality of leadership also affirm that it is within and through community that our spiritual life develops and our vocations are nurtured. In the book *Spirit at Work: Discovering the Spirituality in Leadership,* D. Susan Wisely and Elizabeth M. Lynn discuss the power of community reflection and conversation to discover the larger meaning and purpose of our own work.[49] While chief academic officers, as positional leaders, "can create occasions for that process of reflection, conversation, and renewed action," it is also as participants in that process that they make connections with colleagues and together discover the deep spiritual sources of their collective work.[50] Guided conversation and prayer within a theological school community can enable individual members, including chief academic officers, to understand their distinctive vocations and to see them as inseparable parts of a larger whole. The spirit is nurtured both in solitude and in community.

These reflections on the importance of spiritual development for academic leaders urge us to take a broad, inclusive view of professional development. Who our leaders *are* psychologically, intellectually, and spiritually is critical to what our leaders *do* administratively. Theological schools seeking to support the professional development of their academic officers and other institutional leaders must be intentional about their support of personal development as well. Theological schools whose aim is to foster the personal, intellectual, and spiritual formation of students are challenged to take the same holistic view of those who serve that mission as teachers, scholars, managers, and leaders.

## Conclusion

The preceding discussion of the evaluation and professional development of chief academic officers in theological schools includes principles of effective practice generally and raises several issues for further consideration:

- Professional development relies upon both formal and informal evaluation to identify areas where skill development, growth, and revitalization are needed. Theological school deans place high value on formal evaluation of their job performance as a means of getting reliable and constructive feedback from various constituent groups and as a guide to planning for their professional development. Theological schools lacking formal evaluation processes should consider the multiple benefits of evaluation for individual administrators and their institutions.
- The professional development needs of academic officers, like those of their administrative and faculty colleagues, vary with the aptitudes and interests of individuals, the specific requirements of their positions, and the distinctive challenges facing their institutions. Defining individual needs within the organizational context is the critical first step in professional development.
- The availability of institutional funds to support development activities is a necessary, but not sufficient, condition for effective professional development. Also essential is a supportive framework of institutional

practices that afford deans regular opportunities to assess their needs and to plan appropriate and timely ways to address them.

- There are many resources nationally for academic administrators that focus on the acquisition of managerial skills and leadership development. Research shows that such programs tend to be most beneficial when selected for their applicability to job requirements and to the specific needs of the individual. Conferences and workshops also foster contact with colleagues from other institutions, and relationships are most readily sustained among those who hold similar positions in similar types of institutions.
- Professional development is most effective when it is holistic in approach, recognizing the interdependence of the individual's personal and professional life. Theological school deans noted particularly the importance of intellectual and spiritual development to the quality and vitality of their administrative work. These findings suggest a multifaceted approach to professional development that sees individual needs in the context of organizational life and recognizes administrative development as inseparable from personal growth.

This discussion of administrative evaluation and development concludes on a note of urgency. The Study of Chief Academic Officers has revealed that the majority of deans come to their positions with little or no preparation for their administrative roles and without adequate institutional support for developing the necessary skills once in office. At the same time, there is widespread awareness among theological educators that the challenges facing their schools are not diminishing with time but becoming more daunting and complex. How theological schools meet those challenges will depend in large part on the strength of their leadership. The task of acquiring managerial skills and the qualities of mind and spirit that effective leadership requires should not be left to individual discretion or to chance. The schools themselves—through the denominations, universities, and governing boards that empower them—must encourage and support the continuous development of those who are called to lead.

## Notes

[1] Peter Seldin, *Evaluating and Developing Administrative Performance. A Practical Guide for Academic Leaders* (San Francisco: Jossey-Bass, 1988), 9.

[2] Seldin, 157. See also Charles F. Fisher, "The Evaluation and Development of College and University Administrators," in *Administrative Development in Higher Education,* Vol I, *The State of the Art,* John A. Shtogren, ed. (Richmond, VA: Higher Education Leadership and Management Society, 1978), 1–19. For a brief summary of objections to linking evaluation and professional development, see Robert C. Nordvall, *Evaluation and Development of Administrators.* ASHE-ERIC Higher Education Research Report No. 6 (Washington, DC: American Association for Higher Education, 1979), 6–7.

[3] On the survey, the group of deans that most strongly disagreed with the statement, "I think that performance evaluation for administrators is a waste of time," were those who had served in their positions 11 years or more. On the scale 4=strongly agree – 1=strongly disagree, the mean ratings of respondents were: 1.3 for deans 0–3 years in office; 1.5 for deans 4–6 years; 1.9 for deans 7–10 years; and 1.1 for deans 11+ years.

[4] Findings of the study concerning professional development were published in a previous monograph: Jeanne P. McLean, *Professional Development for Chief Academic Officers. A Call to Action,* Monograph Series on Academic Leadership, vol. 4 (St. Paul, MN: University of St. Thomas, 1996).

[5] The rationale for administrative evaluation in higher education is compiled from several sources: Madeleine F. Green and Sharon A. McDade, *Investing in Higher Education: A Handbook of Leadership Development* (Washington, DC: American Council on Education, 1991), 189–191; Seldin, 24–27; and Nordvall, 4–6.

[6] Seldin, 33.

[7] *Procedures, Standards, and Criteria for Membership,* Bulletin 42, Part 3 (Pittsburgh, PA: The Association of Theological Schools, 1996), 34–35.

[8] Seldin offers a full discussion of effective and ineffective evaluation techniques and provides samples of evaluation forms. He also recommends the use of outside consultants if there is insufficient expertise within the institution. See Seldin, 40–123. Glen Rasmussen's essay, though somewhat dated, discusses decanal evaluation specifically and suggests basic elements of an evaluation questionnaire. Glen R. Rasmussen, "Evaluating the Academic Dean," in *Developing and Evaluating Administrative Leadership,* Charles F. Fisher, ed. (San Francisco: Jossey-Bass, 1978), 23–40.

[9] Data analysis of deans' responses to the statement, "I meet annually with my immediate supervisor for a performance evaluation," revealed that 19.4 percent of deans in freestanding seminaries disagreed with the statement, compared to only 9.7 percent of deans in university-related schools. Denominational analysis showed that deans in Roman Catholic and mainline Protestant seminaries were more likely to meet with their supervisor for annual performance evaluation than were deans in interdenominational, nondenominational, and other denominational seminaries. On a scale 4=strongly agree –

1=strongly disagree, the mean rating of deans in mainline Protestant schools was 3.3 and in Roman Catholic schools 3.2, compared to other means ranging from 2.6 to 2.9.

In response to the statement, "I get regular feedback from my colleagues on how well I am performing my job," deans in freestanding schools (mean 2.7) more strongly agreed than did deans in university-related schools (mean 2.3), and deans 0–3 years in office (mean 2.8) received feedback more regularly than deans serving 4 years or more (means 2.3 to 2.5).

[10] Green and McDade, 192, and Seldin, 32–33, consider the reliance on multiple sources characteristic of successful administrative evaluations.

[11] In response to the statement, "I have input in determining the evaluation criteria for my job," the deans' responses differed according to their length of service. Using the scale 4=strongly agree – 1=strongly disagree, mean ratings were highest for long-term deans: 7–10 years in office (3.5), 11+ years in office (3.4), 4–6 years in office (3.2), and 0–3 years in office (3.0).

[12] Using the rating scale 4=strongly agree – 1= strongly disagree, deans 4–6 years in office had the highest mean rating (3.3) on the statement, "The criteria on which I am evaluated have been clearly explained to me orally or in writing." Other deans had a range of mean ratings from 2.8 to 3.0.

[13] Mean ratings on "ability to be a team player" were 3.7 for deans in freestanding seminaries and 3.4 for deans in university-related schools.

[14] Other items not listed in Table 9 were rated as follows: decisiveness (3.4); capacity for creative, independent thinking (3.3); ability to take risks, stimulate change (3.2); reputation for teaching (3.1); ability to relate well with church and civic communities (3.0); reputation for scholarship (2.9); and ability to raise funds (1.8).

[15] To maintain the fairness and integrity of the evaluation process, evaluation instruments should distinguish between constituents who know of the dean's work directly and those who know it only indirectly. Since the purpose of formal evaluation is to get beyond hearsay and innuendo to an appraisal of administrative performance, evaluators with firsthand knowledge of the dean's work are preferable.

[16] A comparison of results on the survey for the Study of Chief Academic Officers and the 1993 survey of theological school faculties conducted by the Auburn Center shows that deans and faculty agree that "the continued appointment of the academic dean should be subject to faculty review." Using the scale 4=strongly agree – 1=strongly disagree, the mean rating of deans (3.17) and of faculty (3.16) were virtually the same.

[17] Data analysis showed no statistically significant differences on this point based on type, size, or denominational affiliation.

[18] Seldin, 31. Additional guidelines for successful evaluation programs can be found in Seldin, 29–33, and Green and McDade, 191–194.

[19] Madeleine F. Green, ed., *Leaders for a New Era: Strategies for Higher Education* (New York: American Council on Education and Macmillan Publishing Company, 1988; reprint, Phoenix, AZ: American Council on Education and Oryx Press, 1996), 26.

[20] Using the scale 4=strongly agree – 1=strongly disagree, the mean ratings of survey respondents were as follows: "My institution provides adequately for the professional

development of faculty" (mean 2.8), and "My institution provides adequately for the professional development of administrators" (mean 2.4).

Respondents to the Auburn Center survey of theological school faculty had a similar appraisal of faculty development efforts. The statement, "The school in which I teach provides adequately for faculty development," received a mean rating of 2.8.

A recent study of theological school presidents also observed: "In general, theological schools have not established general provisions for the professional development of executive leadership. Only 34% of the presidents report that their institutions make budgetary provisions for their professional development. . . ." Leon Pacala, "The Presidential Experience in Theological Education. A Study in Executive Leadership," *Theological Education* 29, no. 1 (Autumn 1992), 33.

[21] Support for seminars to update and strengthen administrative skills was available to 72 percent of deans in freestanding schools and to 50 percent of deans in university-related schools. Consulting opportunities were available to all women deans and to 72 percent of men deans.

[22] Analysis further showed that support for seminars to update and strengthen administrative skills was least important to deans 7–10 years in office. Using the scale 4=very important – 1=unimportant, their mean rating was 2.5, compared to mean ratings of 3.0 to 3.2 by other deans. Sabbaticals were least important to deans in Roman Catholic seminaries, whose mean rating was 3.4, compared to ratings of 3.7 and 3.8 by deans of other denominations.

[23] Evidence from site visits suggests that deans usually are awarded sabbaticals due to their faculty status and for the purpose of doing scholarly work. Sabbaticals for administrators to address their professional needs as administrators are relatively rare.

[24] Green and McDade, 14–17, 102–103.

[25] Karen M. Ristau, *Challenges of Academic Administration: Rewards and Stresses in the Role of the Chief Academic Officer,* Monograph Series on Academic Leadership, vol. 2 (St. Paul, MN: University of St. Thomas, 1996), 3. On the deans' survey, respondents were asked to rate several factors in terms of their importance in deciding to accept their position. Using the scale 4=very important – 1=unimportant, the statement, "I felt I had the skills," received a mean rating of 3.2 or "somewhat important."

[26] G. Melvin Hipps, "Faculty and Administrator Development," in *New Directions for Institutional Research: Effective Planned Change Strategies,* no. 33, ed. G. Hipps (San Francisco: Jossey-Bass, 1982), 52.

[27] Sharon A. McDade, *Higher Education Leadership: Enhancing Skills through Professional Development Programs,* ASHE-ERIC Higher Education Report No. 5 (Washington, DC: Association for the Study of Higher Education, 1987), 72–75. McDade provides an able summary of the stages of adult development as they apply to an administrative career.

[28] In response to the question, "In which area do you feel most prepared and effective?" 40 percent of survey respondents cited curriculum and academic programs and 16 percent cited academic priorities and planning. When asked "In which area do you feel least prepared?" 39 percent cited fundraising, 14 percent academic budgets, and 10 percent faculty development. In responding to both of these questions, fewer than 10 percent of deans identified other areas of responsibility.

Data analysis revealed that a higher percentage of deans in university-related schools (12 percent) felt least prepared in the area of faculty development, compared to 5 percent of deans in freestanding seminaries. However, a higher percentage of deans in freestanding schools (26 percent) felt least prepared in the area of spiritual formation, compared to 3 percent of university deans.

[29] Seldin, 160.

[30] Growth contracts should not be written in stone. During the years a contract is in effect, changes may occur within the institution or with the dean that necessitate modifying particular objectives and plans. Growth contracts generally are working documents that are most useful if updated annually or at appropriate intervals.

[31] Seldin, 160.

[32] McDade, 72.

[33] More complete listings of development programs for academic administrators can be found in the previously cited books by McDade and by Green and McDade.

[34] McDade, 59.

[35] McDade, 68. The statement includes a quotation from Madeleine F. Green, "Discussion Paper: A Framework for Leadership Development," Unpublished (Washington, DC: American Council on Education, 1988), 8.

[36] McDade, 59.

[37] For an overview of professional development programs and discussion of the difficulty of assessing their impact on career advancement see: McDade, 65; and Jack H. Schuster, "Professional Development Programs: Options for Administrators," in *Leaders for a New Era,* Madeleine F. Green, ed., 201–224.

[38] McDade, 61.

[39] Green, 19.

[40] The Council of Independent Colleges at their annual Deans Institute brings together new deans and experienced deans with three or more years of service who volunteer to serve as mentors. At the conference, mentors introduce new deans to colleagues, attend a joint session, and arrange an hour or more of informal conversation on topics identified by the new dean. The deans are encouraged to remain in contact after the conference. The Fellows Program, sponsored by the American Council on Education (ACE), selects approximately thirty fellows annually for year-long internships in which they work closely with presidents and senior officers of colleges and universities to develop their administrative and leadership skills.

[41] Green, 19–20.

[42] Gordon T. Smith, "Academic Administration as an Inner Journey," *Theological Education* 33 (Supplement Autumn 1996), 66.

[43] Smith, 66.

[44] The sabbaticals available to academic officers tend to have the same requirements for a scholarly project as do those available to faculty and typically are granted to deans by virtue of their faculty status. Among the eleven schools visited for the study, only one was in the process of instituting an "administrative sabbatical," which required a scholarly project but differed in being available less frequently than faculty sabbaticals. At another

theological school, the dean was given a two-month leave during the summer to attend a national leadership development program. Sabbaticals for administrators as administrators appear to be relatively rare in theological education.

[45] Parker J. Palmer, "Leading from Within: Out of the Shadow, into the Light," in *Spirit at Work: Discovering the Spirituality in Leadership,* Jay A. Conger and Associates (San Francisco: Jossey-Bass, 1994), 24–25.

[46] Palmer, 32–37.

[47] Palmer, 38.

[48] Smith, 67.

[49] D. Susan Wisely and Elizabeth M. Lynn, "Spirited Connections: Learning to Tap the Spiritual Resources of Our Lives and Work," in *Spirit at Work,* 100–131.

[50] Wisely and Lynn, 124.

# 8 Academic Leadership: The Challenges Ahead

*"We need a vision of what the academic life is all about."*
*Theological school faculty member*

This final chapter turns our attention from the present realities of academic administration to its future challenges. With the work of the chief academic officer fully before us, we return to an issue with which our inquiry began: Given the increasingly important role of chief academic officers, how will theological schools attract and retain persons with the managerial, leadership, and pastoral gifts needed to meet the challenges of the job? How can theological schools improve current rates of turnover in the office and provide continuity and stability in the academic leadership of the schools?

To address these questions, we begin by considering prevailing attitudes toward academic administration within the theological school community. Whether individuals are attracted to administration and whether chief academic officers, once hired, continue to serve may depend heavily on the perceived costs and rewards of administrative work. First, we examine general perceptions of administration as revealed in the survey and interview findings of this research. Then we consider in more detail the deans' own assessments of their administrative experience: why they accepted their positions, what the satisfactions and dissatisfactions of the job have been, and what would influence them to stay in office or to leave. These general attitudes toward administration and the deans' reflections on their experience in office enable us to identify the incentives and disincentives to administrative service and, thereby, to understand the obstacles confronting theological schools in their efforts to secure and retain effective academic leaders.

Evidence of this research reveals two types of challenges facing the theological education community: the first is to change the prevailing attitude toward academic administration from "a job that somebody has to do" to a vocational choice on a par with scholarship and teaching, worthy of the brightest and the best in theological education; the second challenge is to adopt within the schools policies and practices concerning the chief academic officer position that reflect an understanding of its importance and potential. Such changes of attitude and institutional practice were cited by participants in the study as essential to meeting the demand for strong, effective academic leaders for the future. These changes recognize the emergence of a new form of the office and its critical leadership role in theological education.

## Perceptions of Academic Administration

A generally favorable view of academic administration was evident in two separate surveys of theological school deans and faculty.[1] Both groups "somewhat agreed" with the statement, "Administrative service is a respected professional choice at my institution."[2] However, deans and faculty diverged somewhat in their answers to related questions. Deans responded positively to the statement, "I would encourage others I respect to consider administrative service."[3] In contrast, the majority of faculty, while indicating their respect for administration, were not inclined to choose the deanship for themselves. Faculty "somewhat disagreed" with the statement, "At some point in my career, I would seriously consider serving as an academic dean in a theological school."[4] Clearly, individual faculty may reach this conclusion based on their own lack of aptitude and interest in administration and/or as a result of a negative view of administration itself.

These data illustrate what one seminary faculty member referred to as the "love-hate relationship" with administration: "I love others for doing administration but would hate to do it myself." Interviews with faculty suggest that, with few exceptions, those in leadership positions are respected for doing administration, but this respect essentially can be gratitude for their willingness and ability to do a difficult, often thankless job no one else wants to do. Thus, the positive regard for administrators actually may arise from a negative attitude toward administrative work. As one seminary president explained, "People are aware of the responsibilities and respect administration. Administration is seen as a big burden, and a successful dean carries big burdens well." Administration is burdensome, so administrators are respected for taking it on.

Faculty in our study generally expressed ambivalence about academic administration. On the one hand, many viewed the chief academic officer position as "extremely important and challenging," as one faculty member stated, and some considered the opportunity to be "first among equals" or to earn a higher salary appealing. On the other hand, faculty remarked on the loss of personal time, the hectic pace, the amount of paperwork, the number of meetings, and the stress that comes with mediating conflict and dealing with difficult people. As one dean observed, "Faculty say they don't want my job . . . when they perceive me as caught in the middle of administrators and faculty, faculty and students, or faculty and faculty."

Most frequently, however, faculty lamented what they perceived as two inevitable consequences of accepting an administrative position: the reduced time for teaching and the inability to remain current in their scholarship. As one faculty member explained, "The move to administration is a sign of a colleague's competence, a promotion, but it also generates sympathy because it means less time in the classroom. Administration has a martyr quality to it because it requires leaving teaching." Another faculty member found administration "an unappealing job if you take scholarship seriously," and others agreed it would be difficult, if not impossible, to be on the cutting edge of a discipline and to maintain scholarly productivity while serving as an academic administrator. From a faculty perspective, administration requires sacrifice. As a result, one dean observed, some faculty believe "deaning is a sell-out."

Several participants in the study noted that, because the work of administrators and faculty is fundamentally different and requires different aptitudes and skills, faculty often are neither attracted nor well-suited to administration. The faculty work of reading, writing, and teaching, even when peppered with meetings, is essentially private and allows for considerable personal autonomy and flexibility. Administrative work, by contrast, is public, highly interactive, accountable to others, and largely prescribed by the flow of external events.[5] Whereas faculty focus on the pedagogy and scholarship of the theological disciplines, academic officers deal with matters of administrative organization, institutional policy, and decision making. While chief academic officers generally are expected to have faculty experience, to understand the academic life, and in some settings to be accomplished teachers and scholars, they also are expected to have another set of competencies tailored to their administrative tasks.

The nearly infinite list of attributes desirable in a dean, as discussed in preceding chapters, includes managerial, organizational, political, and leadership skills, abilities to work effectively with diverse groups of people, to manage conflict, to empower others, and to bring them together around a common vision. Such attributes, so essential to the deanship, typically play a lesser role in faculty appointments where competence in the discipline, teaching experience, and scholarly productivity figure prominently. Some faculty noted that administration requires personal stamina and toughness, the need to be thick-skinned and to depersonalize issues—abilities that may engender their respect for administrative colleagues as readily as they strengthen their own disinclination to serve.

Only three of the more than 200 persons interviewed during the study felt that differences between faculty and administrators fostered distrust. As one faculty member stated, "Faculty do not know the complexity of top-level jobs and people misinterpret what they don't know. Academic culture breeds a hermeneutic of suspicion." Just as deans without faculty experience are disadvantaged in understanding the demands of teaching, scholarship, and other aspects of faculty life, so those without firsthand experience of the deanship can have difficulty appreciating the complex requirements of the job and the high-level skills it requires. While distrust between faculty and administrators based on these differences is considered by many endemic to higher education, it was rarely observed in this study. This may be due, in large part, to the relatively small size of theological schools, the distinctive character of their academic cultures, and the frequent blend of administrative and faculty duties in individual positions.[6]

In some instances, the religious and cultural values of a school's denomination also may affect attitudes toward administration and toward those aspiring to administrative positions. A senior administrator interviewed during the study explained that, in some church cultures, "those who are professionally ambitious or interested in administration are cut out because they should not be looking for advancement." In this view, a move to administration is considered career advancement, and it would be unseemly to seek it overtly. As an experienced dean has noted, "Sometimes certain faculty members discover that they like being dean—and sometimes they are good at it. But there is no permission to celebrate that gift. . . ."[7] Just as aspiring to leadership positions may be negatively construed as self-promotion and "careerism," so in other settings it may be considered a religious vocation or call as respected and worthy as any other. Clearly, attitudes shape behavior, and how administration is perceived can affect in powerful, but subtle ways the ability of theological schools to attract able and gifted administrators.

## The Deans' Assessment

With their direct experience of the office, chief academic officers give a more richly detailed and balanced assessment of administrative work. While deans frankly acknowledge the challenges, stresses, and sacrifices of the job, they identify more clearly and strongly than their faculty colleagues the satisfactions and rewards of serving as a senior academic officer. In survey responses and site visit interviews, deans reflected on their path to academic administration and appraised the job's satisfactions, dissatisfactions, and significance in their professional lives. They also cited the factors most influential in their personal decisions to stay or to leave their positions.

### *Becoming Dean*

Individuals become theological school deans for reasons as various as these:

> The seminary was in crisis and I became dean by default and pressure.
>
> My move to administration was "accidental" and followed my job as head of a student residence.
>
> I was recruited from the faculty after an unsuccessful search.
>
> I liked administration and was encouraged by colleagues.
>
> After being nominated by the faculty, I declined the position and then the rector persuaded me to accept.
>
> I got pulled into administration because I was organized and could manage.
>
> I was recruited from outside the seminary to block an internal candidate.
>
> The church called, and I wanted to serve.

This sampling of responses from deans interviewed during the study reveals the combination of circumstantial and personal factors that prompted their move to academic administration. While some clearly sought administrative office and felt they were called, others were persuaded, even pressured, by colleagues to accept their positions, and still others arrived by serendipity or dint of circumstance. Few deans entered administration as a result of deliberate planning or intent.

Findings of the survey of theological school deans offer a more complete picture of the factors important to deans in accepting their current positions. Deans were asked to rate the importance of each of the following items, using the rating scale: 4=very important – 1=unimportant. The factors are listed here in order of their importance to deans.

**Table 13**
**Factors Important in Accepting the Chief Academic Officer Position**

| | Mean Rating |
|---|---|
| I was encouraged by denominational and/or academic colleagues. | 3.3 |
| I felt I had the skills to be an effective administrator. | 3.2 |
| I felt a sense of obligation or duty. | 3.2 |
| I wanted to have greater influence on academic and institutional decisions. | 3.1 |
| I was genuinely interested in administration. | 3.1 |
| I wanted to be of greater service to others. | 3.1 |
| I wanted to work at this particular institution. | 3.0 |
| I considered academic administration as part of my religious vocation or calling. | 2.7 |
| I was looking for a new professional challenge. | 2.5 |
| I wanted to advance my career. | 1.8 |
| I was attracted by the higher salary. | 1.6 |

These ratings are informative in a number of ways. The top seven statements rated (3.0 to 3.3) show the importance of external incentives, such as the encouragement of colleagues and a sense of obligation or duty to others, and of personal factors, such as having the confidence and interest to undertake administrative work and the desire to influence institutional decision making and to be of service.[8] Not surprisingly, theological school deans overall rated career advancement and a higher salary "not very important" in their decision to accept their positions. However, deans in larger schools and deans in inter/nondenominational and mainline Protestant seminaries considered the opportunity to work at a particular school and to receive a higher salary more important than did other deans.[9]

Less predictably, theological school deans rated the sense of religious vocation or call relatively less important than obligation or duty and several other factors. One possible explanation, based on site visit evidence, is that some deans come to their positions unexpectedly and for a variety of circumstantial reasons, and, consequently, a developed sense of administrative vocation, at least initially, is unlikely. On this point, deans differed on the basis of gender: a sense of religious vocation or call was more important to women deans than to men, and a sense of obligation or duty was more important to men than to women.[10] Further analysis showed that deans who considered academic administration part of their religious vocation were more likely than other deans to be looking for a new professional challenge and to want to be of greater service to others. Deans who accepted their positions out of obligation or duty were less likely than other deans to be seeking career advancement.

Site visits revealed that some deans, who had not aspired to administration and accepted their positions reluctantly, nonetheless acquired a sense of calling to administration as they grew more comfortable in their role and discovered the creative potential of the job. With experience, these deans gradually strengthened their commitment to administration and more fully understood its worthiness as a vocational choice. A longitudinal study of the deans' attitudes toward administrative work from the time of hiring and throughout their tenure in office is needed to determine how prevalent this evolution might be.

For the 65 percent of deans who came directly from the faculty, another important factor in their decision to take an administrative position was their prior commitment to theological teaching and scholarship and the adjustment in these areas the move required. Survey results showed that having little time to pursue scholarly or research interests was commonly associated with job stress. While deans readily acknowledged these sacrifices, they responded to them in various ways. Site visits revealed that, while most deans continued to teach and find teaching indispensable to their administrative work, many accepted the decreased time for scholarship matter-of-factly as a consequence of their taking an administrative position. Those who sought to maintain their scholarship usually protected time in their schedules for this work and sometimes made specific contractual arrangements to do so. Other deans who were skeptical of their ability to devote time to scholarship while serving as administrators recommended that persons not consider administration until they had established themselves as scholars and met their personal goals in that area. This advice was particularly apt in the case of one dean who, in his third year of teaching, was strongly encouraged by faculty colleagues and persuaded by the president to accept the deanship. Even after a successful first term, he felt the job had come too soon in his teaching career and deprived him of the chance to do scholarly work. His early entry into administration and his lack of a track record in teaching and scholarship sometimes made it difficult to provide leadership in these areas.

Clearly, an individual's decision to accept an administrative position at a particular time in an academic career has various motivations and incentives and depends upon the ability to reconcile the personal and professional sacrifices it requires with the benefits it promises. Once in the position, as deans gain a more accurate sense of the work, they have opportunities to reassess the balance of costs and rewards and their continuing commitment to administrative service. They also gain perspective on the dissatisfactions and stresses, the satisfactions and rewards of the job.

### *Dissatisfactions and Stresses*

When asked on the survey, "What is the greatest hindrance or barrier to you in carrying out your responsibilities?" chief academic officers focused primarily on practical issues of workload and institutional limitations, but when asked during interviews about the most difficult, least satisfying aspects of the job, they discussed parts of the work that were personally most demanding and stressful. Taken together, these reflections offer a realistic account of the principal challenges confronting theological school deans in their daily work.

Deans most often cited "time and money" or, rather, the lack of both as hindrances to them in doing their job. Many deans expressed frustration with the lack of sufficient time to complete important tasks and the hectic pace of days filled with meetings, calls, appointments, and frequent interruptions. Second only to insufficient time were concerns about limited financial resources and the constraints that placed on their efforts to strengthen programs and develop the faculty. Third, and closely related to the first two, was the lack of adequate support staff to assist the dean and to ease the workload of the office. Inadequate staffing, which often was attributed to a tight institutional budget, tended to exacerbate the difficulty of handling the numerous clerical and administrative tasks of the office. Fourth, deans felt hindered by a variety of institutional problems distinctive to their particular settings, ranging from weaknesses within the administration to aspects of the culture, such as lack of collegiality, distrust, and turf wars, that had become barriers to their work. Some deans felt hampered by their personal inability to manage the workload and deal with these other institutional issues.

When deans were interviewed during site visits and asked about the least satisfying aspects of their work, several mentioned particular activities that were personally unappealing, such as committee meetings, paperwork, repetitious tasks, detail work, and the like. Most deans agreed, however, that dealing with conflict and making negative personnel decisions were the most difficult and stressful parts of the job. Situations of conflict among students, faculty, or administrators, the dismissal of students, the need to give negative evaluations or to deny tenure were inherently difficult and often caused sleeplessness and worry that extended beyond the working day. Half of the deans interviewed acknowledged how hard it was to keep the problems of work from encroaching on their personal lives. The long hours and the all-consuming nature of the work explain, in part, why nearly two-thirds of the deans surveyed indicated that academic administration took a greater toll on their personal life than other jobs they have had.[11]

As an experienced dean observed, "I don't think you can manage with a heart and not find the job stressful." Survey results confirm that 65 percent of theological school deans consider the job stressful.[12] Further analysis reveals, however, that those who find the job stressful, for whatever reason, may nonetheless have several other positive and satisfying components of their work. Many deans who reported job stress had good working relationships with colleagues, felt their concerns were addressed in a timely manner, and indicated they would encourage others they respect to consider administrative service.

Perhaps most significantly, 73 percent of deans agreed the job becomes more manageable the longer they serve. Many deans found that, with time and experience, they became more confident in their role, more skilled in handling the challenges of the job, and better able to keep things in perspective. Many deans learned that coping with stress required that they take care of themselves physically, emotionally, and spiritually. During interviews, deans discussed the importance of developing in their lives habits of regular exercise, a network of professional peers, family, and friends for counsel and support, and a vital spiritual life nourished by worship, daily prayer, and other spiritual practices. Many experienced deans consciously worked to maintain a balance between their personal and professional lives and between the academic and administrative aspects of their professional work. While these challenges were widely shared by deans, the solutions they found were distinctly personal.

### *Satisfactions and Rewards*

Just as the challenges and dissatisfactions of the job can discourage some deans from continued service, so its satisfactions and rewards may provide incentives to academic administration and enhance the retention of chief academic officers.

Among the most stunning findings of this research is that chief academic officers, as a group, have a high level of job satisfaction and find considerable reward in their administrative work. As we have seen, this does not mean they fail to appreciate the personal and professional costs of the job or the difficult, demanding nature of the work. Rather, satisfactions and dissatisfactions coexist and, for the majority of deans in the study, the positive features of the job outweighed the negative. Whatever the daily stresses and frustrations, the job also had deep and lasting rewards.

While many positive indicators of the deans' satisfaction have been noted throughout this book, a review of selected survey findings affords perspective on the nature and range of these satisfactions. Table 14 summarizes survey results in three categories: professional relationships, the quality of institutional leadership and campus climate, and support and recognition. Mean ratings in sections A and B are based on the rating scale, 4=excellent – 1=poor, and means in section C are based on the rating scale, 4=strongly agree – 1=strongly disagree.

**Table 14**
**Indicators of Job Satisfaction**

| A. Professional Relationships | Mean Rating |
|---|---|
| between the chief executive and chief academic officer | 3.7 |
| between faculty and the chief academic officer | 3.5 |
| among senior administrators | 3.4 |
| between the board of trustees and major administrators | 3.3 |

| B. Institutional Leadership and Campus Climate | Mean Rating |
|---|---|
| quality of executive leadership | 3.3 |
| quality of administrative teamwork | 3.3 |
| quality of leadership in academic matters | 3.2 |
| quality of faculty leadership | 3.1 |
| collegiality | 3.3 |
| general campus climate | 3.2 |
| morale | 3.1 |

| C. Support and Recognition | Mean Rating |
|---|---|
| I believe I serve with the full support of the president/chief executive. | 3.8 |
| I believe I serve with the full support of the faculty. | 3.6 |
| Faculty and administrators cooperate effectively in making decisions. | 3.5 |
| I have the opportunity to discuss my professional needs and plans with my supervisor. | 3.3 |
| My administrative work is adequately recognized and rewarded. | 3.0 |

These ratings, between "good" and "excellent," indicate several important sources of the deans' satisfactions. While this list is not exhaustive and, in individual cases, may be balanced by dissatisfactions in other areas, theological school deans as a group are positive in their assessment of their most important relationships, of the quality of institutional life, and of the collegial support and recognition that make their work possible. The fact that deans overall rated their relationships with colleagues so positively is consistent with the personal accounts of deans interviewed concerning the satisfactions and rewards of the job.

Foremost among the rewards of serving as chief academic officer was the opportunity to help faculty and students by solving problems and removing obstacles to their work and by fostering their growth and development. When deans were asked during site visits and focus groups about the most satisfying aspect of their work, they spoke, sometimes passionately, of their role in serving the faculty and the students:

- I just shout at the prospect of being involved in the continuous formation, and sometimes re-formation, of people who are seeking to serve the church. I have no greater joy than that.
- I think the most satisfying aspect is when you come up with a bright idea or engineer an approach that helps somebody. In this job you have that opportunity often. That gives the most immediate pleasure. There also are longer-term pleasures—seeing projects through with faculty, staff, and administrators. In my previous job as dean, the greatest pleasure was seeing faculty blossom. Their publications increased and their fears and weaknesses were dealt with.
- Most satisfying is when you feel you've made a difference, when you impact the lives of people, when you can help students.
- Like musicians, sometimes you know you've played well even before the clapping begins. The position can be rewarding and there are moments when the dean realizes accomplishment, is able to influence a person's career, to set a professional tone, or has created the possibility for these things to happen. A dean gains satisfaction from seeing both faculty and students develop and grow.
- When the faculty knows that you are seeking their best interest and you realize their trust, and when you see the faculty develop as better teachers and have more influence in the wider church, knowing I had a part in that is what keeps me going. I know I am a builder.

These statements describe the dean's role in creating an environment in which the work of faculty and students, individually and collectively, can flourish. Whether deans are solving short-term problems, creating a positive climate for growth, or influencing an individual's career, deans gain satisfaction from knowing their efforts have enhanced the development of faculty and students who, in turn, contribute to the ongoing work of the church. In this way, academic leadership of the seminary for many deans is a form of service to the larger church.

Deans also find other aspects of their job personally rewarding. Some discussed their singular opportunity to work across the disciplines and departments of the school and to gain a sense of the whole. From this vantage point, deans can help colleagues see their individual efforts as part of a single mission and of the larger community. As one dean explained, "I love institution-building . . . there are ways to build a deeper sense of camaraderie and sisterhood and brotherhood here." Others considered it a privilege to have so direct a hand in developing the faculty and enhancing the quality of theological education. Still others enjoyed the variety of tasks and the unpredictability of an average working day. As one dean commented, the work is seldom boring: "You have no idea what will happen during a day. It may be a complete disaster or a stimulating, exciting day." As another dean put it, "You're where the action is."

The nature and scope of the dean's work, so stressful for some, was a source of personal fulfillment for others. One dean noted that the position enabled him to use all his talents and draw upon all his past experience:

> It is a position in which I've been able to bring to bear all the experiences that I've had in the church, in the community, and in the academy into one professional experience. . . . There is a holism about what I do and who I envision myself to be that is quite exhilarating. It's as if my life prepared me for this job. . . . It also gives me a sense of competence and a sense of assurance.

The considerable challenges of the job can have the positive effect of developing the talents and skills of officeholders and stimulating their personal growth. For some, this benefit was quite unexpected. As a dean profiled earlier in the book remarked, "I've been a new person during the last six years [as dean], and it's something I never imagined myself doing."[13]

Administration also can strengthen the spiritual life. When deans were asked on the survey how their original expectations differed from their actual experience doing the job, one dean replied, "I have found the job to be far more spiritually enriching than I ever imagined." In a 1991 interview,

Vincent Cushing, President of Washington Theological Union, elaborated on the spiritual dimension of administrative work:

> There's a spiritual discipline that's built up on some very simple, and almost American virtues. One is persistence, that there's no substitute for staying at the task, day in and day out, out of fidelity to the gospel and out of response to the ministerial vocations that we are personally called to and that we're trying to suggest to others is a worthwhile way of living out life. So persistence and a refusal to trivialize theological education . . . is part of that asceticism too. That's got to be rooted in some ways in a deep openness to the word of God, and to service of the gospel. What really has to pull us forward in this thing is the gospel itself, and the experience of Christ in our lives, given all our own faults and failings and limitations.[14]

The persistence that administration requires, the faithfulness to the gospel and to the ministerial life, presents opportunities for spiritual development. Administration requires a spiritual discipline that is rooted in openness to the word of God. Chief academic officers who recognize in their administrative work the embodiment of principles of their religious faith may find the job to be, as their colleague stated, far more spiritually enriching than they ever imagined.

This potential for personal growth is known principally by those with direct experience of the office. Even a cursory review of the roles, responsibilities, and relationships examined in this book shows the potential of academic administration to draw forth and develop a broad range of personal aptitudes. The challenges are not merely intellectual, or interpersonal, or psychological, or physical, or spiritual, but all of these at once. In the multiple demands of academic administration lies its power to further the growth of the whole person. As observed some years ago by a retiring seminary president, "We also are persons before we are leaders or fillers of any role in institutions."[15] While who we are is independent of any position we hold, the work we do can serve to strengthen or thwart our personal development. As deans testified, those who accept the challenges of the chief academic officer role can discover, sometimes unexpectedly, the stimulating, life-giving potential of administrative work.

### *Reasons to Stay and to Leave*

Beyond assessing the satisfactions and dissatisfactions of the job, deans were asked on the survey about the factors that would most directly affect their decision to stay or to leave their positions. The deans gave narrative responses to two questions: "In the future, what single factor would most strongly influence your decision to continue serving in your current position?" "What single factor would most strongly influence your decision to move on?" Answers to these questions provide clues to both retention and turnover in the chief academic officer position.[16]

Support of colleagues, particularly of the president and the faculty, was cited by nearly half of survey respondents as the single most important factor in the decision to stay in their positions. Conversely, the lack of such support would most strongly influence their decision to leave. While some deans noted the importance of constituent support generally, most referred specifically to the necessity of good relationships with the president and/or faculty, thereby underscoring the integral connection of both parties to the deans' work.

The continued service of deans also depended on other factors. One-third of the deans surveyed indicated the need for institutional changes, ranging from progress in defining the mission and goals of the institution and developing particular programs to quite specific improvements in working conditions, such as administrative assistance or additional financial resources. Beyond these institutional changes, deans noted the importance of remaining personally effective and committed to the work. Several deans stated they would continue to serve as long as they were able to provide leadership and be a catalyst for change. Still others would remain in office for personal reasons, such as their continued satisfaction and fulfillment, God's call to do this work, or their sense of duty. A small percentage of deans would hold their positions until another qualified replacement was at hand.

Factors that would prompt deans to leave their positions closely parallel their reasons for staying. In addition to the primary reason of loss of support for their work, about one-third of deans indicated they would leave if certain institutional problems were not solved. Others would leave if their work was no longer personally fulfilling or if it jeopardized their health and well-being. Some deans would leave if called to another ministry or given an opportunity for a better position. Most striking, however, was that 15 percent of deans would leave administration if they were unable to continue their teaching, research, or pastoral work. In such instances, where these activities were not only desirable but indispensable, retaining academic officers would necessitate that the position accommodate their academic interests and that deans achieve a satisfactory balance between their academic and administrative work.

Research findings further suggest that relatively few theological school deans aspire to other administrative positions within their own schools or at other academic institutions. When asked on the survey, "What are your professional plans after leaving your present position?" the majority of deans indicated they planned either to resume the occupation they had prior to becoming dean or to retire.[17]

**Table 15**
**Plans after Leaving the Chief Academic Officer Position**

| | % of deans |
|---|---|
| Return to teaching/research | 54 |
| Retirement | 21 |
| Church ministry/pastoral work | 10 |
| Academic administration/dean at another institution | 4 |
| President at another seminary/theological school | 4 |
| President at a college or university | 2 |
| Church leadership/administration | 1 |
| President at a nonacademic institution | 1 |
| President at present institution | 0 |
| Other | 6 |

These data indicate that only 12 percent of deans planned to continue in administration after leaving office, and only 6 percent aspired to executive-level positions. Perhaps to the consolation of seminary presidents, none sought the presidency of their own institutions. These reports were somewhat at odds with findings of a 1992 study of seminary presidents showing that 15 percent came to their offices directly from the dean/academic vice president position.[18]

During interviews for this research on chief academic officers, deans and presidents also were asked if being a dean was good preparation for being a president. Their answers were yes, and no. While some acknowledged that familiarity with the institution and experience in administrative leadership would be assets, most observed that the constituent development and fundraising tasks that occupy most presidents today were markedly different from the academic focus of the dean's position, and even of the presidency in its traditional form. In most instances, the jobs require different skills. Consequently, deans with strong ties to the academic life who wish to maintain their teaching, scholarship, and close working relationships with faculty and students rarely found presidential responsibilities attractive. Many would agree with the dean who advised: "[C]hoose to become a dean because you love this special calling, not because you long someday to be president."[19]

This research shows that, with the exception of those retiring, the majority of deans planned to return to their prior occupations.[20] For this group, administration did not displace their prior occupation but was a temporary departure from it. How future plans affected length of service in the chief academic officer position was impossible to determine with the available data. Of particular interest would be whether tenure in office differs for deans who are seeking administrative advancement compared to deans who plan to return to their previous line of work. While these data indicate that most deans do not plan to continue in administration, further study is needed on the range of options available to those with an ongoing commitment to administrative work who seek challenges and opportunities beyond the chief academic officer role.[21] At present, the path is not clear or well charted for the deans seeking other opportunities for professional growth and advancement in administration. As the chief academic officer role grows in scope and complexity, however, options for those seeking to progress in their administrative careers should expand as well.

To summarize, both the prevailing attitudes toward administration examined earlier and the deans' assessments of their work reveal the incentives and disincentives to administrative service. These findings help to identify the challenges facing theological schools in attracting and retaining academic leaders. The testimony of working deans and their colleagues also offers insight into how these challenges can be addressed.

## The Challenges Ahead

Several challenges face theological school communities who take the position of chief academic officer seriously, that is, who understand its potential for leadership and its importance in shaping the academic life of the institution. The emerging role of the chief academic officer described in these pages raises the stakes for theological schools seeking capable, committed academic leaders. No longer is the goal simply to fill a position defined by routine administrative and clerical tasks; rather, it is to find an individual who has the managerial, leadership, and pastoral skills necessary to help the community realize its vision—to lead both from the center and from the heart. Who the chief academic officer is professionally and personally matters greatly. Who assumes administrative responsibility for managing the academic area, building the faculty, developing academic programs, maintaining standards for teaching and learning, and encouraging scholarly productivity has significant consequences for individual schools and for the enterprise of theological education as a whole.

Like other higher education institutions, theological schools do not select their leaders once and for all but face the recurring task of finding chief academic officers who are able to fulfill the formidable responsibilities of office and are willing to serve. Attracting and retaining able academic leaders presents several challenges to the theological education community. While individual schools may be at different stages in recognizing and meeting these challenges, this research suggests they are widely shared.

*The first challenge is to become intentional about leadership succession in the chief academic officer position and proactive in efforts to identify and prepare individuals to assume the role.* A broad spectrum of faculty, administrators, and board members interviewed for the study recommended a shift from the ad hoc approach to administrative hiring, which attends to leadership succession only when vacancies occur, to a planned approach that involves early identification of candidates and their advanced preparation for administrative service. While some schools plan for leadership succession in the presidency, this research suggests that few make comparable plans for transitions in the chief academic officer position. As one administrator explained, "There's no succession planning because there is an attitude that 'God will provide.'" Despite such assurances, participants in the study were increasingly uncomfortable with a laissez-faire attitude toward hiring academic officers, and many urged theological schools to take a proactive stance in identifying and preparing future leaders.

Those interviewed thought succession planning for the chief academic officer position was the responsibility not only of the president but of the current academic officer, the administrators, faculty, and board members of the school.[22] Collectively, their task was to cultivate future leaders: 1) by identifying individuals with an aptitude for administration and actively encouraging their interest; 2) by providing opportunities for them to gain training and experience in administrative work; and 3) by helping them assess their readiness for administrative service.

*Identifying Prospective Administrators.* "We don't always look for deans in the right places," one seminary president noted. When those interviewed considered what the "right places" might be, they overwhelmingly affirmed that chief academic officers should come from the faculty, or at least have significant faculty experience, preferably in theological education. As we have seen, academic credentials and experience give credibility to the office, and understanding academic policy, programs, curriculum, and faculty responsibilities is essential to leadership of the academic area. While the hiring of professional administrators without faculty experience may be gaining acceptability for some administrative positions, it was strongly opposed for chief academic officers. A trustee's observation was widely shared: "The best deans are from the faculty, since they need a strong academic background and knowledge of academic culture. The first problem is to attract good people to seminaries."

Outside of faculty ranks, however, are individuals with faculty experience in their background who may be serving as administrators, denominational leaders, pastors, or in other related ministries. Some of those interviewed felt their combination of academic, administrative, and/or pastoral experience could make them desirable candidates for the deanship. Others encouraged bringing prospective leaders from outside the seminary to lecture or to preach as a way of introducing them to the campus community. Several participants in the study also suggested that administrators and faculty identify graduate students, and even undergraduates, with management and leadership skills and encourage them to consider academic administration at some time in the future. As one seminary president stated, "I wish faculty could be educated not only to encourage young people to get on the faculty but to do administration." A dean echoed this belief: "I have some students who would make good deans down the road. We need to nurture the young to serve." Thus, while those interviewed had strong convictions about the need for academic credentials and faculty experience, several felt that too many schools looked for candidates exclusively within their own faculty and failed to cast the net widely enough and to encourage prospective leaders early enough in their careers.

*Providing Training and Experience.* Some participants in the study believed "the best deans are home-grown," that theological schools should provide opportunities for faculty and students to develop their administrative skills and to gain experience in leadership positions. As noted previously, 76 percent of deans felt they had the primary responsibility for developing faculty leadership, which they typically exercised by giving faculty members opportunities to chair committees and take on other leadership roles.[23] "Administrators should mentor those who have administrative potential," one dean advised; they should be aware of those with an interest in administration, provide opportunities for them to develop their skills, and lend professional and personal support to them for this work. Several participants suggested that, whenever possible, faculty should be supported to attend seminars and workshops to hone their administrative skills and to participate in accreditation visits and professional development programs of the Association of Theological Schools.[24] These initiatives would give encouragement and practical guidance to those with leadership potential.

Several faculty also recommended that graduate students receive formal training in administration and be encouraged to gain administrative experience. One faculty member felt "we need courses on leadership in the theological curriculum," while another lamented that "when training PhDs we do nothing in the administrative area. If we want people who can administer, we have to train them and have to build it into the supervising of doctoral students." The pool of future leaders for theological schools would be strengthened considerably if graduate students received formal training in administration and leadership, opportunities to develop skills in these areas, and encouragement from faculty and administrators to consider administrative service.

*Assessing Readiness for Administrative Service.* When deans in the study reflected on their own path to administration, they frequently discussed the timing of their move to the deanship and its effect, for good or ill, on their professional life. Several felt it important to have met other professional goals, in the areas of teaching and scholarship for example, prior to the deanship, since little time would be available for substantial accomplishment in these areas once the job was underway. Others noted that the most promising future leaders are sometimes tapped too early in their academic careers. As one president observed, "We have catapulted women and minority deans into leadership positions before they are ready." When the deans surveyed cited "the encouragement of colleagues" as the most important factor in their decision to accept their positions, they underscored the significant role that faculty and administrators play in moving individuals toward administrative service. Theological school communities need to take seriously their role in helping prospective candidates assess their personal readiness to serve.

*The second challenge is to develop within the theological education community, particularly among faculty and students, a more balanced and positive view of academic administration.* Our earlier discussion revealed that attitudes toward academic administration held by chief academic officers generally were more positive and more balanced than the attitudes of those without firsthand experience of the job. If, as many deans attest, they have numerous sources of job satisfaction, considerable reward in furthering the work of faculty and students and advancing the mission of the school and the church, and opportunity for personal growth and renewal, it is curious that their colleagues rarely noted these positive dimensions of the work. While faculty were keenly aware of the difficulty of the job and the sacrifices it requires, they seemed less attuned to its satisfactions and rewards. One possible explanation is that positive aspects of the job are both less obvious and less frequently expressed by officeholders. As one seminary president observed, "I don't think we send a lot of good signals to people that this [administration] can be challenging and fun if you're cut out right for it." Perhaps, like so many of us, deans more readily express their troubles and disappointments than their joys. Administration cannot be attractive to faculty or students who receive few, if any, "good signals" about the work.

In some cases, negative attitudes toward administration may result simply from observing deanships that are troubled. If the chief academic officer appears stressed, overworked, and on the verge of burnout, faculty and others may infer, perhaps accurately, that the impossibility of the administrative workload, difficult personnel matters, the lack of time for scholarship, and the like have these dire consequences. In other words, if the job seems not only to require sacrifices but to threaten the health and well-being of officeholders, then colleagues may readily conclude that the chief academic officer position is undesirable and too costly to consider. In such instances, improving attitudes toward academic administration requires changes in the chief academic officer position itself, in the workload and conditions of employment, and in institutional support for individual officeholders.

*The third challenge is to define the chief academic officer position so the role and responsibilities of office are realistic, humane, and adequately supported.* Meeting this challenge may not only affect colleagues' perceptions of the office but may contribute to the recruitment and retention of chief academic officers. In interviews and survey responses, deans discussed the importance of entering the position with a clear understanding of their administrative responsibilities and their role in academic leadership, particularly in relation to the president. As discussed in Chapter Three, the inability of theological schools and presidents to define the job clearly can lead to conflict and confusion between president and dean and can result in deans underperforming or overreaching the presumed limits of their position. While rigid descriptions of duties are impractical given the need to respond flexibly to changing conditions, so, too, uncertain parameters and shifting roles are detrimental to the dean and the work of the office. In such circumstances, deans are hindered in their efforts to balance their various responsibilities and to develop a manageable workload. However, deans can be effective and confident in their work when they have a clear understanding of expectations concerning the role and responsibilities of the office.

The confession of one dean is instructive here: "I feel I have lost control of my life. I continue with my full teaching load, work full-time as dean, and take home $200 more each month."[25] In different ways, several deans expressed a similar frustration with job overload and found themselves unable to keep up with their administrative work while retaining many of their faculty responsibilities. Although most deans teach and many consider it essential to their professional life, a sizable number carry more than half-time teaching loads.[26] Some deans also are committed to their scholarship and seek to maintain their research and writing at some level. Individuals who have these commitments and are selected to serve as chief academic officers must appraise the total workload and discuss with the president ways to balance their academic interests with the administrative requirements of the job. In the theological schools visited for the study, most deans had significantly reduced teaching loads and, while some decided not to attempt major scholarly work during their time in office, others negotiated a schedule that enabled them to devote one day per week to their nonadministrative work and to be eligible for study leaves and sabbaticals. Such accommodations not only made the workload more reasonable and enhanced the deans' satisfaction, but they also sent positive signals to colleagues who might be considering administrative service.

Another means by which theological schools can make the dean's responsibilities manageable is to provide adequate support staff to handle the routine duties of the office. Many of the deans who felt most burdened reported either the lack or inadequacy of clerical and administrative assistance, while those with capable staff credited them with their ability to stay on top of things and keep the office running smoothly.

Deans also cited other conditions that make the job doable. Several commented on the importance of achieving balance between authority and responsibility in their positions. Although deans recognize that shared governance limits their authority in many areas, they consider their ability to make decisions within their jurisdiction without being second-guessed a necessary component of their work. Deans also sought balance between the routine and creative aspects of the job, and between their managerial and leadership roles. Some deans lamented the unexpected preponderance of routine tasks and felt they could not do the job without opportunities to do creative thinking, planning, and problem solving and to exercise leadership. As one dean explained, "Crises don't undo people, the mundane does." While mundane tasks clearly are integral to the management of the academic area and impossible to eliminate entirely, many deans find that the more challenging and creative aspects of their work are what sustains them. Defining the chief academic officer position requires attention not only to the overall quantity of the work and the balance of academic and administrative duties, but to opportunities for creativity and leadership.

Finally, although deans generally expressed satisfaction with their financial compensation, some were disheartened by the fact that their move to administration resulted not only in a heavier workload and a twelve-month contract, but little or no salary increase.[27] One president in the study explained that limited finances prevented him from paying administrators what they were worth. Poor compensation, however, has a higher price: it can make hard-working administrators feel undervalued and can show the rest of the community that academic administration demands yet another personal sacrifice. To some it may seem, as a seminary trustee observed, that "we have a tendency to take people for granted because they work for the church." Considering these consequences, presidents and boards would do well to evaluate employee compensation and make every effort to develop a compensation schedule that is fair internally and commensurate with comparable institutions in theological education.

Participants in the study identified all of the above measures as crucial to attracting and retaining strong candidates for the chief academic officer position. Theological schools that are intentional in their efforts to define the position clearly and realistically, to balance the workload, and to provide adequate and tangible forms of support will make the chief academic officer position more manageable for officeholders and more attractive to those considering administrative service. The short-term benefit of these measures is to make the work of the office more effective and rewarding; the long-term benefit is to create a more positive image and a more favorable climate for academic administration.

*The fourth challenge is to support the personal and professional development of officeholders.* Neither presidents nor deans give high marks to theological schools for their professional development of administrators.[28] Our analysis of chief academic officers on this issue showed that, although professional development opportunities are widely available, theological schools often lack the infrastructure of related practices that enables deans to utilize these opportunities effectively. The most notable example was the scarcity of sound evaluation practices, so critical to identifying individual needs and planning specific ways to address them. The president, as supervisor of the chief academic officer, is key to establishing the practices that will encourage the acquisition of needed skills and support the dean's professional and personal development.

Why is this so important to the future of the deanship? First, in order to attract well-qualified and gifted administrators, the deanship must be perceived as an opportunity for new challenges and professional growth. Highly competent people rarely seek positions that offer little chance to utilize their talents or to acquire new skills. While some may be attracted by the challenges of the job, many more will be concerned about having the support and resources necessary to meet them. A supportive president and good professional development practices help to assure deans that their time in office will not be a professional loss but a stimulating, even exciting period of professional growth.

Second, chief academic officers, in particular, need assurance that the professional activities that nourished them in the past can continue, and that new forms of renewal will come with the job. Since deans typically come to administration by way of other professional work, many deans care deeply about maintaining their prior activities, such as teaching, scholarship, or pastoral work, at some level. Many deans give as their primary reason for doing so the fact that these activities nourish them intellectually and spiritually and, without those resources, they could not effectively handle their administrative work. Many deans also discover that administration itself offers unexpected rewards, such as an expanded network of colleagues, new relationships, new knowledge, and opportunities for spiritual growth.

Third, explicit attention to the professional and personal development of administrators serves the school in supporting individual efforts to do quality work, and it serves individuals by demonstrating that their professional and personal vitality are valued. Particularly in settings where past deans have not always fared well, their successors need to know they will not be used up, burned out, and discarded, but that the president and other colleagues will support their growth and enrichment and protect them from job burnout. Professional development, in its many forms, is a means of providing opportunities for personal renewal, and therein lies its potential to retain capable people in the chief academic officer position.

*The fifth challenge is to address the problem of job turnover and to strengthen the stability and continuity of academic leadership in theological schools.* The statistics on turnover reported earlier indicate that approximately one-quarter of ATS member schools have a personnel change in the chief academic officer position each year.[29] Consistent with these findings, deans responding to the survey had served an average of 3.8 years in their positions. While the optimal rate of turnover may vary with the circumstances of individual schools, in general, frequent changes in leadership are disruptive and can have a destabilizing effect on the community. Personnel changes in senior administrative positions can shift priorities, alter communication, decision-making practices, and relationships, advance or derail ongoing projects, and require new methods of working together. While change itself can be beneficial, changes occurring too frequently can be detrimental. As one dean observed, "In general, a school is not well run if there is regular turnover."

Frequent turnover in the position presents difficulties from the dean's perspective as well. Several deans and presidents acknowledged that it takes two to three years to get used to the job and at least five years to learn the culture, earn credibility, and get things accomplished. As one dean explained, "It is important to have continuity. There is a long learning curve, contacts to be made, an institutional culture and grammar to learn." All of this, so necessary to good administration, takes time. When deans serve only three or four years, they leave the position precisely at the point when they could be most effective.

While the causes of frequent turnover in the chief academic officer position are many and often specific to individuals and their institutions, this research identified several factors that seem to play a prominent role. One likely suspect is the term limits that attach to the position in some seminaries. Findings of the study reveal, however, that term limits generally do not account for these rates of change, since over half the deans surveyed did not have specified terms; those who did typically had terms of three to five years in length that were renewable, on average, for 2.4 terms.[30] These data suggest that most deans who were performing adequately could continue to serve six years or more. In a related finding, the majority of theological school deans and faculty did not believe the deanship should rotate among the faculty.[31] This is consistent with the view that special aptitudes and skills are required for the managerial and leadership responsibilities of the office and continuity in these functions is important.

Participants in the study identified several other factors they believe contribute to frequent turnover. The first is that some individuals who accept the deanship may not be administratively inclined and, after some experience in office, may realize their abilities are not well matched to the requirements of the position. Their expectations may not have been consistent with the reality of the job, and they may not find it professionally rewarding.[32] Second, the institution itself may be troubled. For example, one administrator felt the structure of the school was dysfunctional, which was a source of considerable frustration. Another dean believed his predecessors had left due to the lack of a solid working environment; "the right hand didn't know what the left hand was doing," he explained. Serious institutional difficulties, whether they be cultural, structural, or financial, can create instability and adversely affect the retention of senior administrators.

A third factor that contributes to frequent turnover relates to the deans' experience of the job. Deans on the survey who responded positively to the statement, "I am anxious to complete my administrative tour of duty," also were the deans who found the job stressful and felt it took a greater toll on their personal life than other jobs they have had. Several administrators noted in interviews that deans are undertrained for the work and simply are not well equipped to handle the job. One dean observed that people left their positions either because "change was too rapid and they couldn't cope, or because there was no change and the job was boring." Evidence of this study suggests that, for most theological school deans, it more likely would be the former than the latter. Finally, deans may leave their positions because they do not feel supported by colleagues or sufficiently appreciated and rewarded for their work.

If participants in the study have rightly identified at least some of the principal causes of turnover in the chief academic officer position, there is reason for hope. Theological schools can solve many of these problems by adopting more effective hiring practices, by defining the position clearly and realistically, and by offering timely and appropriate professional development support to officeholders. While a more systematic study is needed of the reasons deans actually leave their positions, these observations afford a starting point and identify specific institutional practices that need to be assessed in schools where job turnover is a problem.

The balance between too much change and too little is a delicate one and highly variable for individuals and institutions. As a seminary president remarked, "If you stay too long, you get stale. You lose your fastball." If you leave too early, as we have seen, not much can be accomplished. The optimal point is to serve long enough to know the job and be effective and to leave before you and the job get stale. There is no litmus test and no rule. Based on this research, the primary challenge for theological schools is to improve turnover rates and to strengthen the retention of academic leaders, thereby providing greater continuity and stability in the academic leadership of the schools.

*Finally, and most importantly, the sixth challenge is to develop within the theological education community a sense of administration as an academic vocation.* When asked how theological schools in the future will attract and retain good academic administrators, several faculty members, deans, and presidents expressed the need for an enlarged understanding of the academic vocation. As one president observed, "Many take on administration when their heart is someplace else. They do not see administration as a vocation." This dilemma is exacerbated by the fact that faculty experience is widely, and rightly, considered a prerequisite for the chief academic officer position. Consequently, the first call for many deans is teaching and scholarship, and this always may be where their heart is. More direct routes to academic administration generally are discouraged, since the work of managing and leading the academic area depends heavily on an in-depth understanding of teaching, learning, scholarship, and the practices of the academic life. Under these circumstances, administration almost inevitably comes in second.

However, as noted earlier, some deans find that once in office they grow to love the work and to sense God's call to this special service. One dean who had come to administration from the faculty acknowledged, "Administration is what gets me up in the morning, it's what I live for." Others spoke of their personal transformation, their unexpected fulfillment in administration that increasingly made them feel called to the work. Sometimes this sense of call comes gradually. One seminary president, who suggested "reconstruing the deanship as a call, a special vocation," noted that it often takes time for individuals to realize they can do administration and are called to the work. Frequent turnover and a brief tenure in office may eclipse that process.

Two faculty members from different schools proposed a rethinking of the notion of the academic life and what a call to that life might be. Both suggested that when we think of the academic vocation exclusively as teaching and scholarship, we circumscribe it too narrowly, and we create the false assumption that administration is separate and apart, different from the academic life and its vocation. "We need to rethink the notion of academic vocation," one faculty member stated. "We need to help faculty see administration as part of the faculty job." The other faculty member took an even broader view: "We need to view the community as a whole and see administration as dealing with problems we all care about, but at a different level and in a different way. We need a vision of what the academic life is all about."

What these faculty members propose is an enlarged understanding of the academic community and the academic vocation. In this view, administration, like teaching and scholarship, is an integral part of both, and together they represent different facets of the community's work to fulfill its educational mission. Administration, teaching, learning, and scholarship simply serve the shared goals of the academic community at different levels and in different ways. A call to the academic life may be a call to teaching, scholarship, and/or administration, each of which is embraced by individuals differently according to their aptitudes and interests, and may be the focus at different times in a person's professional life.

Consequently, the shift from serving primarily as a teacher to serving primarily as an administrator is not a change *of* vocation, but a change *within* a vocation. The academic vocation is rich in the options it holds.

Administration is not a sell-out or a loss of that vocation, but simply another way of responding to the call to the academic life and to service of the theological school community. To rethink the notion of academic vocation in this way could help the administrators, faculty, and students of theological schools see their various kinds of work as interrelated parts of a single community.

One practical consequence of this view would be the inclusion of administrative service as a component of the academic reward system. As a university dean suggested, "Administration should count equally with scholarship and teaching, so it has credibility and people want to do it." If that were the case, then administrative work at various levels of the institution would "count" when it came to promotion, tenure, and other types of advancement and reward.[33] Still others have made a compelling case for administration as a form of teaching and scholarship, thereby demonstrating it is not different from these academic practices but an essential part of them.[34] Now that administrative work and the high-level skills it requires are better understood, it is time for theological schools and other higher education institutions to reevaluate the place of administration within the academy and to establish policies and practices that reflect an enlarged and deepened understanding of the academic life. Administration is not a vocation apart. It is a call to the academic life. It is a call to lead and to serve.

Perhaps the greatest challenge, as one dean stated, is this: "We have to help people grasp that these positions are ones in which people can serve and can serve productively, that they can find joy, and that this work is worthy of our best and highest service."

## Notes

[1] The survey of theological school deans was conducted for this study, and the faculty survey was part of the Auburn Center's Study of Theological School Faculty. The latter included administrators with faculty status. The two surveys had several questions in common.

[2] Using the scale, 4=strongly agree – 1=strongly disagree, deans gave this statement a mean rating of 3.2 and faculty 3.0.

[3] Using the rating scale above, deans gave this statement a mean rating of 3.3. Deans differed in their ratings according to school size: deans in seminaries with a student FTE of 150 or higher more strongly agreed with the statement than did deans in smaller schools.

[4] Using the scale in note 2, faculty gave this statement a mean rating of 2.1.

[5] A similar version of the differences between faculty and administrative work is discussed in an earlier publication of this research: Karen M. Ristau, *Challenges of Academic Administration: Rewards and Stresses in the Role of Chief Academic Officer,* Monograph Series on Academic Leadership, vol. 2 (St. Paul, MN: University of St. Thomas, 1996), 2. This entire chapter builds on Ristau's previous discussion of the costs and rewards of the job.

[6] See Chapter Two, 49.

[7] Barbara Brown Zikmund, "The Role of the Chief Academic Officer in Theological Education," *Resources: Issues in Theological Education.* A publication of the Association of Theological Schools in the United States and Canada. Issue 8 (October 1984), 3.

[8] Being encouraged by colleagues was most important to deans in the smallest schools (student FTE 75 or less) and least important to deans in mid-sized schools (student FTE 76–150).

[9] "I was encouraged by denominational and/or academic colleagues" was most important to deans in small schools (student FTE 75 and lower) with a mean rating of 3.6, and least important to deans in mid-sized schools (student FTE 76–150) with a mean of 3.0.

"I wanted to work at this particular institution" received mean ratings as follows: 3.3 inter/nondenominational seminaries, 3.1 mainline Protestant, 2.7 Roman Catholic and other seminaries.

"I was attracted by the higher salary" received mean ratings of 1.9 inter/non-denominational seminaries, 1.8 mainline Protestant seminaries, and 1.5–1.3 Roman Catholic and other seminaries. Interestingly, satisfaction with financial compensation was consistently positive among deans across denominations. Although rated low overall, interest in a higher salary was most important to deans in the largest schools (student FTE 500 and higher) and least important to deans in small schools (student FTE 75 and lower), with mean ratings ranging from a high of 1.9 to a low of 1.3.

[10] "I considered academic administration as part of my religious vocation or call" received the mean ratings: 3.5 women, 2.6 men. "I felt a sense of obligation or duty" received mean ratings: 3.3 men, 2.7 women.

Data analysis further shows that obligation or duty was most important to deans in small schools (student FTE 75 or less) and least important to deans in mid-sized schools (student FTE 76–300). We might deduce that deans in small schools would feel a greater sense of obligation or duty, particularly if academic officers were appointed from the small pool of faculty; however, this interpretation is muddied by the fact that it was deans in mid-sized schools and not deans in large schools (student FTE 301 or more) who found duty least important in their decision to accept their positions.

Deans in Roman Catholic seminaries and in inter/nondenominational schools were less likely than other deans to consider academic administration part of their religious vocation. Their mean ratings were 2.3–2.6, compared to ratings of 2.9–3.0 by all other deans.

[11] Using the rating scale above, the statement, "I have found that academic administration takes a greater toll on my personal life than other jobs I have had," received a mean rating of 2.9.

[12] The statement, "I find this job very stressful," received a mean rating of 2.8.

[13] See Chapter One, 23.

[14] "Recipe for Presidency: A Conversation," *In Trust* 3, no. 1 (Easter 1991), 13.

[15] Donald W. Shriver, Jr., "Visions and Nightmares: The Leader's Call to See Reality—and Change It," *In Trust* 3, no. 3 (New Year 1992), 18.

[16] The causes of turnover among chief academic officers would be assessed most accurately by an exit interview or polling of those who leave their positions each year. With access only to current officeholders, this research identifies probable, not actual, causes of turnover in the position.

[17] Some deans indicated the possibility of more than one future occupation. This table reports the combined total for each item. Fifteen percent of survey respondents did not answer this question.

[18] Mark Allyn Holman, *Presidential Search in Theological Schools: Process Makes a Difference* (Oakland, CA: 1993), distributed by agreement with the Association of Theological Schools in the United States and Canada, 25.

[19] Elizabeth C. Nordbeck, "The Once and Future Dean: Reflections on Being a Chief Academic Officer," *Theological Education* 33 (Supplement Autumn 1996), 32.

[20] Gender analysis shows that future career plans are similar for men and women deans.

[21] Russell E. Richey, upon reviewing this manuscript, first raised this issue in relation to the view of administration as an academic vocation. Those who make a long-term commitment to administration may well be concerned about what follows the deanship. Richey raised several questions: "How should the academic dean envision his/her career? What would logically build on the experience and expertise [of the deanship]? Would persons stay longer in the post or stronger candidates assume it were schools and/or the church to identify or create an appropriate sequel?" These important questions are an outgrowth of this research but unfortunately beyond its scope to address.

[22] Except in unusual circumstances, succession planning should include the current chief academic officer who knows firsthand what academic leadership requires. To

exclude the academic officer from such planning could fuel suspicion of an untimely departure.

[23] See Chapter Four, 121.

[24] See Appendix C for a selected list of professional development opportunities for academic administrators.

[25] The dean made this comment in response to a narrative question on the survey: "In what ways did your original expectations about academic administration differ from your actual experience doing the job?"

[26] Survey results show that of the 93 percent of deans who teach, an estimated 14 percent carry 6 or more credit hours per year.

[27] See note 9.

[28] See Chapter Seven, note 20.

[29] See Introduction, note 1.

[30] Forty-three percent of survey respondents had term limits, but indicated their terms were renewable. Term limits were most common in university-related schools, where 68 percent of deans had terms, compared to freestanding schools, where 41 percent had terms. Although the response rate on the renewability of terms was low, respondents indicated they could serve two terms or more. Nonrespondents appeared either to have no limits on the number of terms or to be unaware of what those limits might be.

[31] The statement, "The academic deanship should be a position that rotates among the faculty," received a mean rating of 1.87 (scale: 4=strongly agree – 1=strongly disagree). Theological school faculty, responding to the Auburn Center survey, agreed with the deans and gave this statement a mean rating of 1.92 on the same scale.

Interestingly, specified terms were more common in university-related schools than in freestanding schools (see note 30), and deans/academic officers in university schools were more likely than other deans to favor rotation in the position. University deans gave the statement above a mean rating of 2.7, compared to a mean of 1.8 for other deans. The available data offer no definitive explanation for this difference. One result that initially seemed promising was that 70 percent of the university deans surveyed were required or expected to produce scholarly work, compared to only 40 percent of deans in freestanding schools. Shorter administrative terms would be less disruptive of ongoing scholarly work. However, data on the actual tenure of deans in office shows little difference between deans in freestanding and university-related schools, suggesting that neither specified terms nor a preference for rotating deanships translates into more frequent changes in the position.

[32] On the survey, respondents who were anxious to leave their positions tended not to find the work professionally rewarding.

[33] Giving due credit for administrative experience could help to ameliorate the problem experienced by some junior faculty, who spend considerable time and effort on committee work and other administrative assignments only to find they do not count for much at the time of promotion and tenure. See Barbara G. Wheeler, "Tending Talents: The Cultivation of Effective and Productive Theological School Faculties," in *Tending Talents.* The Second in a Series of Reports from a Study of Theological School Faculty, Auburn Studies, No. 4 (New York: Auburn Theological Seminary, 1996), 13.

[34] In his book on the seminary presidency, Neely McCarter discusses the numerous teaching functions of the presidential office. His idea of the president as educator could be adapted readily to other senior administrative offices. See Neely Dixon McCarter, *The President as Educator: A Study of the Seminary Presidency* (Atlanta, GA: Scholars Press, 1996), 43–62. In a 1993 article, Raymond Rodriguez states that "the most effective administrators remain practicing scholars, whether the content of their scholarship is related to their disciplines or to their administrative duties." He argues persuasively that an expanded notion of scholarship can legitimately include "the scholarship of administration," and that such scholarship can be documented and subjected to peer review like any other. See Raymond J. Rodriguez, "Campus Administrators as Practicing Scholars," *The Chronicle of Higher Education* 39, no. 26 (March 3, 1993), B3.

# Afterword
# Advice to Prospective Deans

In a book intended to bring the experience and insight of chief academic officers to their faculty and administrative colleagues, to their fellow deans, and to others interested in theological education, it seems fitting to conclude with practical wisdom expressed in the deans' own words. Deans participating in the study were asked: "What advice would you give to a person considering academic administration in a theological school?" Their responses give a realistic, candid, sometimes humorous account of what academic leadership requires. Their statements do more than advise prospective deans; they open the window on their world a bit wider for us all.

- Be clear about your objectives.
- First, serve as a faculty person. Unless you understand and, at least to a degree, honor faculty concerns, trouble will be yours as the sparks fly upward.
- Undertake a preparatory, deputy role in academic administration to observe, gain perspective and critical distance. Certainly teach to know faculty challenges and concerns, as well as students' objectives and needs.
- Do you really want to put individual scholarship and teaching on the back burner? Can you find ways to express these through corporate administrative leadership?
- Be certain of a sense of call, vocation, to academic administration. Be certain of the support of each key player—chief executive officer, faculty, board of trustees.
- Examine whether you have the gifts and calling from God.
- You will need: 1) strong administrative skills, 2) a lot of common sense, 3) patience, 4) a sense of humor, 5) time.

- Check carefully the true expectations of the position to see if there is authority commensurate with the responsibilities. Seek to discover if there is congruence between one's own vision and that of other key players.
- Only get into this business if you love it and have gifts for it. Know what being an administrator will cost you, be clear about your limits and what you'll pay, and be able to walk away when it gets too much. You must respect and esteem your colleagues, and they must respect and come to trust you. Do this work because you care deeply about the people affected by it, otherwise stay out.
- Be sure you are comfortable with conflict, able to listen, and willing to be alone, for the job is often "in between" faculty and administration.
- Don't pretend you are in charge of General Motors.
- It is an honorable profession. Consider it prayerfully. Have a realistic picture of your abilities. . . . Develop spiritual and physical disciplines for yourself, including reality checks on joy in your work.
- Be sure that your vision and goals (personal and institutional) are sufficiently compatible with those of your administrative and faculty colleagues so that you can work together and not at cross-purposes. Be absolutely straight with people, refusing to get caught up in trivial games. Answer your mail and return calls. Say thank you—a lot—to everybody.
- Consider if you are willing to be a servant.
- Know yourself and be willing to find yourself in crossfires of competing issues and demands. Love people, even cantankerous ones. Love your work but be able to be done with it after working hours are through. Take seriously your work but do not take yourself, as a worker, very seriously at all. Know why you are doing what you are doing and gain joy from attempts to bring to fruition those efforts. Build a support system outside your institution. Leadership, itself, can be very lonely.
- Get a thick skin.
- Make sure you have a supervisor who will guarantee your success.
- You must like administration and know your support system. Don't take confrontation personally, and never predict what faculty will do.

Don't expect glory or power. Keep in touch with your professional discipline. Be committed to the school's purpose.

- Keep in good physical shape—you'll need to. Consult with faculty on decisions. Be prepared for successes and frustrations. Make sure you preserve time for reading and writing.
- You can always qualify a no, but you can't qualify a yes. There are certain things you put in writing and certain things that you don't.
- As an African American, I would encourage other persons of color to look seriously at academic administration as a vocation. It is a ministry that deserves to be chosen, rather than thrust upon you.
- Go for it! But realize it is a high-stress position which may take its toll personally, professionally, physically. Find ways to protect these aspects of life, achieve a healthy balance.
- Can you take heat and not personalize it? Can you say no when necessary? Do you have to be liked by everyone? Can you honestly say you like problem solving and can do it under time constraints without 100% certainty you are right?
- The fact that one is an effective faculty member does not necessarily mean that he or she possesses the requisite skills, drive, and leadership which are important in academic administration. Of particular importance is the ability to motivate people, to create an esprit de corps, to cast vision, and to relate to the institution's several constituencies. . . . Lastly, I would discuss the reality of loneliness. Academic leadership produces significant isolation.
- Be willing to: determine the needs the faculty and curriculum have early on; address those needs; expect to make hard decisions; if you are from the faculty, realize your relationships to the faculty will change; learn about budgets; keep your faculty and president well informed, avoid dropping bombshells; maintain a bit of distance from the job, don't overinvest; make certain you are kept well informed; maintain impartiality in relationships to faculty, expect to nurture some, applaud others, rein in still others; listen to gossip but don't enter in; let the faculty know you are *with* them and *for* them in what you do as well as what you say; interpret the major actors to each other—students, faculty, administration; stay in touch with the student body.

Take it on as a calling, not as "less than teaching"; remain compassionate but firm; make hard decisions as they affect people with soul searching, but make them; take a good vacation.

- Gain the respect of the faculty. Do not attempt this role without their support.
- Do not take it on unless you can do it with enthusiasm. This involves seeing administration as a valuable contribution to theological education. If one's heart is really in teaching, then one should not become an administrator.
- My only aphoristic response is: "Listen, propose, listen, revise, listen, decide."
- Make sure you have faculty and administrative support. Be sure you have enough authority to succeed or fail.
- Only take on the challenge if you can see it as an arena for the exercise of your own creative gifts.
- Invest some years in teaching and involvement in committee work. Learn to balance work with leisure, companionship, personal development. Foster a sense of humor and realism: the world and your institution existed before you and will continue to do so long after you retire.

# Appendix A
# The Study of Chief Academic Officers in North American Theological Schools

The following information on the Study of Chief Academic Officers supplements the general overview of the project provided in the Introduction. Each of the four main components of the research—the survey, site visits, focus groups, and commissioned essays—are described in detail to elucidate the research design, policy issues, and selected findings. A summary of all participants in the study concludes this report.

The project encompassed the 219 theological schools which in 1993–1994 had accredited, candidate, or associate status with the Association of Theological Schools in the United States and Canada (ATS). Characteristics of these schools are described in the survey respondent data below. Chief academic officers in theological schools have various titles depending on institutional structures and traditions. Among the 219 schools included in this research, titles are distributed as follows: Provost, 6 schools (2.7%); Vice President for Academic Affairs, 18 schools (8.2%); Academic Dean, 145 schools (66.2%); other titles, 25 schools (11.4%); and academic/executive officers combined, 25 schools (11.4%). In this study, the most common term "dean" is used generally to refer to all who hold the chief academic officer position.

Lilly Endowment Inc. supported the planning, research, and dissemination of this study. The project was based at The Saint Paul Seminary School of Divinity, University of St. Thomas (MN), and the research was conducted over two years from 1993 to 1995. Jeanne P. McLean served as project director, and other researchers were Karen M. Ristau, Mary Abdul-Rahman Baron, and Paula J. King.

The project Advisory Committee held three one-day meetings between 1993 and 1997, two during the developmental phase of the project and one during the dissemination phase. They consulted on overall project design, research policy, the development of research instruments, and dissemination efforts. They also offered critical review of portions of the book manuscript. Advisory Committee members were a distinguished group of scholars and leaders, representing theological schools and other areas of higher education: Estela M. Bensimon, Robert Birnbaum, Madeleine F. Green, James Hudnut-Beumler, Garth M. Rosell, Thomas P. Walters, and Barbara Brown Zikmund.

## I. Survey of Chief Academic Officers

The survey instrument was designed by the research team in consultation with the project Advisory Committee and other consultants. The instrument was pretested with six theological school deans from different types of institutions prior to its general distribution. In October 1993, researchers distributed the written survey to the chief academic officer in each of the 219 ATS-related theological schools. The purpose of the survey was to acquire a general statistical profile of chief academic officers and their work from a broad cross section of theological schools. Survey data revealed general trends in the deanship and provided a framework for interpreting findings from site visit interviews and focus group discussions. With a response rate of 75 percent, survey results afforded a reliable picture of theological school deans serving in 1993–1994.

### *Content of the Survey*

The survey included 360 numerical items and four narrative questions. The main body of the survey solicited both factual data about individual deans and their responsibilities, as well as their attitudes and opinions on a variety of issues related to their work. The survey included the following topics: 1. Background on Current Deans: education, prior experience, demographic information, reasons for taking position; 2. Role of the Dean: responsibilities and influence, views of leadership, governance, professional relationships, academic policies and practices, institutional life; 3. Institutional Policies concerning Academic Officers: hiring, terms of appointment, evaluation, professional development; 4. Administrative Service: length of service, attitudes toward administration.

The four narrative questions were: 1) What is the greatest hindrance to you in carrying out your responsibilities? 2) A. In the future, what single factor would most strongly influence your decision to continue serving in your current position? B. What single factor would most strongly influence your decision to move on? 3) Based on your experience, what constitutes effective academic leadership? 4) What advice would you give to a person considering academic administration in a theological school?

### *Survey Respondents*

*Rate of Survey Response:* 75% (actual 74.88%), with 164 of 219 schools responding. Among the 11% of schools listing no chief academic officer, 8% returned surveys completed by chief executive officers whose positions combined academic and executive functions.

*Categorical Analysis of Survey Respondents.* The two columns below compare the entire population of theological school deans in ATS-related schools in 1993–1994 (left column) with the group of deans who responded to the survey (right column). This comparison shows that survey respondents are highly representative of the entire population of ATS deans in all categories.

| | All Deans | | Survey Respondents | | |
|---|---|---|---|---|---|
| *Gender:* | | | | | |
| Men | 197 | 90% | 46 | 89% of all respondents | 74% of all men |
| Women | 22 | 10% | 18 | 11% of all respondents | 82% of all women |
| *ATS Schools by Status:* | | | | | |
| Accredited Schools | 189 | 86% | 147 | 90% of all respondents | 78% of all accred. schools |
| Candidate Schools | 7 | 3% | 6 | 3% of all respondents | 86% of all candidate schools |
| Associate Schools | 23 | 11% | 11 | 7% of all respondents | 48% of all assoc. schools |
| *ATS Schools by Denomination:* | | | | | |
| Protestant, mainline | 81 | 38% | 56 | 34% of all respondents | 81% of all Protestants |
| Roman Catholic | 52 | 24% | 42 | 26% of all respondents | 81% of all Catholics |
| Inter-/Nondenom. | 39 | 18% | 33 | 20% of all respondents | 85% of all Inter/Nondenom. |
| Other | 47 | 20% | 33 | 20% of all respondents | 70% of all Other |
| *ATS Schools by Type:* | | | | | |
| University-related | 26 | 12% | 21 | 13% of all respondents | 81% of all Univ.-related |
| Independent | 193 | 88% | 142 | 87% of all respondents | 74% of all Independent |
| *ATS Schools by Size (Student FTE):* | | | | | |
| Up to 75 | 56 | 26% | 37 | 23% of all respondents | 66% of group |
| 75–150 | 64 | 29% | 50 | 30% of all respondents | 78% of group |
| 151–300 | 52 | 24% | 39 | 24% of all respondents | 75% of group |
| 301–500 | 25 | 11% | 21 | 13% of all respondents | 84% of group |
| 500–2,656 | 17 | 8% | 14 | 8% of all respondents | 82% of group |
| Data Missing | 5 | 2% | 3 | 2% of all respondents | 60% of group |

## II. Site Visits

The project director and one of three members of the research team visited a representative group of eleven theological schools in the United

States and Canada in 1994 and 1995. Through personal interviews in the campus setting, we sought to learn firsthand about the work of chief academic officers, to examine concepts and practices of academic leadership and governance in diverse institutional contexts, and to study how theological schools cultivate and support their academic leaders.

During the three-day campus visits, the research team interviewed an average of twenty people at each site, including the chief academic officer, the chief executive officer, and representatives of the senior administration, the faculty, students, board of trustees/advisors, and church leaders. In consultation with the Advisory Committee, researchers developed interview protocols for each group to facilitate comparison of findings across institutions. The protocols contained some questions common to all and others tailored to their distinctive roles within the school. The interview protocol for the chief academic officer was pre-tested. Interviews on site ranged from three hours in length (over two days) for the academic officer to one hour or more with other individuals and groups. Participation in interviews was completely voluntary. As a matter of policy, the names of the schools and individuals interviewed were confidential.

### *Criteria for Site Selection*

The criteria for selecting the eleven theological schools for site visits aimed at achieving broad representation and balance among ATS schools. The criteria included factors such as institutional size, denomination, type (independent/university-related), geographic location, and racial/ethnic identity. Among academic officers, researchers sought gender balance and representation of various lengths of service. Only schools that were accredited by the ATS and whose academic officers had completed the survey for the study were eligible for site visits. Invitations were issued in writing to theological school presidents who accepted on behalf of their institutions.

### *Characteristics of the Schools Visited*

The eleven schools participating in site visits had the following characteristics:

*Denomination:* 2 Roman Catholic, 4 mainline Protestant, 4 Interdenominational, 1 Other. Among these 11 schools, 3 identify themselves as evangelical.

*Type:* 8 Independent; 3 University-related.

*Location:* 9 United States, 2 Canada.
*Size* (based on student FTE): 3 schools (150–250 FTE), 4 (251–350 FTE), 2 (351–450 FTE), 2 (451 and higher FTE).
*Predominant Race:* 10 White, 1 Black

Within these schools, the chief academic officers had the following characteristics:

*Gender:* 8 Men, 3 Women
*Length of Service:* 2 deans: 0–3 years; 3 deans: 4–6 years; 5 deans: 7–10 years; 1 dean: over 10 years.

## III. Focus Groups

In order to foster interinstitutional dialogue on the central issues of the study, we convened five focus groups during the research period: two focus groups of deans, and one group each of faculty, presidents, and trustees. The focus groups served to broaden the range of schools participating in the study and to stimulate conversation and interaction among peers from different institutions. Researchers developed focus group protocols for each group. All considered the role of the dean and other constituents in institutional governance, concepts and practices of leadership, and criteria for effectiveness in academic administration. Other questions were tailored to the role of each group and their relationship to the chief academic officer.

Following is the schedule of focus groups and the number of participants in each.

| | | |
|---|---|---|
| Deans' Focus Group #1 | June 1994 | 7 participants |
| Deans' Focus Group #2 | May 1995 | 7 participants |
| Faculty Focus Group | April 1995 | 7 participants |
| Presidents' Focus Group | June 1994 | 7 participants |
| Trustee Focus Group | September 1994 | 6 participants |

## IV. Commissioned Essays

The study commissioned six reflective essays of chief academic officers at different types of theological schools and at different stages in their administrative service: two deans in their first three years, two with four to six years of experience, and two with seven or more years. The essays afforded an inside view of the dean's daily work, its difficulties and rewards, the lessons learned, and the vocation of academic administration. These essays were commissioned in response to a need frequently expressed by academic officers to know more about their peers at other schools and how they meet the challenges of the job.

The six essays were published in Theological Education, volume 33, Autumn 1996 Supplement under the general title, "The Study of Chief Academic Officers in Theological Schools: Reflections on Academic Leadership." An address by James L. Waits, executive director of ATS and a former dean, delivered at the ATS Conference for New Deans in October 1995, was included in this collection. Authors and titles of the six essays written for this project are:

James Hudnut-Beumler, "A New Dean Meets a New Day in Theological Education"
Brian O. McDermott, "Of Force Fields and Aspirations: Being an Academic Dean in the Nineteen-Nineties"
Elizabeth Nordbeck, "The Once and Future Dean: Reflections on Being a Chief Academic Officer"
Russell E. Richey, "To a Candidate for Academic Leadership: A Letter"
Gordon T. Smith, "Academic Administration as an Inner Journey"
Jane I. Smith, "Academic Leadership: Roles, Issues, and Challenges."

## V. Summary of Participants

The research activities involved a total of 388 participants, 248 of whom participated in personal interviews or focus groups. A total of 165 chief academic officers participated in the study. In calculating these totals, individuals involved in more than one activity are counted only once.

Below is an itemized account of the number of participants in each of the research activities.

| | Site Visit Interviews | Focus Groups | Survey | Essays |
|---|---|---|---|---|
| Chief Academic Officers | 11 | 14 | 164 | 6 |
| Chief Executive Officers | 10 | 7 | | |
| Senior Administrators | 37 | - | | |
| Faculty | 93 | 7 | | |
| Students | 35 | - | | |
| Board of Trustees/Advisors | 19 | 6 | | |
| Church Leaders | 11 | - | | |

# Appendix B
# Profile of Chief Academic Officers in Theological Schools, 1993–1994

This profile is based on data collected on the Survey of Chief Academic Officers, conducted in October 1993 as part of this research. Survey respondents represented 75 percent of the total population of ATS schools in 1993–1994 and, as indicated in Appendix A, were well distributed across those schools.

Note: Percentages may not total 100% if not all categories are reported or percentages are rounded to the nearest whole percent.

**Gender**

| | | |
|---|---|---|
| 146 | (89%) | Men |
| 18 | (11%) | Women |

**Race/Ethnicity**

| | | |
|---|---|---|
| 155 | (94.5%) | White/Caucasian |
| 3 | (1.8%) | African American/Black |
| 2 | (1.2%) | Native American |
| 2 | (1.2%) | Asian American/Asian |
| 1 | (.6%) | Mexican American/Chicano |

**Education**

| | |
|---|---|
| 98.2% | Doctoral degrees: Ph.D. 66.5%; Th.D. 12.8%; S.T.D. 8.5%; D.Min. 3.7%; Ed.D. 1.8%; other 4.9% |
| 58.5% | M.Div. |
| 48.2% | M.A. |
| 20.1% | S.T.M., Th.M., M.Th. |
| 15% | S.T.L. |

**Ordination**

| | |
|---|---|
| 85% | Ordained (93% of men; 22% of women) |
| 15% | Not ordained |

**Age**

| | |
|---|---|
| 52 years | Average age |
| 36–72 years | Age range |

**Experience**

| | |
|---|---|
| 88% | Faculty experience in theological or higher education (average 8 yrs.) |
| 44% | Administrative experience in theological/higher education (average 3 yrs.) |
| 59% | Ministerial or pastoral work for church (average 8 yrs.) |
| 10.7 | Average number of years at present institution |
| 17.6 | Average number of years in theological education |

**Household Status**

| | |
|---|---|
| 68% | Married |
| 24% | Single |
| 5% | Single (divorced or widowed) |
| 1% | In partnership |

**Where Deans Come From: Positions Immediately Prior to Deanship**

| | |
|---|---|
| 65% | Faculty members: 60% in theological schools; 47% at same institution |
| 21% | Academic administrators: 18% in theological schools; 11% at same institution |
| 6% | Ministers, pastors |
| 7% | Other |

**Terms of Appointment**

| | |
|---|---|
| 43% | Have specified terms; data on renewability of terms is incomplete |
| 87% | Have faculty rank (92% of schools rank faculty): Professor 56%, Associate 20%, Assistant 5%; other 5% |
| 75% | Have tenure (68% of schools grant tenure) |
| 93% | Teach (73% each term; 16% once a year) |

Teaching is: 38% required, 38% expected, 20% optional
Scholarship is: 3% required, 40% expected, 56% optional

**Years of Service as Dean**

| | |
|---|---|
| 3.8 years | Average length of service |
| 57% | Served 3 years or less; 23.2% were new deans in 1993 |
| 24% | Served 4–6 years |
| 19% | Served 7 years or more |
| 7% | Served 11 years or more |

**Where Deans Plan to Go After Leaving Office**

Strong correlation with work immediately prior

| | |
|---|---|
| 54% | Return to teaching/research |
| 21% | Retirement |
| 10% | Church ministry/pastoral work |
| 6% | Presidency in theological/higher education (0% at present institution) |
| 4% | Academic administration elsewhere |

# APPENDIX C
# SELECTED RESOURCES: ANNOTATED LIST OF SUGGESTED READINGS AND PROFESSIONAL DEVELOPMENT PROGRAMS

These selected resources for chief academic officers include in Part I an annotated list of suggested readings, and in Part II a description of professional development programs for academic officers available nationally.

## I. Suggested Readings

### *Leadership*

Bensimon, Estela M., Anna Neumann, and Robert Birnbaum. *Making Sense of Administrative Leadership: The "L" Word in Higher Education.* ASHE-ERIC Higher Education Report No. 1. Washington, DC: School of Education and Human Development, The George Washington University, 1989.

This book is an invaluable guide to theories of leadership and organizations. It offers a critique of these theories and discusses their implications for effective administrative leadership in higher education. As the authors explain, one of the best ways for leaders to deal with the complexity of their institutions is "to develop awareness of the various theories of leadership and conceptual models of organizations so that they can generate multiple descriptions of situations and multiple approaches to solutions." (p. 73)

Conger, Jay A. and Associates. *Spirit at Work: Discovering the Spirituality in Leadership.* San Francisco: Jossey-Bass, 1994.

The premise of this collection of essays is that the workplace today is for most of us a place of connection and a primary source of community. The book discusses both personal and organizational processes for cultivating the spiritual dimension of our lives and includes several essays that inform the leadership role of theological school deans.

Green, Madeleine F. and Sharon A. McDade. *Investing in Higher Education: A Handbook of Leadership Development.* Washington, DC: American Council on Education, 1991. Reprint, Phoenix, AZ: American Council on Education and Oryx Press, 1996.

This handbook is an invaluable guide to leadership development. Beginning with an introduction to the basic principles of leadership development, the authors present concise, easily referenced discussions of practical strategies for developing leaders at every level of the organization, including governing boards, senior and mid-level administrators, faculty, and managers and professional staff. Particularly helpful is a complete annotated list of national and regional development programs and a discussion of on-campus initiatives. The book is well researched and, although some of the program information is dated, it remains the best reference book on leadership development in higher education.

Heifetz, Ronald A. *Leadership Without Easy Answers.* Cambridge, MA: The Belknap Press, 1994.

The model of leadership Heifetz proposes most adequately captures the role of chief academic officers emerging from this study. Although Heifetz's examples are drawn primarily from the political arena, the general principles of the theory are readily applicable to the academic setting. This book makes an important contribution to our understanding of leadership practice.

### *Chief Academic Officers/Academic Deans*

Austin, Michael J., Frederick L. Ahearn, and Richard A. English, eds. *The Professional School Dean: Meeting the Leadership Challenges.* New Directions in Higher Education, no. 98. San Francisco: Jossey-Bass, 1997.

This collection of essays discusses various aspects of the dean's leadership role. Many of the case examples are drawn from the field of social work, with reactions and applications offered by deans in other professional schools. An essay by Clarence G. Newsome of Howard University School of Divinity discusses the dean's role in leading from the heart of the school and "leveraging the spirit of a school for growth." (p. 106)

Brown, David G., ed. *Leadership Roles of Chief Academic Officers.* San Francisco: Jossey-Bass, 1984.

This collection of essays by various authors contains several essays on working with faculty to foster their leadership and development. Other topics include planning and budgeting. Many of the essays are brief and intended as catalysts to thinking strategically about important issues.

Ehrle, Elwood B., and John B. Bennett. *Managing the Academic Enterprise. Case Studies for Deans and Provosts.* New York: American Council on Education/Macmillan Publishing Company, 1988.

Through twenty-five case studies, the book "directly and concretely addresses the leadership, management, and administrative concerns of deans and provosts. . . ." (vii) The case studies deal with practical problems—with finances, personnel, programs, and the like—to which deans and provosts offer responses based on their different leadership styles. Although the cases are formulated for academic officers in colleges and universities, almost all are interesting reading and suggest approaches to situations that could arise in theological schools.

Gould, John Wesley. *The Academic Deanship.* New York: Teachers College Press, Columbia University, 1964.

Presenting results of one of the few research-based studies of academic deans, Gould's book discusses the role, responsibilities, and professional relationships common to the deanship in higher education. This book draws upon results of a questionnaire and personal interviews with 260 college and university deans and is laced with direct quotations and stories. Although its language is somewhat dated, the type of research conducted and the topics discussed closely parallel this study of theological school deans.

Tucker, Allan, and Robert A. Bryan. *The Academic Dean: Dove, Dragon, Diplomat.* 2d ed. New York: American Council on Education/Macmillan Publishing Company, 1991.

The authors discuss the role of academic dean in a university setting. Based on their own experience, they offer practical advice on how to deal with the array of problems arising in the course of the dean's work.

*Administrative Issues*

Bensimon, Estela M., and Anna Neumann. *Redesigning Collegiate Leadership: Teams and Teamwork in Higher Education.* Baltimore, MD: The Johns Hopkins University Press, 1993.

This book is an excellent resource for deans, presidents, and others interested in developing effective teams. Based on a study of leadership teams at fifteen institutions, it makes a strong case for the importance of team leadership, it identifies difficulties that may impede team building, and it offers practical guidelines on how to establish and utilize teams effectively. The book is thorough in its analysis and indispensable for the sound advice it offers.

Chait, Richard P., and Associates. *Trustee Responsibility for Academic Affairs.* Washington, DC: Association of Governing Boards of Universities and Colleges, 1984.

Recognizing the need to help trustees oversee the academic area "without interfering with the president or usurping the prerogatives of the faculty" (p. x), the Association of Governing Boards commissioned a study of "The

Role of the Trustee in Academic Program and Personnel Planning." This book includes essays by the study group and findings of their research. Particularly helpful to chief academic officers are discussions of the role of Academic Affairs Committees and practical guidelines for how to work with them on personnel and program issues.

Creswell, John W., et al. *The Academic Chairperson's Handbook.* Lincoln, NE: University of Nebraska Press, 1990.

Much of the advice offered here applies to academic deans as readily as to department heads. The authors take a practical approach to working with faculty and offer concrete, specific suggestions on creating a positive work environment for faculty, improving teaching and scholarship, orienting new faculty, refocusing faculty, and dealing with personal issues.

Holton, Susan A., ed. *Conflict Management in Higher Education.* New Directions for Higher Education, no. 92. San Francisco: Jossey-Bass, 1995.

Holton offers a practical guide to understanding and dealing with basic types of conflict that occur in higher education. This collection of essays includes faculty-to-faculty conflict, student conflicts, administrator-faculty conflicts, and institutional conflict. Holton believes conflict is an inevitable and necessary part of academic communities, and the task is not to eliminate it but to learn to manage it. The book also lists conflict management programs available in the United States.

Lucas, Ann F. *Strengthening Departmental Leadership: A Team-Building Guide for Chairs in Colleges and Universities.* San Francisco: Jossey-Bass, 1994.

While this book focuses on leading an academic department, its advice about working with faculty is equally applicable to deans. Lucas offers helpful discussion of such topics as motivating, evaluating, and rewarding faculty members, supporting effective teaching, enhancing scholarship, building teams, managing conflict, and strengthening leadership. The author is attuned to the complexity of interpersonal relationships and group dynamics.

Marchese, Theodore J., and Jane Fiori Lawrence. *The Search Committee Handbook: A Guide to Recruiting Administrators.* Washington, DC: American Association for Higher Education, 1988.

This handbook offers practical advice to academic institutions searching for senior administrators. It discusses each of the principal stages of the search process from the announcement of vacancy to making the appointment. This concise, easily referenced guide would be particularly useful to schools conducting a national search.

McDade, Sharon A. *Higher Education Leadership: Enhancing Skills through Professional Development Programs.* ASHE-ERIC Higher Education Report

No. 5. Washington, DC: Association for the Study of Higher Education, 1987.

This examination of the professional development of leaders in higher education discusses research on career paths, administrative responsibilities, and the implications of both for professional development. In addition to a survey of national institutes, conferences, and workshops, the book discusses the uses, benefits, and problems of professional development programs. This book is less comprehensive than the Green/McDade handbook above, but probes many of the issues relating to administrative development.

Palmer, Parker J. *The Courage to Teach: Exploring the Inner Landscape of a Teacher's Life.* San Francisco: Jossey-Bass, 1998.

An excellent text for reflection with faculty colleagues on the vocation of teaching and the passion, integrity, and sense of identity it requires. This book focuses not on teaching methods but on the inner work good teaching requires. Particularly helpful to deans is Parker's discussion of teaching and learning in community and how positional leaders can make that possible.

Seldin, Peter. *Evaluating and Developing Administrative Performance.* San Francisco: Jossey-Bass, 1988.

Seldin firmly establishes the link between professional evaluation and development, discusses the rationale for each, examines successful and unsuccessful programs in both areas, and offers examples to guide institutions planning to initiate or strengthen administrative evaluation and development. The book references other research in these areas and presents ideas in a readily accessible format.

## II. Professional Development Programs for Academic Administrators

Professional development programs are listed in three areas: a) programs for theological school chief academic officers, b) programs for deans and provosts in higher education, and c) programs for leadership development. Information on the programs was obtained directly from the sponsoring organizations.

### *A. Programs for Theological School Chief Academic Officers*

Sponsored by the Association of Theological Schools in the United States and Canada (ATS), 10 Summit Park Drive, Pittsburgh, PA 15275-1103. Tel. (412) 788-6505; Fax (412) 788-6510; e-mail: ats@ats.edu; website: www.ats.edu

**Annual Seminar for Chief Academic Officers**

Contact: ATS

Based on previous biennial conferences for new and veteran deans, ATS inaugurated in March 1999 an annual seminar for chief academic officers in theological schools. Presenters include experienced administrators in theological education, researchers, and ATS staff. The seminar considers topics such as the dean's relationship with other senior administrators and the faculty; faculty recruitment, selection, and development; educational evaluation and planning; and the vitality and professional development of deans. The seminars are intended to foster an ongoing professional organization and a community of peers. Registration is open to chief academic officers in all ATS-related schools. Deans pay travel expenses and a registration fee.

**Programs for Deans Offered by the Faculty Resource Center**

Contact: Loretta Groff, Faculty Resource Center, ATS. e-mail: frc@ats.edu

The program for deans previously offered by the Faculty Resource Center concluded in December 1998, and the next program cycle is scheduled to be announced early in 1999.

**Women in Leadership in Theological Education**

Contact: Kathryn Hepfer, Program Coordinator, ATS

This four-year initiative has been designed to increase the number and enhance the tenure of women in administrative leadership positions in ATS schools. The project includes leadership development training programs and consultations, networking support, and a referral service. Stipends are available for other activities. These programs are intended for women currently in upper level administrative positions in theological schools or in mid-level management positions and committed to administration, and for women who have leadership potential but little or no administrative experience. Seminars are held in March and October each year, and professional development awards are announced and distributed each fall.

## *B. Programs for Academic Deans and Provosts in Higher Education*

These programs typically attract participants from colleges and universities according to the focus of the sponsoring organization. Topics tend to be relevant to the work of theological school deans, though some translation to the seminary context may be required. Individuals are encouraged to contact coordinators for more information on program content and its applicability to their setting.

**American Council on Education (ACE), Workshops for Division and Department Chairs and Deans**

Contact: Center for Leadership Development, ACE, One Dupont Circle, NW, Suite 800, Washington, DC 20036; Tel. (202) 939-9410

These two-day workshops focus on departmental leadership and encourage institutional teams of deans and heads of departments, divisions, and programs to attend. The three workshops, held at separate locations each year, include sessions on evaluating college teaching, conflict management, legal issues, team building, and stress and time management. Content varies among the three workshops. Registration fees for nonmember institutions in 1998 ranged from $690 to $715 per person.

**American Conference of Academic Deans (ACAD)**

Contact: Eliza Jane Reilly, Executive Director, ACAD, 1818 R Street NW, Washington, DC 20009; Tel. (202) 387-3760; Fax (202) 265-9532; e-mail: reilly@aacu.nw.dc.us

ACAD is a national organization of academic officers from a wide range of colleges, universities, and community colleges that emphasize the liberal arts and undergraduate education, though participation from others is welcome. ACAD sponsors an annual national conference, with sessions and workshops focused specifically on the needs and interests of academic officers, and a preconference workshop for new deans. Members have access to an on-line discussion group, and The Handbook for Deans is available January 1999. In 1998, membership dues were $40-$60 per person.

**Seminar for New Deans, Council of Colleges of Arts and Sciences (CCAS)**

Contact: Richard J. Hopkins, Executive Director, Council of Colleges of Arts and Sciences, College of Liberal Arts and Sciences, Arizona State University, P.0. Box 873901, Tempe, AZ 85287-3901; Tel. (602) 727-6064; Fax (602) 727-6078; e-mail: rhopkins@asu.edu.

The two-and-a-half-day seminar is held twice annually, in Williamsburg, VA, in June and in San Diego, CA, in July. Presenters are experienced deans who focus on practical issues in academic administration. Topics in the 1998 seminars included: getting started in the job, setting goals and planning, legal issues, budget and resource management, building good relationships with chairs and academic vice presidents, and development and fundraising. Seminars are limited to forty participants who are primarily, though not exclusively, from colleges of arts and sciences. Registration is $375 per person.

## *C. Programs for Leadership Development*

**Carnegie Mellon University, Academic Leadership Institute**

Contact: Deborah G. Corsini, Director of Executive Education, The Heinz School, Carnegie Mellon University, Pittsburgh, PA 15213-3890; Tel. (412) 268-6082

This two-week summer program is primarily designed for men and women in leadership positions in colleges and universities. Topics include: leadership; strategic management and planning; legal and ethical issues; political, economic and technological trends; and modern management concepts and techniques. The program is participatory in nature, using small study groups and discussion. A seminary dean who recently attended found it informative and helpful, although it was necessary to translate issues to the seminary context. The comprehensive fee for tuition, room, and board in 1998 was $4,000.

**Harvard University, Graduate School of Education**, sponsors three programs for leadership development. All are intensive, residential summer programs, two to three weeks in length, held annually at the Harvard University campus. Sessions are conducted by experienced faculty and tend to be highly interactive, with frequent use of case studies and discussion. A limited amount of financial aid is available.

Contact: Tacy San Antonio, Senior Program Coordinator, Harvard Graduate School of Education, 339 Gutman Library, Cambridge, MA 02138; Tel. (617) 496-1818

1. **Management Development Program (MDP):** This program prepares mid-level administrators in colleges and universities for responsible management and leadership. The goal is to prepare administrators to develop effective solutions to the problems they encounter and to give perspective on higher education issues. Participants are from a broad range of higher education organizations in the United States and abroad. The curriculum includes topics such as leadership, diversity and community, financial management, team building, human resource management, and legal issues in higher education. In 1999, the comprehensive program fee of $3,900 included tuition, room and board, and all instructional materials.

**2. Institute for the Management of Lifelong Education (MLE):** This program is designed for skilled, experienced administrators—deans and directors, provosts and vice presidents—who will help their institutions adapt to a changing future. It is designed for those whose role is to think strategically about where their institution is going—about new alliances and partnerships, the impact of new delivery mechanisms, and how to serve new student populations. MLE is particularly useful as a source of mid-career renewal. Participants work with seminar faculty and each other testing new ideas and developing new strategies for leading their institutions into the future. The comprehensive fee for this two-week program in 1999 was $3,900.

**3. Institute for Educational Management (IEM):** The institute is designed to meet the professional development needs of senior administrators in higher education. The program sharpens the strategic, integrative, and decision-making skills required of campus leaders. IEM focuses on case studies of current and emerging issues at colleges and universities. The goals of the program are to challenge routine thinking, improve management and leadership practices, clarify institutional mission and vision, and improve the quality of higher education. In 1999, the comprehensive fee for this three-week program was $5,900.

**Bryn Mawr College/Higher Education Resource Services (HERS) Mid-America Summer Institute for Women in Higher Education Administration**
Contact: Betsy Metzger, Assistant Director, HERS Mid-American, University of Denver, Park Hill Campus, 7150 Montview Blvd., Denver, CO 80220; Tel. (303) 871-6866; Fax (303) 871-6897; email: bmetzger@du.edu
This three-week institute offers women faculty and administrators intensive training in educational administration. Its focus is both on management and leadership issues as well as personal career development. Participants are typically faculty members or middle-level administrators who are interested in senior management positions. The curriculum includes units on the academic environment, the external environment, the institutional environment, professional development, and other issues defined by participants. The 1999 fees for the institute included a nonrefundable application fee of $75 and a comprehensive fee for participants of $5,700 for residents and $4,700 for nonresidents.

# APPENDIX D
# REFERENCES

## I. Publications of the Study of Chief Academic Officers in Theological Schools

*Academic Leadership: A Study of Chief Academic Officers in Theological Schools.* Monograph Series. 5 vols. St. Paul, MN: University of St. Thomas, 1996–1998.

Volume 1. McLean, Jeanne P. Leading from the Center: The Role of Chief Academic Officer, January 1996.

Volume 2. Ristau, Karen M. Challenges of Academic Administration: Rewards and Stresses in the Role of the Chief Academic Officer, March 1996.

Volume 3. Abdul-Rahman, Mary. Career Paths and Hiring Practices of Chief Academic Officers in Theological Schools, May 1996.

Volume 4. McLean, Jeanne P. Professional Development for Chief Academic Officers, November 1996.

Volume 5. McLean, Jeanne P. Dean-Faculty Relationships: Meeting the Challenge, October 1998.

"The Study of Chief Academic Officers in Theological Schools: Reflections on Academic Leadership." *Theological Education* 33 (Supplement Autumn 1996), 1–76.

Hudnut-Beumler, James. "A New Dean Meets a New Day in Theological Education," 13–20.

McDermott, Brian O. "Of Force Fields and Aspirations: Being an Academic Dean in the Nineteen-Nineties," 47–59.

Nordbeck, Elizabeth M. "The Once and Future Dean: Reflections on Being a Chief Academic Officer," 21–33.

Richey, Russell E. "To a Candidate for Academic Leadership: A Letter," 35–45.

Smith, Gordon T. "Academic Administration as an Inner Journey," 61–70.

Smith, Jane I. "Academic Leadership: Roles, Issues, and Challenges," 1–12.

Waits, James L. "Developing the Community of Scholars. An Address to New Academic Deans in ATS Schools," 71–76.

## II. Other Sources Cited

American Association of University Professors Committee on College and University Government. "Faculty Participation in the Selection, Evaluation, and Retention of Administrators." *Academe* 67 (October 1981), 323–324.

Ammerman, Nancy T. *Baptist Battles: Social Change and Religious Conflict in the Southern Baptist Convention.* New Brunswick, NJ: Rutgers University Press, 1991.

Austin, Michael J., Frederick L. Ahearn, and Richard A. English, eds. *The Professional School Dean: Meeting the Leadership Challenges.* New Directions in Higher Education, no. 98. San Francisco: Jossey-Bass, 1997.

Bass, Dorothy C., ed. *Practicing Our Faith: A Way of Life for Searching People.* San Francisco: Jossey-Bass, 1997.

Bennis, Warren G. *On Becoming a Leader.* New York: Addison-Wesley Paperback Edition, 1994.

Bensimon, Estela M., Anna Neumann, and Robert Birnbaum. *Making Sense of Administrative Leadership: The "L" Word in Higher Education.* ASHE-ERIC Higher Education Report No. 1. Washington, DC: George Washington University School of Education and Human Development, 1989.

Bensimon, Estela M., and Anna Neumann. *Redesigning Collegiate Leadership: Teams and Teamwork in Higher Education.* Baltimore, MD: The Johns Hopkins University Press, 1993.

Blum, D. E. "24 Pct. Turnover Rate Found for Administrators: Some Officials Are Surprised by Survey Results." *The Chronicle of Higher Education* (March 29, 1989), A1-A14.

Bolman, Lee G., and Terrence Deal. *Modern Approaches to Understanding and Managing Organizations.* San Francisco: Jossey-Bass, 1984.

Borsch, Frederick H. "Faculty as Mentors and Models." *Theological Education* 28, no. 1 (Autumn 1991), 71–75.

Boyer, Ernest L. *Scholarship Reconsidered.* Princeton, NJ: The Carnegie Foundation for the Advancement of Teaching, 1990.

Briggs, Kenneth A. "The Costs of Money Trouble: Two Presidencies Done In by Financial Woe." *In Trust* (Summer 1994), 13–17.

Brown, David G., ed. *Leadership Roles of Chief Academic Officers.* San Francisco: Jossey-Bass, 1984.

Canary, John F. "The Spiritual Care of a Seminary Faculty." *Seminary Journal* 1, no. 3 (Winter 1995), 12–19.

"Catholic and Baptist Faculty Fired." *In Trust* 6, no. 4 (Summer 1995), 24–25.

Chaffee, Ellen E., and William G. Tierney. *Collegiate Culture and Leadership Strategies.* Washington, DC: American Council on Education/Macmillan, 1988.

Chait, Richard P., and Associates. *Trustee Responsibility for Academic Affairs.* Washington, DC: Association of Governing Boards of Universities and Colleges, 1984.

"Changing Scenes." *In Trust* 2, no. 1 (Easter 1990), 27.

Clarke, Erskine. "Leadership: The Study of the Seminary Presidency in Protestant Theological Seminaries." *Theological Education* 32 (Supplement II, Autumn 1995), 1–110.

Conger, Jay A., and Associates. *Spirit at Work: Discovering the Spirituality in Leadership.* San Francisco: Jossey-Bass, 1994.

Creswell, John W., et al. *The Academic Chairperson's Handbook.* Lincoln, NE: University of Nebraska Press, 1990.

Curran, Charles E. *Faithful Dissent.* Kansas City, MO: Sheed and Ward, 1986.

DePree, Max. *Leadership Jazz.* New York: Doubleday, 1992.

"Describing the New Leader: What's Needed in a Theological School President Today. A Conversation." *In Trust* 8, no. 4 (Summer 1997), 20.

Dupont, Gerald E. "The Dean and His Office." In *The Problems of Administration in the American College.* Roy J. Deferrari, ed. Washington, DC: The Catholic University Press of America, 1956.

Dykstra, Craig. "Vision and Leadership." *Initiatives in Religion* 3, no. 1 (Winter 1994), 1–2.

Falender, Andrew J., and John C. Merson, eds. *Management Techniques for Small and Specialized Institutions.* New Directions for Higher Education, no. 42. San Francisco: Jossey-Bass, 1983.

Glassick, Charles E., Mary Taylor Huber, and Gene I. Maeroff. *Scholarship Assessed: Evaluation of the Professoriate.* San Francisco: Jossey-Bass, 1997.

Gould, John Wesley. *The Academic Deanship.* New York: Teachers College Press, Columbia University, 1964.

Green, Madeleine F. "Developing Leadership: A Paradox in Academe." In *Academic Leaders as Managers.* Robert Atwell and Madeleine Green, eds. New Directions for Higher Education, no. 36. San Francisco: Jossey-Bass, 1981.

———, ed. *Leaders for a New Era: Strategies for Higher Education.* New York: American Council on Education and Macmillan Publishing Company, 1988; reprint, Phoeniz, AZ: American Council on Education and Oryx Press, 1996.

Green, Madeleine F., and Sharon A. McDade. *Investing in Higher Education: A Handbook of Leadership Development.* Washington, DC: American Council on Education, 1991.

Greenleaf, Robert K. *Seminary as Servant.* Indianapolis, IN: The Robert K. Greenleaf Center, 1980.

———. *Servant: Retrospect and Prospect.* Indianapolis, IN: The Robert K. Greenleaf Center, 1980, 1988.

Heifetz, Ronald. *Leadership Without Easy Answers.* Cambridge, MA: The Belknap Press, 1994.

Hipps, G. Melvin. "Faculty and Administrator Development." In *New Directions for Institutional Research: Effective Planned Change Strategies,* no. 33. G. Melvin Hipps, ed. San Francisco: Jossey-Bass, 1982.

Holman, Mark A. *Presidential Search in Theological Schools: Process Makes a Difference.* Oakland, CA: 1993. Distributed by agreement with the Association of Theological Schools in the United States and Canada.

Holton, Susan A., ed. *Conflict Management in Higher Education.* New Directions for Higher Education, no. 92. San Francisco: Jossey-Bass, 1995.

"How Free Should Teachers Be? Academic Freedom, Tenure, and Keeping the Faith: A Conversation." *In Trust* 3, no. 3 (New Year 1992), 10–15.

Jarvis, Donald K. *Junior Faculty Development: A Handbook.* New York: The Modern Language Association of America, 1991.

Kahle, Roger R. "Learning to Work Together: Boards, Faculties, and the Benefits of Collaboration." *In Trust* 7, no. 4 (Summer 1996), 12–14.

Kaiser, Walter C., Jr. "Pluralism as a Criterion for Excellence in Faculty Development." *Theological Education* 28, no. 1 (Autumn 1991), 58–62.

Kaplowitz, Richard A. *Selecting College and University Personnel: The Quest and the Questions.* ASHE-ERIC Higher Education Report No. 8. Washington, DC: Association for the Study of Higher Education, 1986.

King, Gail Buchwalter, ed. *Fact Book on Theological Education 1993–1994.* Pittsburgh, PA: The Association of Theological Schools in the United States and Canada, 1994.

Kuh, George D., and Elizabeth J. Whitt. *The Invisible Tapestry: Culture in American Colleges and Universities.* ASHE-ERIC Higher Education Report No. 1. Washington, DC: Association for the Study of Higher Education, 1988.

"Leadership: The Study of the Seminary Presidency. Reflections of Seminary Leaders." *Theological Education* 32 (Supplement III) 1996.

Leonard, Bill J. *God's Last and Only Hope: The Fragmentation of the Southern Baptist Convention.* Grand Rapids, MI: Eerdmans, 1991.

Lucas, Ann F. *Strengthening Departmental Leadership: A Team-Building Guide for Chairs in Colleges and Universities.* San Francisco: Jossey-Bass, 1994.

Lynn, Robert Wood. "Living on Two Levels: The Work of the Academic Dean in North American Theological Education." *Theological Education* 24 (Autumn 1987), 75–85.

Marchese, Theodore J., and Jane Fiori Lawrence. *The Search Committee Handbook: A Guide to Recruiting Administrators.* Washington, DC: American Association for Higher Education, 1988.

McCarter, Neely D. *The President as Educator: A Study of the Seminary Presidency.* Atlanta, GA: Scholars Press, 1996.

McDade, Sharon A. *Higher Education Leadership: Enhancing Skills through Professional Development Programs.* ASHE-ERIC Higher Education Report No. 5. Washington, DC: Association for the Study of Higher Education, 1987.

Mech, Terrence. "The Managerial Roles of Chief Academic Officers." *The Journal of Higher Education* 68, no. 3 (May/June 1997), 283–298.

Moore, Kathryn M., and Susan B. Twombly, eds. *Administrative Careers and the Marketplace.* New Directions for Higher Education, no. 72. San Francisco: Jossey-Bass, 1990.

Nason, John W. *Presidential Search: A Guide to the Process of Selecting and Appointing College and University Presidents.* Washington, DC: The Association of Governing Boards of Universities and Colleges, 1980, 1984.

Neumann, Anna. "The Thinking Team: Toward a Cognitive Model of Administrative Teamwork in Higher Education." *The Journal of Higher Education* 62 (September-October 1991), 485–513.

Nordvall, Robert C. *Evaluation and Development of Administrators.* ASHE-ERIC Higher Education Research Report No. 6. Washington, DC: Association for the Study of Higher Education, 1979.

Nouwen, Henri J. M. *In the Name of Jesus: Reflections on Christian Leadership.* New York: The Crossroad Publishing Company, 1989.

Pacala, Leon. "The Presidential Experience in Theological Education: A Study of Executive Leadership." *Theological Education* 29, no. 1 (Autumn 1992), 11–38.

Palmer, Parker J. *The Courage to Teach: Exploring the Inner Landscape of a Teacher's Life.* San Francisco: Jossey-Bass, 1998.

Patrick, Anne E. *Liberating Conscience.* New York: Continuum, 1996.

*Procedures, Standards, and Criteria for Membership.* Bulletin 42, Part 3. Pittsburgh, PA: The Association of Theological Schools in the United States and Canada, 1996.

Rasmussen, Glen R. "Evaluating the Academic Dean." In *Developing and Evaluating Academic Leadership.* Charles F. Fisher, ed. San Francisco: Jossey-Bass, 1978.

"Recipe for Presidency. A Conversation." *In Trust* 3, no. 1 (Easter 1991), 12–17.

Rodriguez, Raymond J. "Campus Administrators as Practicing Scholars." *The Chronicle of Higher Education* 39, no. 26 (March 3, 1993), B3.

Rosovsky, Henry. "Deaning: A Short Course." *In Trust* 2, no.1 (Easter 1990), 19.

Rost, Joseph C. *Leadership for the Twenty-First Century.* Westport, CT: Praeger Publishers, 1991.

Sagaria, Mary Ann. "Administrative Mobility and Gender: Patterns and Processes in Higher Education." *The Journal of Higher Education* 59, no. 3 (May/June 1988), 306–326.

Schuster, Jack H., Daniel W. Wheeler, and Associates. *Enhancing Faculty Careers: Strategies for Development and Renewal.* San Francisco: Jossey-Bass, 1990.

Schuth, Katarina. *Reason for the Hope: The Futures of Roman Catholic Theologates.* Wilmington, DE: Michael Glazier, Inc., 1989.

Seldin, Peter. *Evaluating and Developing Administrative Performance: A Practical Guide for Academic Leaders.* San Francisco: Jossey-Bass, 1988.

Shriver, Donald W., Jr. "Visions and Nightmares: The Leader's Call to See Reality—and Change It." *In Trust* 3, no. 3 (New Year 1992), 16–21.

Shtogren, John A. *Administrative Development in Higher Education.* Vol. I: *The State of the Art.* Richmond, VA: Higher Education Leadership and Management Society, 1978.

Stackhouse, Max L. "The Faculty as Mentor and Model." *Theological Education* 28, no. 1 (Autumn 1991), 63–70.

Stein, Ronald H., and Stephen Joel Trachtenberg. *The Art of Hiring in America's Colleges and Universities.* Buffalo, NY: Prometheus Books, 1993.

Strohm, Paul. "Toward an AAUP Policy on Evaluation of Administrators." *Academe* 66 (December 1980), 406–413.

Strom, Jonathan, and Daniel Aleshire, eds. *Fact Book on Theological Education 1996–1997.* Pittsburgh, PA: The Association of Theological Schools in the United States and Canada, 1997.

Taylor, Barbara E. *Working Effectively with Trustees: Building Cooperative Campus Leadership.* ASHE-ERIC Higher Education Report No. 2. Washington, DC: Association for the Study of Higher Education, 1987.

*Theological Education* 24, no. 1 (Autumn 1987); 27, no. 1 (Autumn 1991); 31, no. 2 (Spring 1995).

*Theological Education.* The Study of the Seminary Presidency: Reflections of Seminary Leaders. 32 (Supplement III 1996).

Trotter, Thomas F. "Trustees and Academic Affairs." In *The Good Steward.* Washington, DC: Association of Governing Boards of Universities and Colleges, 1985.

Tucker, Allan. *Chairing the Academic Department.* 3d ed. Phoenix, AZ: American Council on Education and Oryx Press, 1993.

Tucker, Allan, and Robert Bryan. *The Academic Dean: Dove, Dragon, or Diplomat?* Washington, DC: American Council on Education, 1987.

Wheeler, Barbara G. "Shaping Theological Faculty for the Future: How Academic Deans Can Help." Address given at the Conference for Theological School Chief Academic Officers, Pittsburgh, PA, October 1997.

———. *True and False.* The First in a Series of Reports from a Study of Theological School Faculty. Auburn Studies No. 4. New York: Auburn Theological Seminary, 1996.

Wheeler, Barbara G., and Mark N. Wilhelm. *Tending Talents.* The Second in a Series of Reports from a Study of Theological School Faculty. Auburn Studies No. 5. New York: Auburn Theological Seminary, 1997.

Wister, Robert J. "The Effects of Institutional Change on the Office of Rector and President in Catholic Theological Seminaries,1965 to 1994." *Theological Education* 32 (Supplement I, Autumn 1995), 47–160.

Yuker, Harold E. *Faculty Workload: Research, Theory, and Interpretation.* ASHE-ERIC Higher Education Report No. 10. San Francisco: Jossey-Bass, 1984.

Zikmund, Barbara Brown. "The Role of the Chief Academic Officer in Theological Education." *Resources: Issues in Theological Education.* Issue 8 (October 1984), 1–8.

Zikmund, Barbara Brown, and William McKinney. "Choosing and Nurturing Faculty for an Unconventional Seminary." *Theological Education* 31, no. 2 (Spring 1995), 13–26.

# Acknowledgements

This book is a small part of the Lilly Endowment's efforts, over many years, to support and strengthen theological education. Like others before me, I am grateful to the Endowment for the financial support and good counsel that made this work possible. In particular, I would like to thank Craig Dykstra and Fred Hofheinz for recognizing the need for a study of chief academic officers and for giving me and my colleagues the privilege of doing it.

The research on which this book is based relied on the voluntary participation of chief academic officers and their colleagues throughout theological education. In whatever forum they contributed, chief academic officers were unfailingly generous, candid, and thoughtful in response to our questions. I am indebted to the eleven theological schools visited for the study whose administrators, faculty, students, trustees, and church leaders graciously received the research team and contributed immeasurably to an understanding of the context for the dean's work. Participants in the five focus groups conducted for this study brought a breadth of perspective and an exchange of ideas on central issues that was most helpful. Special thanks are due to the six chief academic officers who offered written reflections on their administrative experience: James Hudnut-Beumler, Brian O. McDermott, Elizabeth C. Nordbeck, Russell E. Richey, Gordon T. Smith, and Jane I. Smith. Whatever insights this book offers are due entirely to the members of the theological education community who contributed so generously to this study.

Many persons played a role in conducting this research. My colleagues, Mary Abdul-Rahman Baron, Paula J. King, and Karen M. Ristau, served as members of the research team and made invaluable contributions to the project. Their partnership in conducting site visit interviews and focus groups particularly enriched this study. I am grateful, also, to Project Advisory Committee members Estela M. Bensimon, Robert Birnbaum, Madeleine F. Green, James Hudnut-Beumler, Garth M. Rosell, Thomas P.

Walters, and Barbara Brown Zikmund, for their encouragement and sound advice at critical stages of the project. Their collective wisdom as teachers, administrators, and scholars was an extraordinary resource. I also want to thank Mary Ellen Drushal, Victor Klimoski, Katarina Schuth, and Wilson Yates who served as readers and informal advisors during the study, and Lorman Lundsten, Jeff McLean, Johanna Baboukis, Amy Garbacz, and Kris Raggozino whose expertise in data management was indispensable.

From the initial planning of this research through its dissemination, the staff of the Association of Theological Schools in the United States and Canada (ATS) has been enormously helpful. Especially, I would like to thank Deena Malone and Nancy Merrill for their assistance with data and publications, and Michael Gilligan and Daniel Aleshire for their collaboration on programming for ATS deans. The Saint Paul Seminary School of Divinity at the University of St. Thomas served as the research site. Rectors Charles Froehle and Phillip Rask, the faculty and staff of the seminary provided a hospitable and supportive environment for this work.

During final preparation of the book manuscript, I was fortunate to have the able assistance of Nicholas Cafarelli who edited the text, Johanna Baboukis who developed the index, and Cathy Slight who provided administrative support. I am grateful for the skill and precision each of them brought to the task. Several colleagues—Robert Birnbaum, James Hudnut-Beumler, Diane Kennedy, Russell Richey, and Garth Rosell—graciously provided a critical reading of the book manuscript in its final stages and made helpful suggestions.

Finally, I owe special thanks to my family and friends whose interest, support, and welcome diversions sustained me through it all. Above all, I am grateful to my husband, Jeff, whose insightful readings (and rereadings) of the text and steady encouragement were greater gifts than he knows.

# INDEX

Numbers in parentheses refer to page number of text associated with the note mentioned.